THEY RODE INTO EUROPE

Zue Funsprugg.

Das Teutsch gestech

THEY RODE INTO EUROPE

The Fruitful Exchange
in the Arts of Horsemanship
between East and West

by

MIKLÓS JANKOVICH

Translated by

ANTHONY DENT

GEORGE G. HARRAP & CO. LTD

LONDON · TORONTO · WELLINGTON · SYDNEY

To Ilona

Originally published in German under the title
" Pferde, Reiter, Völkerstürme "
© BLV Verlagsgesellschaft mbH
München · Basel · Wien 1968

First published in Great Britain 1971
by GEORGE G. HARRAP & CO. LTD
182-184 High Holborn, London WC1V 7AX

English translation © George G. Harrap & Co. Ltd 1971

ISBN 0 245 50412 5

Composed in Monotype Dante type and printed by
William Clowes and Sons, Limited, London, Beccles and Colchester

Made in Great Britain

Author's Foreword to English Edition

This book was written in Hungarian but first published in German at Munich in 1968, as *Pferde, Reiter, Völkerstürme*. The present edition is a translation of that text, and has been rendered by Mr Anthony Dent, who is himself a writer on horses and their connection with history, and who has bred horses. He has supplemented the original text with his own interpolations (which are marked as such) in those passages which have a special bearing on conditions in Britain and North America. In thanking him for his valuable co-operation I am also expressing the conviction that together we can offer our English-speaking readers an original work on equestrian history that will satisfy a need wherever in the world horses are ridden and the English language spoken.

Original Foreword

Those important developments in the history of mankind which led in Europe to travel on horseback and to mounted warfare had their origin among the peoples of the steppes. Materials on their characteristic culture have been accumulated over the centuries abundantly in Hungarian archives. From a study of these, and from the results of research in the fields of history, ethnology, archaeology, and the study of horses I have been able to frame a coherent picture of the horseman's civilization and its diffusion throughout the world.

One fact alone has endowed the horse with historical significance: the horse enabled the Eurasians to travel overland from the Atlantic to the Pacific seaboards of the Old World, thus permitting contact between distant centres of civilization, and facilitating that exchange of ideas and inventions which is a fundamental requisite of human progress. Everything that we now revere as the triumph of the human spirit has been bought somewhere, at some time, not only with human blood and tears but also with the sweat of horses.

With the progress of technology the machine took the place of the animal as the source of power. The horse, which was the most loyal and self-sacrificing auxiliary of the human race, has vanished from our everyday life, within the memory of a generation still living, who can report from their own experience what life in the Equestrian Age was like. It is primarily to that generation that I dedicate this book.

But in it I have also something to say to the present generation, who live not only physically but also spiritually in the Machine Age. To them it often seems that bygones are bygones, and what is obsolete must be valueless. And yet youth is still drawn to animals, particularly to the horse. Hence we have in this mechanized generation a regeneration of riding for pleasure. And so this book is also dedicated to all those who are committed to sports on horseback. Sport is an inescapable function of civilization, and for them some knowledge of the equestrian past is an essential background element in their understanding of the horse–man relationship.

Lastly, the writing of this book has left me with the revived memory of many horses and many men—men with whom I have ridden and with whom I have served, for some of whom horses were a profession, for some a passion. I think now of many a horse whose footfall I would know again by ear after all the years, and of many a horse that has paid me its tribute of sweat under saddle or between the shafts. And for every word that I have written in the following pages, in memory I stroke them still, and pat their steaming necks.

M.J.

Translator's Preface

It is difficult for Europeans living west of the Rhine, and doubly difficult for the inhabitants of the British Isles, to appreciate the full force and significance of those waves of horsemen out of Asia that broke again and again on the (metaphorical) shores of Europe for centuries before the birth of the Roman Empire and for further centuries after its demise, reaching one of their peaks in the period following the death of Charlemagne, and finally turning to the ebb only with the unsuccessful siege of Vienna by the Turks. They left behind, on that last occasion, a useful piece of equine flotsam in the shape of the Byerly Turk, that magnificent Oriental stallion snatched from the undertow by a mercenary captain in the service of Prince Eugène, and brought home by him to serve as a charger at the battle of the Boyne, and become one of the Founding Fathers of the *General Stud Book*.

There you are; the maritime metaphor comes easiest to the lips of the Anglo-British islander. For us the Fury of the Norsemen is real enough; it is part of our history that sticks out like a sore thumb in every other place-name north of the Trent. The menace of the Blackamoors too has its place in our folklore here and there, as in the mummers' play of St George, simply because the last repercussions of the Turkish invasions were sea-borne, and the farthest range of the marauding galleys from the Barbary coast brought them now and again to the southern coasts of Britain, to snatch some luckless shepherd or fishwife from a lonely headland in Cornwall or Cork and haul them off to the slave-market of Tangier. But behind these pirates from the shores of Tripoli there stretched an unending chain of conquest and invasion, victory and defeat, a vortex of mounted strife that had its storm-centre far away in the steppes of Central Asia. There were brewed devastating gales that blew where they listed, sometimes to the south against Persia and India, sometimes to the east against the Chinese Empire—and one-third of the time against what came to be known as Christendom. Gaul and Iberia lay under the lee of steep mountains and thick forests that would diminish the force of such gales; only Britain lay behind salt water that would bring them to a dead stop.

Of all these terrible bowmen from the steppe, none learned, luckily for us, the art of combined operations, or how to transport light cavalry by sea. They were of many races and many tongues—Scythians, Sarmatians, Parthians, Huns, Alani, Tartars, Turks, Patzinaks, Mongols, and many more. Of such it was written by the prophet Habakkuk: "Their horses also are swifter than the leopards, and are more fierce than the evening wolves, and their horsemen shall spread themselves, and their horsemen shall come from afar: they shall fly as the eagle that hasteth to eat. They shall come all for violence." For all their diversity of racial origin, they had but one uniform way of life. There was no natural function that they could not and did not perform without dismounting—and one unnatural one. They could shoot faster and straighter from the saddle than any Westerner on foot, though not so far.

In popular English speech we have only two memorials of these horse-borne (all but horse-born) raiders—to 'catch a Tartar', which is to have a bull by the horns, and the word 'ogre', which is the English adaptation of the Old French variant of *Hongrois*—Hungarian. Mr Jankovich knows all about ogres because his forefathers have lived among them since the seventeenth century, when they were displaced from Croatia (now Yugoslavia) by the invading Turks. During the past three hundred years there has been a Jankovich of every generation serving in the Hungarian Army as an officer of Hussars. In the middle of the tenth century Hungarian raiders reached the Atlantic coast at the mouth of the Loire, and then turned south away from it—while the English were barely aware of their presence.

Yet the indirect influence of these fast-shooting Eastern badmen, even on the inhabitants of sheltered Britain, was astonishingly widespread and powerful in every field of transport and communications before the first or steam-driven mechanical revolution. These were the people who invented the riding-saddle (though perhaps not the pack-saddle) and the stirrup. They also invented the relay system of mounted messengers which is the progenitor of every postal service in the world. Their type of saddlery was the cause (and also partly the effect) of a style of horsemanship which utterly displaced the Celtic method of equitation, that in antiquity had been almost universal in Europe, and was derived ultimately from the driving style of the charioteer. For these nomads had no heroic tradition of chariot-driving; only a tradition of mounted herdsmen and hunters and bow-bearing warriors. Yet when they did take to the wheel, using the wagon as a means of victualling the marauding horse-archers and transporting the abundant booty, they produced two more useful innovations—the free-turning fore-axle and the 'bogy' system that was early applied to the design of railway engines; that is, small wheels in front and larger 'driving' wheels behind. This was a feature of the charac-teristic Hungarian vehicle, the *kocsi*, from which in the seventeenth century both the word and the thing—the English 'coach'—were derived. Only a people in-timately acquainted with the mechanics of equine power could have invented this system of large wheels behind and smaller wheels before; it is a mechanical imi-tation of the anatomy of the horse, whose massive hind-legs drive him forward at speed, while his lighter fore-legs merely assist in steering, and support his head and forepart.

In warfare the steppe-born art of mounted bowmanship was learned by few Western peoples, and the British were not among them. But some short time after 'villainous saltpetre' made its debut on the military stage the Hungarians began to specialize as mounted hand-gunners, known as hussars, doing what the mounted archer had done before them. A cruder and slower imitation of the hussar, made in Germany, soon spread through the West, and under the name of 'Reuters' were employed as mercenaries by Henry VIII. These pistoleers were the ancestors of the British dragoons, but, being mounted on the wrong type (and altogether the wrong quality) of horse, they never had the handiness or the speed of the genuine Magyar article. During the Seven Years War the combination of mobility and fire-power which this arm offered impressed itself on British commanders, and 'light dragoons' using Hungarian-type saddles and mounted on a better class of troop-horse began to appear in the Army List. As a result of the Napoleonic Wars these light dragoons reverted as near as might be to the original Danubian type, even going so far as to adopt the name Hussar; so much so that the Light Brigade of Balaclava fame had the clothing, the saddlery, and the accoutrements partly of Polish Ulani (in the Lancer regiments) and partly of Hungarian light horsemen.

Once the machine-gun and barbed wire between them had made nonsense of the horse as a vehicle for fighting-men, and the internal-combustion engine had robbed the coach-horse of what little utility the steam-engine had left it, the equine and the equestrian spheres of influence were confined more and more to ceremony and sport. As to ceremony, the major State occasions in the English-speaking world in the first four months of 1969 were the funeral of ex-President Eisenhower and the State reception of the Italian President at Windsor Castle. In the former not only was the coffin carried on the only horse-drawn 75 mm gun-carriage behind the only team of artillery horses that the U.S. Army has left, but a charger, fully accoutred and saddled, with jack-boots pointing backward in the stirrups, was led in the cortège. I once had the honour to serve under General of the Army Dwight D. Eisenhower, but I never saw him on horseback, and nobody else ever did either. It is just that horses are still inseparable from really first-class funereal pomp. The saddle-cloth on this horse was of the Hungarian pattern. At Windsor the ceremonial march-past was led by the bands of the Household Cavalry, which in turn was led by the drum-horse, accoutred in the Turkish manner and bearing brass kettle-drums ultimately of Turkish or Tartar design. Also on parade was the King's Troop, Royal Horse Artillery, in their full-dress uniform of Hussar (that is, Hungarian) pattern.

In the field of sport, horse-racing, which, as opposed to chariot-racing, is also probably an invention of the mounted nomads of the steppe, has never been so popular, and is diffused throughout the world. It depends on the thoroughbred racehorse, an amalgam of equine races evolved in England, but, as our author demonstrates, containing besides Arabian elements more than a measurable trace of Turkish and other Central Asiatic blood. Other equestrian spectacles, including Olympic events, dressage, and show-jumping in general, are a synthesis, in terms of the horses ridden and style of riding employed, of Eastern and Western elements. And the nodal point at which these traditions met and mingled is the lower Danube valley, among the Magyar horsemen.

The author is singularly well equipped to expound this highly original study of mobility in Eurasiatic societies before the advent of the machine, and its survivals today—first by reason of his access to records in the Magyar language which are beyond the reach of the West European student and layman alike, and second because in early life he himself herded colts on horseback on the Hungarian plains, in living contact with the traditions that go back to those of the earliest horse nomads. His work has opened a new vista for me on this far-reaching avenue of history, and I am glad that the opportunity has been afforded to reveal it to the eyes of an English-speaking public.

Contents

Part I Man and the Horse

Man as Breeder

In the course of prehistoric development it became ever clearer to man that he could exploit various animal species with less labour and peril than by hunting: by taming and breeding them. Of course, it was many thousands of years before all the implications of this were realized, and its realization took many different forms, depending on the parts of the world and species of animal concerned.

It is well known that the first animal to be domesticated was the dog. Even if there were no archaeological proof, this would be evident from the ease with which young puppies can be tamed, and from the fact that the dog eats the same sort of food as the diet of hunting and food-gathering men. Later we find hunting peoples who keep other animals of the cat and weasel tribe (cheetah, ferret) as well as falcons and eagles to hunt for them, and a few aquatic birds like the cormorant to fish for them. In such cases man and beast are only doing what both would do 'naturally' on their own account; only now side by side.

But when we come to the domestication of grazing animals and poultry a new element comes into play which tends to alter the life of the humans as well as the animals concerned. These animals are man's unrestricted and permanently available property, ensuring a supply of food and clothing and important raw materials for tool-making; some also provide a source of labour. So that many more new possibilities arise from the exploitation of these animals than by keeping auxiliary hunters such as hawk and hound.

But side by side with this potential, man is faced with new demands, primarily of a mental order. Now he is saddled with the care and protection of flocks and herds, with the provision of grazing in summer and fodder in winter, with protection against wild beasts and robbers. This amounts to much more work for the stock-keeper, involving also the division of labour and committedness. A balance had to be struck between the profits and the obligations of keeping animals—as it still has today. This was one of the most important stages in human progress.

Prehistorians up to now have been unable to form a clear and uniform picture of the earliest stages of domestication. In the absence of evidence they must have recourse to speculation, which is dangerous. It is generally assumed that the first grazing animal to be domesticated in Eurasia was the reindeer. In post-glacial times changes of climate and associated migrations of some animal species, and the extinction of others, led to a substantial spread of domestication, which became specialized, because independently developed, in different regions. Thus in the earlier phases of the history of domestic animals a limited number of wild species were tamed one by one.

Therefore in our view the archaeological material available up to now has only local relevance, and does not offer the basis of a comprehensive picture of the beginnings of stock-breeding. Such partial and local evidence is afforded, for instance, at Stellmoor, in North Germany, for domesticated reindeer in the eighth millennium B.C. or at Qualat Jarmo, in Iraq, for the keeping of sheep, cattle, and onagers in the fifth millennium.

We have no precise information about the earliest stages in the domestication of the horse. The one thing certain is that the earliest horse-keepers came from some hunting tribe in North Eurasia many thousands of years ago. The earliest archaeological find illustrating this in Northern Europe belongs to the end of the Neolithic—that is, between 4000 and 3000 B.C.

Man and the Evolution of Transport

As soon as man, by learning to walk upright, was sundered from the quadruped world he began to pay heavily for this privilege. It not only reduced his speed, but walking and running took up more of his energy. This was a grave disadvantage in the struggle for existence, for which only his increased mental capacity could compensate. Of course, the upright posture favoured his mental development. A man standing upright has a wider range of vision, his powers of observation are increased, he is able to absorb more experiences. This is allied to an increase in capacity and shape of the brain, and makes greater structural adaptability possible.

It took many hundreds of thousands of years to perfect this advance on the 'original' condition of man, and on this followed an improvement in human communications, travelling becoming less demanding in terms of effort, and more rewarding in proportion.

The great mountain ranges throughout the world acted as barriers between individual cultures, while waterways connected them. It is not by chance that the first traces of early civilizations are to be found on the banks of rivers or along sheltered stretches of coastline, where man found it easiest to provide for his daily needs, and to solve the problems of transport and communications. Even in primeval times men were able to take advantage of transport by water, to exploit the power of wind and tide; the raft, the dugout canoe, and at last the ship were what broke down the isolation of tribes and clans, enabling human contacts to be established over great distances. Thus larger human communities arose, and the exploitation of natural energy can be regarded as the first step in human progress.

The next step can be shown to depend directly on the further perfection of communications and the conquest of distance. Man used the energy of animals to facilitate transport by land. This led to contact between hitherto isolated communities.

In Europe and in those parts of Asia where wild Equidae lived, the horse for thousands of years held the primacy among those species of animals used for transport, until in very recent times the discovery of coal and oil and the way to exploit these new sources of energy opened up new possibilities in the field of transport and communications, undreamed of before. But even these possibilities are not the end of the road. In our day nuclear energy is shaping the beginning of a new era of transport.

The Beginnings of Horse-breeding

The single-hoofed animals grouped under the generic title of Equidae inhabited both the Old and the New World in pre-glacial times, or rather their ancestors did so. But at that time they still had more than one toe and were only the height of a dog. Apart from that, they bore little resemblance to the horse of today. It took some fifty to sixty million years before the emergence in North America of Pliohippus, and another ten million before the true horse evolved. Severe conditions during the Ice Age tended to restrict rather than favour the spread of the race geographically. It is only a few thousand years since the last of the American horses died out or migrated into Siberia across what is now the Bering Strait. From then onward they were present only in the Old World.

Three original races of true Eurasian horses are known: the pony (*Equus abeli*); living on the fringes of the forest zone of Western Europe; the Tarpan of Eastern Europe of the border of forest and steppe (*Equus gmelini Antonius*); and the Asiatic wild horse, which may or may not be extinct, but was last seen wild in Djungaria, on the borders of Soviet Asia and Mongolia. This third race was called in the local languages Kertag or Tach or Taki, and its scientific name is *Equus przevalskii Poliakoff*. Whether or not it survives in the wild state, there are about a hundred specimens alive in the zoos of the world. The Tarpan has been extinct for the last century. There are no surviving herds of ponies which are wild, in the strict sense in which zoologists use the word.

These three races are closely allied to each other, in both their habits and bodily structure. None of them exceeds (or exceeded) 13 hands in height. It is difficult to assess the part played by the original wild pony and by the Tarpan as the foundation stock of domestic horses, because living specimens are not available for study.

The least evolved forms of Equidae are the two species of ass still found wild south of the Mediterranean; then come the Asiatic wild asses such as the Persian and Indian onagers and the Kulan and the Kiang of Turkestan and Tibet. Of these only the Mesopotamian sub-species of onager was domesticated in antiquity, but was displaced by the horse. They all inhabit the steppe region of Central Asia, and thus overlap the original habitat of the horse, but are adaptable to more arid zones.

A third group of Equidae still living wild in tropical and sub-tropical Africa are the various species of zebra. Of these the Grévy's Zebra is the largest, having a height of 15 hands, a greater stature than that of all the wild asses and horses. All species of zebra are prized as a source of meat by African tribes; but we know of no attempt by them to domesticate any of the species, although it has been demonstrated that both the zebra itself and the mule which is produced by crossing it with, for instance, the Basuto Pony, can be trained to work, and is easily kept.

Systems of classification of the ancestors of the domestic horse have been frequently revised since before the days of Darwin, and the current scheme, based on physical characteristics but also on feeding habits, is expounded in the various works of Dr Skorkowski in Poland, J. G. Speed in Scotland, and H. Ebhardt in Germany. It presents two wild species of pony and two wild species of horse, with different but overlapping habitats, and has replaced the threefold division mentioned above. Their characteristics shown in the accompanying sketches were as follows.

Pony Type I. Unspecialized, broad forehead, wide nostrils, straight (but in some northern varieties S-curved) facial profile, short ears, broad croup, height at withers 12 hands–12 hands 2 in. Approximately the Exmoor of today.

Pony Type II. Stoutly built, coarse, heavy head, pendulous lower lip, straight facial profile inclining to convex, ears of medium length, split up behind, height at

withers 14 hands–14 hands 2 in., reminiscent of modern northern cold-blooded types.
Horse Type III. Long in the back, long, narrow skull, Roman nose, very long ears, sloping croup, height at withers 14 hands 2 in.–15 hands, slab-sided.
Horse Type IV. Refined, short in the back, short head, wide nostrils, concave facial

Pony Type I   Pony Type II

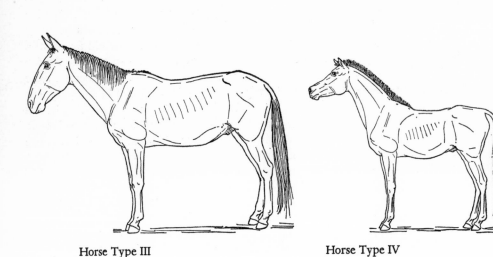

Horse Type III   Horse Type IV

The Four Types of Wild Horse and Pony, according to H. Ebhardt
Drawn by E. Trumler

profile, small, short ears tufted at the tip, very narrow croup with the tail set on high. Height at withers 11 hands 2 in.–12 hands; represented today by the Arab type.

Although the scientific attitude to the question of ancestral horse types has not finally crystallized, we shall in the following pages argue along the lines laid down by Ebhardt, because they are supported by practical research, and because they

2   The Treasure of the Oxus
    Massagetic chariot-and-four, third century B.C.
    British Museum

3   Four-wheeled Wagon in Clay,
    excavated at Buda Kalasz, Hungary.
    Third millennium B.C.
    National Museum, Budapest

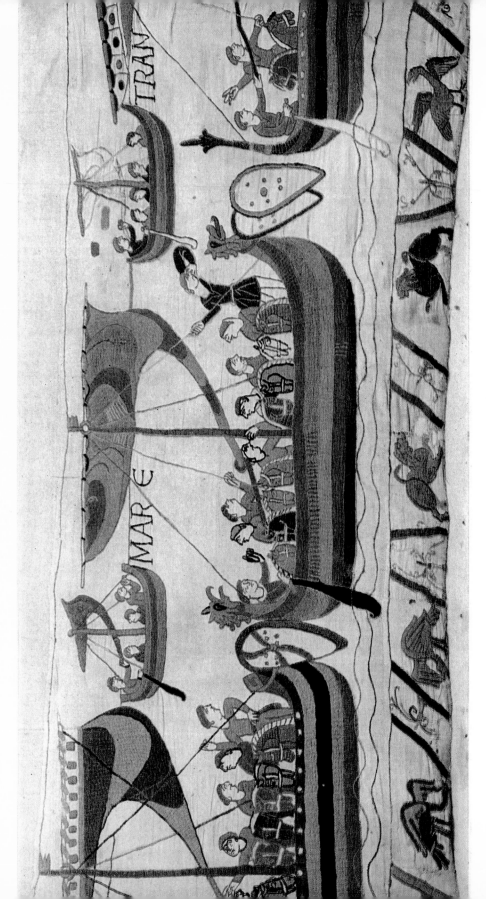

4 The Bayeux Tapestry. Horses transported by sea.

facilitate a decisive step forward in the solution of fundamental problems. The sole deviation from this classification that is justified is in connection with Arab and allied breeds, since today and in historical times they have been represented by a taller type of saddle horse.

In Eurasia these four types were initially bred by prehistoric man solely for meat, like his other domestic animals. This is brought out by the Scandinavian discoveries mentioned above, and by later discoveries from other parts of Eurasia. It was not until a later stage in the history of the animal-taming hunter that the horse entered on its historic role in the progress of mankind, by the exploitation of its strength. On the basis of the archaeological finds made up to the present, scientists have drawn the conclusion that initially the horse was only worked in harness, and not ridden for some thousand years after that. (But it must be taken into account that identifiable remains of carts and cart harness are much more likely to have been preserved over long periods than the rawhide bridle which probably constituted the sole equipment of the first riders.) The reindeer in harness first appeared in Eurasia in the third millennium B.C. The transition to the harness horse took place in the second millennium, and to the 'saddled' horse long after that.

The situation in Southern Eurasia and North Africa, collectively known as the Ancient East, was very different. As early as the fifth millennium, in various parts of the region, with its shared cultural traditions, the most important pack and draught animals were the ox, the onager, and the Nubian Ass (oxen carrying packs appear in early Saharan rock drawings; asses carrying packs in rock drawings in the Eastern Desert of Egypt about the same time; draught oxen, and later onagers harnessed to chariots, in early Mesopotamian art). In this region neither the reindeer nor the horse was found in the wild state. The use of the onager in harness ceased in Mesopotamia in the second millennium [but there are textual references to onager-drawn chariots among the Indian allies of the Persian Great King much later than that, and at least one wall painting of the Egyptian New Kingdom shows a chariot drawn by a pair that may be onagers or else mules, the progeny of an onager and a mare. Tr.]. Everywhere the onager was displaced as a harness animal by the horse, and its name was erased from the roster of domestic animals. Riding, as opposed to driving, did not become common throughout the Ancient East until the first millennium.

E. J. Ross in 1946 opened up a new archaeological perspective of the exploitation of animal tractive power, with his finds at Rana Gundai, in Northern Baluchistan, which showed domestic animals being kept between the fourth millennium and the middle of the first, including the horse derived from Central Asia and the ass derived from North Africa. This at a period in which such use had hitherto been considered impossible in that part of the world. Some scholars are still inclined to reserve judgment on this sensational discovery pending further assessment of the age of the bone material. [The presence of the horse and ass, both domesticated, would, of course, allow the possibility of mule-breeding then and there, but the first written mention of mules occurs later, and farther west, in the laws of the early Hittite kings—fifteenth century B.C. Tr.].

The only conclusion that we shall therefore draw from the Rana Gundai finds is that in the light of present knowledge the question of domestication of animals in Eurasia is still an open one, and must remain so for a long time. This is especially true of Central Asia, which is among the regions considered by scholars to have been the original home of mankind, but where archaeological research is still in its infancy, since the area is a very large one. The final answer to the question of the earliest farming and herdsmanship, both here and in the Afghan/Baluchi region, has yet to come.

For our solution to the problem of when and where animal tractive power was first exploited, we shall look to another quarter. Certainly it was response to an economic challenge, closely allied to the manner in which domestic animals were kept, and can best be studied in the light of practical experience. The choice before the primeval stock-keeper was either to graze his herds on the open range or to keep them in enclosed fields or stables. (This choice was open even to the pig-keeper; the swine could either be kept in styes or 'at pannage' in the forest.)

The difference between the two styles of agrarian life becomes sharpest in winter-time, when steppe nomads drive their cattle to what is called the winter pasture. Here in swamps and marshes or in the shelter of the woods they can always find something to eat. The forest trees provide shelter from the snow-storms. Herds thus are strangers to both halter and manger, and graze for themselves in summer and winter alike, just like wild animals—only that they are guided and guarded by herdsmen.

All over Eurasia where climate and terrain are suitable—that is, provide adequate winter pasture—we find traces of prehistoric herdsmanship in the forest and tundra of the sub-arctic zone with its reindeer-moss, swamps, and marshes for cattle (Camargue), low-lying meadows and deciduous woods for sheep, horses, and goats. This migration with the herds by which he gets his living makes no particular demands on the wandering stockman. There is no ceiling to the number of cattle he can breed, provided he has the sole use of the grazing-grounds.

The sedentary peasant, on the contrary, must spend at least part of the summer cultivating and harvesting fodder and forage for the winter, as well as crops for his own consumption; between grazing seasons—say from October to April—his cares are multiplied. He must bring his stock into stables and byres, or at least into a yard, and he must ration out his feed-stuffs. Even in normal seasons there is a limit to the number of head he can feed over the winter; after a hard winter and a late spring, when all the hay is eaten before the grass begins to grow, his lot is worse than that of the nomadic herdsman. Internal parasites are also a greater menace to the stock of the settled farmer than to that of the nomad. The latter can always move on when the grazing becomes tapeworm-infested or 'horse-sick'; the farmer cannot.

Climatic and topographical factors also play their part. The Russian scientist Popatov has established that the ox cannot be kept north of 51 degrees North. And for every animal that the nomad keeps or could keep there is a similar limit, both north and south. Thus for the horse 51 degrees is not the limit, north of which it must be stabled (it can winter out well to the north of the 60th parallel), but it cannot support life in some southern latitudes where cattle flourish, partly owing to the ravages of such plagues as African 'horse-sickness'.

The northern/southern limits between which the herding of grazing animals is practicable are identical with those between which the same animal was originally found in its wild state. Beyond these limits the animal must either be stabled or at least hand-fed (the classical example being the horse in Arabia). Theoretically there is no limit, geographically, to the 'artificial' keeping of grazing animals—at the beginning of this century Shackleton's expedition took Siberian ponies to the Antarctic. The only limits are economic ones. In time we shall be able, technically, to keep cows in interplanetary spaceships; but it will never pay to do so.

With the spread of settled agriculture and the stabling of cattle a significant breakthrough in agrarian economy took place—some animal species overstepped, as a result of domestication, the northern and southern bounds which Nature had set them in the wild—and this was to have the most important consequences for all mankind, as more and more tribes came into possession of poultry, cattle, pigs, goats, sheep—and horses.

This is by no means to imply that in the early stages of domestication animals were kept exclusively in herds in the open. [Obviously the dog was not, even though the Eskimo dog-team is a sort of wolf-pack, and does not sleep in the igloo. *Tr.*] The case is rather the contrary. The keeping of herds on free range is not more 'primitive' than the other method, nor is it more sophisticated. It is simply a quite different approach to the problem, which did not become widespread until after the rise of sedentary farming.

The above considerations about the keeping of livestock in general are also valid for the exploitation of animal-power by the two kinds of farmers—sedentary and pastoral. To begin with, the sedentary peasants used their animals only in harness, while the nomad herdsmen only rode them. (But probably both used them under the pack-saddle.)

This can be proved as follows. It is notorious that the "Battle-axe" people of Chalcolithic times, who perhaps can be equated with the Indo-European language group, did not ride but only drove carts or chariots, and the memory of such exclusive use of animals in draught is reflected in vocabulary and usage of some Indo-European languages, in historical times. Either they led the wagon team or drove it from the cart or the sled, and even when their cloven-footed cattle were replaced by single-hoofed equines they still did not ride, principally because their way of herdsmanship did not necessitate the risks inherent in riding. [That these risks were preserved in memory long after riding had become an everyday activity —at least of the aristocratic classes—is evident from one of the earliest Anglo-Saxon poems, the *Rune Poem*: "[Rād] byþ on recyde rinca gehwylcum/sefte..." "Riding seems easy to every warrior while he is indoors, and very courageous to him who traverses the highways on the back of a stout horse." *Tr.*]

Matters developed very differently among the wandering herdsmen. Animals only carried the rider or the pack among the peoples of Central Asia, with their Turkish or Mongolian way of life, in this first phase of exploitation of animal power. The herding and protection of half-wild bands of cattle and horses demanded more care and skill on the part of the herdsman than the winter-long care of stalled and hand-fed beasts. The only way to catch up and recover a herd which has panicked is to ride after them on something faster than they are, be it a camel, horse, donkey, reindeer, or even ox. But even droving requires judgment and practice.

Among wild or feral gregarious mammals it is mostly the older and more experienced individuals who are the leaders. The leader lays down the direction and the pace of march to pasture or water-hole, or of flight from enemies. This is especially noticeable in the case of sheep. The bell-wether leading the flock is proverbial.

The same principle applies to all other herd animals, but is less obvious among those which have long been domesticated and kept in enclosures.

The social life of horses has only a very scanty literature devoted to it. In the case of South America the English reader will think of W. H. Hudson's *A Little Boy Lost*, but G. Dadányi, a former cavalry officer of the Hungarian Army, also wrote a book about his experiences as a herdsman in Paraguay, in which he described how the half-wild bands of horses were led by a *mandrina* or bell-mare in the direction desired by the herdsmen. As a young boy I too was employed in herding colts, and have had similar experiences. (Note 1.)

In the case of domesticated horses the leadership function is commonly taken up by an elderly mare, usually conspicuous for her bad temper. If there are several contenders for the title a duel ensues. In the herd itself an interesting reflex action may be observed. If one of the horses is frightened it runs to the leader, while the others graze on unperturbed. But if the leading horse itself is alarmed, then the rest of the herd will gallop off after it.

But these observations are true only of domestic herds, from which stallions are usually absent. The bell-mare is a substitute, but in wild herds or herds which closely resemble the truly wild band of primeval horses (as on Exmoor) the most alert and aggressive adult stallion is the leader. [Only on Exmoor in the absence of an adult stallion the senior entire colt will not automatically succeed to the leadership, but some crafty and cantankerous old mare. *Tr.*] The Polish scholar W. Pruski (1959) in his book about the admixture of Tarpan blood in East European horses observes that domestic horses were often to be seen in the Tarpan herds, but these were all runaway mares, or mares that had been enticed away by Tarpan stallions. On the other hand, nobody had ever seen a runaway stallion take to the steppe and possess the Tarpan mares. Not only would the nearest wild stallion have torn him to shreds, but even if there were none present the wild mares would never accept him as a trustworthy leader of the herd, because he had lost the qualities essential to self-preservation which all born-wild horses possess, male and female alike.

The King Stallion's part does not consist only in holding the herd together and leading it to the best pasture and water. The duelling between stallions, the victor's mastery of the mares, is something essential for the natural selection of the best sire, and herd instinct was the force that created and maintained the communal life of horses in the wild. (Note 2.)

The foregoing explains why the early herdsman began to ride. It identified him, so to speak, physically with the equine leader, from whose back he could keep his herd together or lead it in the right direction rather than drive it, and this was so in the case of camels and cattle as well as horses. The roots of this procedure lie in the pleasure which young children take in romping with young animals. It was reported of the Huns that their children rode calves and foals, the smallest ones even sheep and goats. Thence to the mounting of adult animals by adults was but a step.

This is not to say that the nomad herdsman rode only stallions, and from the examples given above we see that this was not necessary. As the practice of our day demonstrates, the experienced horse-herder may employ the right sort of old mare for this purpose, especially if the herd is not only led but 'whipped-in' from the rear.

Thus riding and driving proceed from two different techniques of stock-keeping. Riding was a decisive aid to pasturing herds in the open country, and driving carts became necessary as permanent occupation of fields demanded more transport. As time went on the extreme forms of exclusive riding and exclusive driving became rarer. Transitional forms arose, in which the drivers occasionally rode their animals, and the riders occasionally harnessed theirs. And from this the point was reached in the history of transportation at which the Equestrian Era begins.

The Primary Centre of Nomadic Stock-breeding

The broad steppe region of Central Asia, which stretches north-west from the Great Wall of China to the mountain ranges of Outer Mongolia, is believed to be the place where nomad horse-breeding had its origin. This preliminary hypothesis rests neither on traditions of historical happenings nor on the fact that the last herds of truly wild horses survived there until recently. But the circumstance that this part of Asia has over the centuries been the storm-centre from which great swarms of horsemen have emerged means that horse-breeding there has been of great historical importance.

Down to our day the nomadic way of breeding horses is still practised in Mongolia, though now only a remnant of what it has been. Nature has provided extraordinary opportunities for stock-breeding, primarily because this was the habitat of three species of wild mammal of great importance to the human economy: the reindeer, the horse, and the camel.

A unique feature of the region is the presence of reindeer. [Only one such anachronistic pocket is known in Western Europe—in Caithness and Sutherland, in Northern Scotland, the reindeer survived into Viking times. *Tr.*] The natural territory of this animal in the wild lies between the 60th and 80th parallels of latitude. Its occurrence in the Sayan Mountains of Mongolia, along the 51st Parallel, is only to be explained by the fact that the highest mountains, rising to 6000 feet, of the Sayan range still support the characteristic flora of the Ice Age, including isolated colonies of reindeer-moss.

Reindeer-mounted Archer. Rock drawing from Tepsei, on the Upper Yenesei, first century B.C.
From Hančar, 1955

In our sketch above of Hančar's theory we have pointed out the crucial role of the reindeer in primitive stock-raising. How do scholars regard the progress of domestication of this deer? During the Ice Age the reindeer was widely distributed in what was then the cooler part of the North Temperate Zone, as is proved by numerous excavations and by the abundance of reindeer pictures in the cave art of France and Spain. Climatic changes at the end of this period led to a northward displacement as well as a shrinking of territory on the part of this and other Cervidae. The reindeer migrated northward to the border of the coniferous forests with the tundra, to which it is still confined, except for some herds in Scandinavia which migrate as far south as Hardanger Vidda. This hardy, abstemious, and easily tameable deer was, according to archaeological evidence, among the first animals to be domesticated.

The Sayan reindeer is, therefore, together with the moss on which it feeds, a survival from the Ice Age. In contrast to the archaeological evidence, written accounts of reindeer-keeping begin comparatively late, in the East. While the reindeer economy of Northern Scandinavia is mentioned in some detail by King Alfred in his translation of Orosius (round about A.D. 900), it is not until the thirteenth century that we have in Marco Polo's account of the Empire of Cathay and his journey to it by land some mention of tribes north of the Great Wall 'who ride on stags'. But other accounts did reach the West by different channels, as in Eden Richet's book published in 1555, where the forest-dwelling 'Scyths' along the wooded shores of Lake Baikal are described as riding cloven-hoofed animals the size of a mule which he calls 'reen'. [But as this is wooded country, as the reindeer is only the size of a rather small mule, and as the elk—the moose of North America —when it has no horns, as in the castrated male, looks much more like a mule, and is nearer to it in size than the reindeer, Richet's 'Scyths' may have been elk-borne. He is quoted by Carruthers in *Unknown Mongolia*, 1913. Incidentally, Peter the Great passed an edict against the capture alive and taming of elk; the reason for this *ukas* was that political exiles had been known to escape from Siberia on elk-back. *Tr.*] The attention of scholars was not drawn to this reindeer culture of Mongolia until rather late in the day, and these people are still little known to the ethnologist. Their way of life is that of primitive herders and hunters, at about the Neolithic level. What its significance is, in the development of pastoral and economic technique, we shall presently see. Russians made the first research into their language and way of life, but these descriptions, which were published early in the present century, aroused little interest. In 1911 Douglas Carruthers travelled from Minusinsk to Mongolia via the Sayan Mountains, and in the course of his journey met the mountaineers, in the forests. His journal contains a detailed ethnographical description of them. Unfortunately, two world wars and the intervening events hindered the continuation of his researches. In 1959 Miklós Gábori visited the reindeer-breeding hunters of the Khardyl-Sardik Mountains south of the Sayan. He published his findings in scientific periodicals, and in his account of Mongolia. Although these are not primarily concerned with reindeer-breeding, and do not give adequate answers to all the questions that arise in our inquiry into the history of transport, they will serve as a basis for a summary of the environment of the Sayan reindeer-herders.

These forest-dwellers, who call themselves Uryanchai, belong to the Altaic (Turkic-speaking) family of peoples and seem to be related, on linguistic grounds, to the neighbouring Soyets and South Siberian Karagasses. At the outset of this century there were 2000 of them or more; now there are only a few hundreds left.

They wander about in bands consisting of two or three families. They are chiefly occupied in hunting. Summer and winter they are out in the wooded Sayan hills, and the Khardyl-Sardik range. Their only domestic animal is the reindeer, which also occurs wild in the area; they milk it, ride it, and carry pack-saddles on it. They do not, like the Lapps, use sledges. They will eat reindeer meat only in the direst extremity.

Their stock-economy is of the Central Asian pattern. In summer the herds pasture on the grassy clearings of the upper slopes. On the march to fresh pastures the herdsman rides a reindeer at the head of the herd, while another mounted herdsman 'whips in' at the rear. They also use the reindeer for hunting elk, wild reindeer, chamois, and bear, since the boggy ground is for the most part impassable for horses, with their solid hoofs, but tolerable going for the reindeer, with its splayed cloven hoof. When they come within range they shoot the game with rifles from the saddle, but formerly they did so with the bow, according to Gábori.

The more characteristic nomad way of herding comes out more clearly in winter. When the upper slopes are covered with snow they do not drive their herds down the mountain but to exposed places where the wind sweeps the reindeer-moss clear of snow. From a historical point of view, this proves that their economy was limited by the occurrence of this moss. We shall have occasion later to refer to economic pressures of this nature.

The riding equipment of the Uryanchai herdsmen approximates to that of equestrian peoples, but is more primitive. They have neither bridle nor bit; the deer are steered by a thong which leads from the rider's hand to a loop round the neck. Their saddles, on the other hand, are a primitive variation—perhaps the original form—of the wooden saddles of equestrian peoples. The horizontal bars which rest on pads on either side of the animal's spine are not joined by arches, but

Mounted Archer, about 1200 B.C.
Rock drawing from Ladak, after C. Diem, 1941.

by two X-shaped forks, and the seat is a leather sling between these two forks. As in the horseman's saddle, the stirrup-leathers are attached to the bars on either side.

All signs indicate that thousands of years ago the transition from reindeer to horse as a riding animal took place here and under these special conditions. Proof is found not only in the typological development of the horse saddle from the reindeer saddle but also in the findings of archaeology and ethnology. In the shamanistic religion of people of Turkic/Mongolian culture the cult-ceremonies of the horse-sacrifice and the reindeer-sacrifice are very similar. The most striking evidence for the transition is in the change in the method of exploitation. In the whole polar zone of Eurasia, from Norway to the Bering Strait—that is, in the main body of its natural post-glacial habitat—the reindeer is used in draught, but it is not ridden, and where it is milked this can be shown to be due to the influence of neighbouring cattle-milkers to the south. In the Sayan, on the contrary, it is exclusively ridden and milked—so that the method of exploitation by nomadic horsemen and Uryanchai reindeer herdsmen is the same. Herodotus in the fifth century mentioned among other Scythian customs that of drinking mare's milk.

But in use for transport there is one other factor which points to a connection between the reindeer and the horse in this region, and perhaps here alone. The Lapps of Arctic Europe, and also the Voguls, Ostyaks, Samoyedes, Chukches, and Koryaks of Arctic Asia, all have a common history in the past of dog-drawn sleighs, dog-power having presumably first been used to supplement the tractive power of men (or more likely women) in sleigh harness. The dogs in turn were displaced by reindeer. Their methods of harnessing and guiding reindeer are all similar. The Tungus, neighbours of the Uryanchai, have been exposed to twin influences, those of riding and driving, so that they both ride their reindeer and use them in draught, as do the Yakuts.

As mentioned above, the Uryanchai only ride their reindeer and use them under the pack-saddle, never in harness. But a peculiar thing about their economy is that they have no dogs, a surprising lacuna among a hunting people. In the absence of the link, in northern latitudes, between the man-drawn sledge and the reindeer team an entirely different line of development was followed, and the possibility of riding and driving arising from a common source is excluded.

Now, to return to the traces of nomadic pastoralism as formerly practised in Mongolia. Besides horses, herds of camels and flocks of sheep were bred; these three species gradually became indispensable for life on the steppes. The only bovid was the Himalayan variety, the yak, imported from Tibet and also used for riding and pack traffic, the yak cows being milked. Later domestic cattle were introduced from China, bringing with them the two-wheeled ox-cart.

Mongolia, the original home of nomadic pastoralism, did not only stamp its impression on stock-breeding; its effect, however indirectly, on the political history of Eurasia was even more important. Knowledge of the evolution that led from nomadic reindeer-breeding through horse-keeping to the riding of the horse is the answer to the question why Mongolia over the centuries has been again and again the calm heart of the hurricane out of which the storms of horse archers have blown so devastatingly. When the economic factors are also taken into consideration, it becomes even more apparent that it was the mounted warrior who during that momentous period known as the Migration of Peoples was solely responsible for wrenching the world off its hinges.

"The Centre of the World"

Travellers in their descriptions of political and economic life among the Central Asian peoples during the nineteenth century are unanimous in emphasizing that the quarrels among the nomadic tribes who were then living under primeval conditions were principally due to economic causes. The historian and ethnologist Armin Vámberi says of the Turkomans in the heart of Turania during the seventies:

> Added to external pressure [he means conquest by Tsarist Russia] was internal strife, almost always about grazing grounds and irrigation canals branching off from perennial rivers. Water and grazing are here indispensable, and this explains the bitterness with which for instance Yomuds and Tekkes (near the Akhal oasis) fought each other for centuries . . .

The Swiss H. Moser said the same thing ten years later, though by 1888 the political independence of these nomadic tribes was vanishing. Only the final triumph of Tsarist power brought an end to these sanguinary struggles for water and grazing in Central Asia. Moser describes the traditions which individual tribes had inherited of the earlier migrations. Thus the Kirghiz still vividly remembered that they had once lived much farther east. When their stock was threatened by lack of grazing they set off westward, driving out the Kalmucks from the grounds which they then occupied.

Historical traditions of earlier periods are all of a piece with this. Thus Arab sources record the Seljuk Turks as having once run their herds on the grasslands round Bokhara, Khorasan, and Khoresmia, which they had gained by force. Again and again in Hungarian chronicles stress is laid on the importance of grazing and water. The scouts preceding the Magyar invaders were always on the lookout for good grass and abundant pure water, and this motif occurs in the legend of the White Horse, in which the Magyar chiefs ask Prince Sviatopolk in exchange for a splendidly caparisoned horse only a bundle of grass and a jug of Danube water. Later they interpreted this exchange of gifts to mean that the symbolic grass and water entitled them to graze their herds all over the Danubian plain and water them in the river—in practice, to take possession of Sviatopolk's country. The same procedure was repeated with the Bulgarian prince, asking of him water from the Tisza, sand, and grass from Alpar. The same motives kept the Huns on the move, as a Chinese source of the first century A.D. mentions them moving across the steppe in search of grazing and water.

The gain or loss of watering-places and pasture made a difference, for the nomad, between riches and poverty, even between life and death from famine. Their herds had increased, as shown above, in proportion as they learnt better animal husbandry by experience, but this very increase led to friction between flock-masters of the kind described often in the patriarchal chapters of the Old Testament. For instance:

> And the land was not able to bear them, that they [Lot and Abram] might dwell together; for their substance was great, so that they could not dwell together.
> And there was a strife between the herdmen of Abram's cattle and the herdmen of Lot's cattle: and the Canaanite and the Perizzite dwelled then in the land. (Genesis, xiii, 6, 7.)

[Here we have the added complication, which had its counterpart in Central Asia, of the settled farmers—the Canaanites and Perizzites whose demands on grazing would be less, but who at certain seasons would consume as much water as the herdsmen; moreover, their arable fields would lie along the river-banks. Such tensions arose between proprietors of 'great substance', because to pastoralists at this stage there is no such thing as over-stocking. One could, of course, have eaten or sold or exchanged the surplus cattle, but then that would be the end of one's reputation as 'the Man with a Thousand Cows', even though the remaining stock would have been in better condition. It is quantity of livestock, not quality, which confers prestige in such societies. *Tr.*]

The almost infinite perspective of early tribal wanderings in Central Asia has not yet been the subject of exhaustive research. Where historical and archaeological inquiry will not suffice, the findings of allied sciences may help the solution of some questions.

Before Columbus demonstrated the globular shape of the world and Magellan's crew came back from its first circumnavigation people thought of the earth as a plate-like disc: the centre of its surface, therefore, would be 'the middle of the world'. Although various rationalizations at different times and places attempted to locate it, this Navel of the World, even at the time when it was most seriously believed in, remained a mystical concept. It was possible to see it as the point of departure of centrifugal forces that for many thousands of years had determined human history. Just as a stone thrown into a pond sets up concentric rings of waves, so forces originating at the centre of the region where pastoral economy was first practised set up waves represented by the increase of herds and pressure on grazing facilities, which finally set in motion the Migration of Peoples. Neighbouring tribes came to blows, and in each case the loser had to vacate his pastures and his homestead, unless he were to face utter extermination. His only recourse was to drive his herds off, into the territory of some weaker pastoral tribe, which in turn he would displace and overpower. This pressure was not exercised solely on the tribes immediately involved, but its effects were apparent among distant peoples, especially among the weaker or less sophisticated.

It is highly probable that these movements originated among reindeer-breeders; but with the appearance of horse-breeders they reached their zenith. The nomad soon learned the advantages which being mounted on reindeer or horse brought, both in herding and in hunting, and he learned to apply these to warfare. As this mode of fighting was brought to perfection it became apparent that harmony between rider and mount was as important as the strength and valour of the rider. Thus a new chapter in the history of warfare came to be written.

The spread of nomadic pastoralism in prehistoric times was always governed by certain geographical and climatic limitations as to its direction. This is evident in the traces of migrations initiated by the reindeer-herders. The Uigurs, practising nomadic reindeer-breeding in the Sayan range, forced the Tungus out of their neighbouring hunting and grazing grounds, and the Tungus in turn drove the Siberian Yakuts northward, displacing the Samoyedes to the north-west and the Koryaks and Chukches to the east; the object of the displaced being all the time to find new winter pasture for their herds—that is, tracts of ground where the reindeer-moss grew. (Note 3.)

Here we come to another interesting fact: the Eskimo of North America came

5
Horseman of the ♦
century B.C. Num♦
from Pazyryk bar♦
Altai Mountains
Hermitage Museum
Leningrad

24

6 The Taki or Mongolian Wild Horse

7 The same, believed to be the only one photographed under a rider. Askania Nova, 1907
Ziemsen Verlag Wittenberg

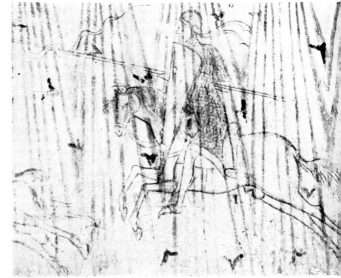

8 Detail from Fresco in Apse of Cathedral at Aquileia: Knight with Pointed Shield and Lance, pursuing . . .
Acta Archaeologica Hungarica

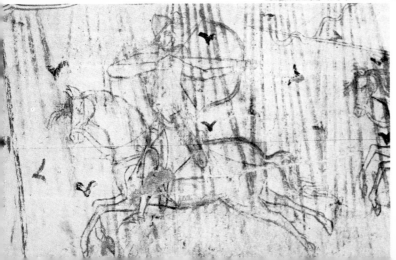

9 . . . Hungarian Raider mounted on Gelding, armed with Bow and Sabre, virtually without Body-armour. *Twelfth century or earlier*
Acta Archaeologica Hungarica

10
Uryanchai Girls riding
Reindeer bareback

11
Reindeer showing
Uryanchai Pattern of
Saddle

12   Mongol herding
Camels

13   Reindeer Mask from Pazyryk
Hermitage, Leningrad

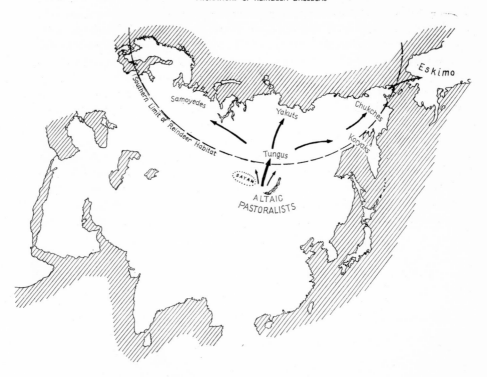

from North-east Asia, the first of them in Mesolithic times, but in many waves since then, and these later crossings of the Bering Strait by Eskimo and Amerindian tribes may have been due to the pressure of the expanding reindeer-breeders of East Siberia. To this day the Eskimo practise a hunting and fishing economy, and their only domestic animal is the dog. The reindeer, in its American form of the caribou, was present in the new continent, but the fact that the Eskimo never attempted to domesticate it must point to their having crossed the Strait at a time before reindeer-herding had become general in Northern Siberia, and so they have remained specialized as hunters and fishermen. [At these callings they have reached a high level of technical skill. Like other North Eurasian hunting tribes since Mesolithic times, they used a composite (wood and horn or whalebone) bow, and before the introduction of firearms some tribes on the west side of Hudson's Bay used a crossbow of such penetrating power that it would even pierce the tough frontal bone of the musk-ox. *Tr.*] The southward migrations of the later waves of Eskimo, in their turn, touched off further migrations among other Amerindian tribes [but these were of a different kind, since flocks and herds were not involved; nor were the Eskimo warlike. Probably as hunters they were more efficient; they did not expel the Indian tribes by conquest; the latter just could not compete with them once the 'easier' meat animals had been killed off, and the Eskimo—but not other races—were able to make a living off what remained. *Tr.*]

The expansive force moving northward in the eastern part of Asia began to slow down when the reindeer-riders of the Mongolian region went over to horse-riding, since they could not then pass the northern limits of the natural habitat of

25

the wild horse (see p. 16). Now the expansion had to take place east and west. Throughout historical time the pattern is the same—the swarms of horsemen, Huns, Ephthalites, Avars, Turks, and Mongols, from the Pacific to the Atlantic, only operated between certain parallels of latitude, which were a prolongation east and west of the home of Przewalski's Horse. Their entry on the agrarian scene brought a novelty, in the form of horse-breeding in herds on open ranges, to Eastern Europe.

[By contrast, it is worth noting that military conquest *by charioteers* overstepped the natural boundaries of the wild-horse habitat as early as the second millennium B.C. *Tr.*]

The pressure exercised by the equestrian tribes had its effect not only to the east and to the west but also to the north and to the south. This particularly affected people whose way of life was not materially affected by changes of climate. Among such were the Indo-European language group, which perhaps may be equated, archaeologically, with the "battle-axe" people who in the third millennium B.C. were moving out of the Central Asian region. Some of them turned south, and

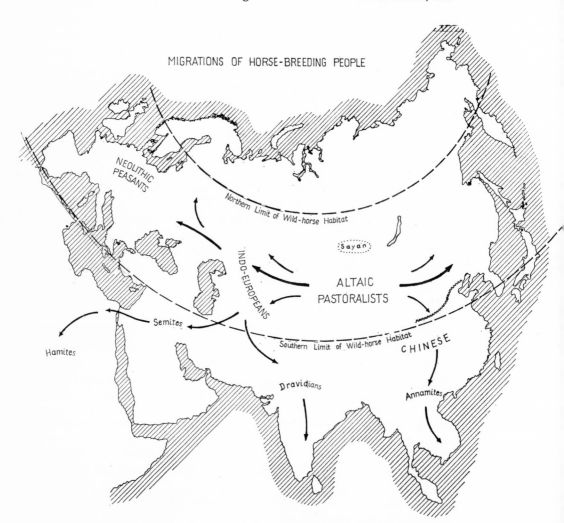

MIGRATIONS OF HORSE-BREEDING PEOPLE

under the name of Aryans conquered India and Persia; the Hittites, Kassites, and Mitannians entered Asia Minor, while the Celts and later the Germans penetrated North and West Europe. All these were chariot-driving, not originally riding, aristocracies.

These movements in their turn all put to flight or subjected peoples of other stock and language. In the south the Dravidians who had originally peopled all India were driven down towards Ceylon, and even into the islands of the Indian Ocean. The Hittites pressing on into Anatolia subjugated the Sumerians, the Mitannians and Kassites overcame the Semitic tribes or drove them back into the Arabian peninsula, and this Semitic recoil had its repercussions among Hamitic peoples farther south. The advance of the Celts and Germans into Europe displaced the Finno-Ugric peoples towards the Baltic, who pushed the European Lapps into Northern Scandinavia.

The mounted herdsmen who were the prime cause of these migrations at last appeared on the scene of historically recorded events, but we do not know the actual date of their 'explosion'. We can only infer it by reference to the time when the sedentary farmers began to be displaced. But the Far East soon began to be the scene of new changes. The full weight of nomadic expansion turned westwards exclusively as soon as the Chinese Empire had become a great political power, in the second half of the first millennium, and was at last able to offer successful resistance to the Asiatic Huns. The hard-hitting Chinese armies and the Great Wall together barred the way to nomad peoples seeking expansion to the east and south-east. They recoiled in the direction of Europe, in the end penetrating as far as the Atlantic. This invasion left visible traces on the ethnographic map of Europe.

The last swarm of horsemen was the Mongol expansion under Jenghis Khan. Although the economic causes of these migrations had continued secondary effects, in that the search for grazing and water still led to war and unrest in the Oriental regions, after the Mongol invasions the displacements at last came to a halt. The superiority of the horseman in battle progressively lost momentum in the same measure as the peoples attacked adopted the technique and tactics of the invaders themselves, and began to use the horse as a weapon, or at least as a weapon-carrier. No longer was riding a monopoly of the warrior-herdsman.

The re-establishment of strategic equilibrium brought back order and stability to the disordered ranks of the Eurasian family of nations. The horse that once had borne the apocalyptic riders out of the heart of Nomad's Land had acted out the last line of his historical role. From now on horses were not only at the service of the warrior but the aides of creative man, supporting his advance to higher things.

Migrations and the Mounted Warrior

Tolstov called the social organization of the pastoral peoples a military state with the institution of slavery. The herdsmen were not only masters in their exploitation of animal resources; in the course of centuries of warfare they acquired more and more the taste for the exploitation of human labour. The mounted warrior's most valuable booty came to be the prisoner of war who could be enslaved. As the economic interests of many pastoral tribes widened they came to include an organized slave-trade.

Over the centuries of chronic war and migration riding technique had reached a high state of perfection. Among the nomads this high standard of horsemanship marked great advances in the arts of transport, communications, and warfare. The military superiority of equestrian nations was made manifest in the Migration of Peoples.

Among the nations first exposed to attack by mounted enemies, the predominant reaction was defensive. Its most impressive monument is the Great Wall of China, along the northern frontier. Remains of a similar defensive line have been found north-east of Kabul, on what was once the Bactrian frontier. It consists of a series of brick walls 17 metres broad traversing uninhabited territory, up hill and down dale, like similar defensive works of which traces have been found at intervals all the way from there to the Hungarian plain.

A self-contained defensive system has also been unearthed in the deserts of Kara-Kum and Kyzyl-Kum. This sterile wilderness was in antiquity, and still in the Middle Ages, a highly developed civilized region, dependent on irrigation canals which distributed water from the tributaries of the Amu-Darya as they flowed out of the Afghan mountains. The attention of scholars has only recently been directed to this ancient civilization. Air photography has supplemented the excavations by Soviet archaeologists before 1939. The plains are covered with drifted sand, underneath which are the remains of a dense network of irrigation channels and the settlements of the first Khoresmian farmers.

But the chief significance of this discovery is military. As well as displacing the agrarian population, the drifting sand has preserved the remains of a peculiar system of defensive works which are the relics of the wars between the Khoresmian settlers or Massagetes, and the nomads. The *Zend-Avesta*, or teaching of Zarathustra, contains many traditions of the centuries-old Khoresmian civilization. According to it, the Massagetes lived in fortified settlements which are known in archaeological parlance as *gorodyishche*. These were so laid out that their four sides were used as living-quarters, while cattle were kept in the central courtyard. As a defence against repeated attacks by mounted enemies the outer walls contained loopholes for archery, and there were towers on them. Finally, from the first century B.C. onwards, fortresses were built whose sole purpose was defence.

The Massagetes were crop farmers at a high level of civilization. According to the *Avesta*, they were organized socially, about the second millennium B.C., in three classes; priests of fire, warriors, and commoners (farmers). The warrior caste was called *rataista*, a word which originally meant 'charioteer', and is derived from the common Indo-European root *rad-*, meaning wheel, though at this time we may assume that riding was gaining ground among them. Herodotus describes them as a heavily armed nation of horsemen, similar in costume and customs to the Scyths. They fought on foot and on horseback, their horses being armoured.

Riding spread to their western neighbours even later, the chariot still being in use in Eastern Europe at a time when the Massagetes were already fighting on horseback. In the lands about the Black Sea this was still true in the times of Herodotus, who says: "The limitless plains beyond the Lower Danube are peopled by the Sigynnes, who dress like the Medes. The winter coat of their horses is five fingers thick, but they are small; they are blunt-nosed and are only driven in harness, being too small to carry a man."

In the Carpathian basin, home of the Tarpan (p. 13) and still inhabited by its tame descendant the *Hucul* pony, riding can only be shown to have been practised after the time of the Sarmatians, and in more westerly regions later than that. According to Tacitus, some Germanic tribes still fought from the chariot in the first century A.D., and only gave up this technique on entering Roman employment as auxiliaries. In the century before that the British force which opposed Caesar's invasion consisted partly of mounted men, partly of chariots. [Chariots were still found in the Caledonian host which opposed the army of Agricola in A.D. 84, somewhere in the Scottish highlands. They were still in use in Ireland in the time of St Patrick. *Tr.*]

But the transference from the chariot to the saddle did not automatically give the newly converted squadrons parity with their adversaries, even in single combat. It took time to learn equitation, and to master the individual arms that went with horsemanship, as opposed to chariot-fighting, let alone the elements of squadron tactics. The Western equipment was rather defensive as opposed to the armament of the Eastern horsemen, which consisted of a short bow that could be used from the saddle, and a sabre. Horse and rider had to be armoured against the arrows.

Armourers came predominantly from the ranks of those peoples who were threatened by mounted enemies. Thus the armour made at Merv by Massagetic smiths was famed in antiquity, and much prized.

But it was precisely armour which impeded the adoption of the highly mobile tactics of nomad warfare. The pike and the javelin suitable for close combat remained in use after the agricultural levies had become mounted. However, in conformity with mounted service they were transformed into the lance, which was effective in the hands of massed armoured horsemen, but only if these were organized in large squadrons.

For a long time armoured mounted troops fought the mounted archers on equal terms, but in the end both armour and heavy non-missile weapons were laid aside, and the tactics of the Eastern cavalry adopted.

The Bactrian or Turanian Horse

Chinese sources are the first to mention this horse. In 126 B.C. Imperial envoys reported that in the distant land of Taiyuan marvellous blood-sweating 'heavenly' horses were bred.

This land of the wonderful horses was the Bactrian kingdom, at that time an important centre of central Asiatic civilization, on the northern slopes of the Afghan mountain ranges. That part of it which lay round the upper Syr-Darya river was called Ferghana, in Chinese Taiyuan; and the most important trade-route of antiquity, the Silk Road, traversed it from east to west. Bactra, the capital of the kingdom, had as its city badge a galloping horse, the symbol of traffic. Its lively trade with foreign countries had been since the fourth century in the hands of Greek (specifically Macedonian) colonists.

But the origin of Bactrian horse-breeding goes back further than that. When Alexander the Great was on his way to the conquest of India he remounted his cavalry on Bactrian horses, before the Chinese became aware of their existence. He also employed Bactrian mercenary cavalry. But even before that, in the time of the Achaemenid dynasty which began in 599, when Bactria had been a dependent satrapy of the Persian Empire, such Bactrian troopers served in the Persian army.

The Persian word *asp*—horse—is found at the time of the earlier independent Bactrian kings, the house of Kavanida, in the names of legendary heroes such as Aurvataspa and Vitaspa, and the ancient royal seat of Bactria was called Zariaspa. The tribal names Zariaspai and Arimaspai mean 'golden horses' and 'well-schooled horses' respectively.

Coin of King Eutractides of Bactria
From Rowland 1961

In the reign of King Yuë-chi (to give him his Chinese name) of Bactria the Chinese Emperor sent repeated embassies to him, seeking to buy horses, but in vain. At last he sent him a thousand gold pieces and a horse of solid gold, to help change his mind. But even this did not have the desired effect. Yuë-chi threw the envoys into prison and had them executed for attempting to escape. So now the Emperor Wu tried what force of arms would do. His first assault was beaten off. At the second attempt Yuë-chi was besieged in his palace. The spoils of this campaign included 30 blood-sweating horses, and 3000 half-bred mares and stallions. With this stock the Chinese Emperor set up stud-farms and covering centres, which according to Sven Hedin were the beginning of serious Chinese horse-breeding.

But the Chinese were not the only beneficiaries of this dispersal. Their records in the second century B.C. mention that the king of the Asiatic Huns, Tuman, possessed a 'thousand-mile' horse which after his death the people of Tung-hu demanded for themselves. We may assume that this horse was a widely known stallion with the conformation and characteristics of the 'heavenly' horses.

From this document, and from the anxiety of the Chinese to obtain horses of quality, we may conclude that the most dangerous enemies of the Chinese, the Huns, owed their superiority not to their valour but to the superior stamp of horse they rode. Eventually the Imperial forces were able to match the superiority of the Huns in matters of horsemanship. The Huns were turned westward largely because of the increased efficiency of Chinese cavalry, who came to be mounted on better horses once the remount studs began to feel the effect of better breeding-stock derived from exotic hot-blooded strains.

The Pazyryk Burial

There are still many uncertainties for archaeology to clear up concerning stock-breeding in early historical times, but so far as horse-breeding in Central Asia is concerned much valuable data has been obtained from one source alone.

Westward from Mongolia, in the high valley of Ulagan in the Altai mountains,

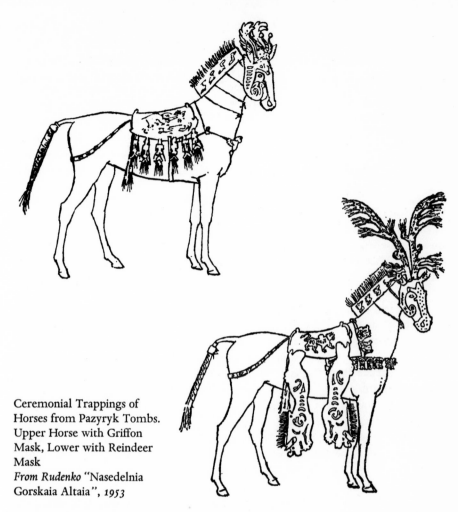

Ceremonial Trappings of
Horses from Pazyryk Tombs.
Upper Horse with Griffon
Mask, Lower with Reindeer
Mask
*From Rudenko "Nasedelnia
Gorskaia Altaia", 1953*

near Pazyryk, the graves of rich herd-owners who died in the middle of the first
millennium B.C. were discovered by Russian explorers and fully described by S. I.
Rudenko.[1] The tombs, known as *kurgans* or barrows, were shafts of rectangular
section revetted with solid beams such as are used to build wooden houses in the
same region today, and lined with felt hangings as the walls of the inmate's own
houses must have been lined in life. By a strange and probably unrepeatable combination of climatic accidents, masses of ice formed in the tombs soon after inter-
ment, thus preserving organic material of all kinds in a deep-freeze. Corpses, leather,
textiles, furs, horn, bone and wooden objects, food both human and animal, were
preserved almost unaltered by decay. Thus where in other finds we only have bits
and buckles, here we have whole bridles. Where elsewhere we have only the skele-
tons, and rarely the whole skeleton, of horses, here we have hair and hide and flesh.
For anything between seven and fourteen horses were found in each grave-shaft.
This unique find enabled 69 more or less perfect horse cadavers of the fifth century
B.C. to be recovered, including even the stomach contents. The only comparable

[1] Published by J. M. Dent, 1969.

finds are the frozen mammoths of an earlier Siberian age, and the mummified corpses from the Danish bogs, which so far have been exclusively human, so that no contemporary European horses are available for comparison with those of Pazyryk.

The height of these at the withers varied from nearly 13 to 15 hands in the adult. [No foals were found, but some of the clothing was trimmed with foal-fur. *Tr.*] On the basis of stature and build they could be divided into four groups. Comparison of a horse from the first group with one from the fourth showed distinct evidence of the breeding of different types, one of which we should today call highly bred, the other a common sort of utility horse. The following peculiarities were noted, among others:

Group I was from 14 hands 3 in. high, to 15 hands. Their common characteristic was an impressive head, with concave profile and high neck carriage, short in the back, strong, 'dry' limbs with well-developed joints. The readiest comparison among present-day light-horse breeds is with the Arab, despite the coarser skeletal build of the Pazyryk horse. All were light-coloured, mostly golden dun, with black mane and tail. Since bridles and saddles were buried with them, they were obviously riding-horses. They correspond to Ebhardt's Type IV, though taller.

The height of horses in Group IV (Pazyryk), or the common horses, was about 13 hands 1½ in. They had short necks attached low to the body, long backs, with relatively short legs. They were buried with harness, and were intended to draw the four-wheeled living-wagon which had been used as a hearse. They resembled closely Ebhardt's Pony Type II. Examination of the stomach contents provided interesting results. They consisted partly of grain, showing that the horses had been kept in stables. The geldings had all been castrated before they were fully grown—evidence of systematic breeding.

This find tends to confirm the testimony of Chinese records, according to which the equine stock of Central Asia was up-graded by a highly bred strain. Furthermore, the remains prove that this up-grading took place shortly before the Hunnish on-slaught on China.

The saddles and bridles found were identical in pattern with that shown in the gold plate on Plate 20, which is Siberian, but not from the Pazyryk site. In general the scarcity of breakable objects such as pottery points to a nomadic tradition as does the general style of their equipment and accoutrements; the great plenty of felt and furs and leather goods of all kinds, especially saddle-bags; and the fact that all the textiles except felt can be shown to be imports. The Bactrian influence in horse-breeding, and hence on horsemanship, is demonstrably more recent than the wagon-borne way of life that lay in the immediate past of these Altaians. The historic role of the Bactrian horse appears all the clearer in the light of modern horse-breeding experience and practice.

Medieval and Modern Times

Very little is known about Bactria in the period following the reign of Yüe-chi. It is mentioned in the sixth century as forming part of the Ephthalite confederacy of states. This was a league of nomads that covered a vast area, but endured only until the years 563–567, when the Turks of Central Asia left their tribal territory and set up a new nomad empire in the area between the Great Wall and the Don. At this

14 Upper Palaeolithic *Art Mobilier*—Statuette of 'Quality' Horse from Lental in Württemberg

15 'Quality' Horses in the Cave Paintings of Altamira

16
Akhal-Tekke Stallion
from Turkmenistan

17
Mare from the Akhal
Oasis, Turkmenistan

18
Onager-drawn Quadriga
from Tell Agrab, about
2600 B.C.
Oriental Institute, University of Chicago

19   Assyrian War-chariot from Tell Agrab

20 Siberian Gold Plate, First
Millennium B.C.
Hermitage, Leningrad
(Peter the Great's Siberian collection)

21 Hunnish Horseman of Migration
Period, dragging Prisoner by the
Hair
Gold vase from Nagyszentmiklos, in
Hofschatzkammer, Vienna

time Bactria split up into several independent principates. About the state of horse-breeding in these we have no immediate information. But the Turkmenian or Turanian horses bred in the adjoining territory of Turkestan prove the survival of this breed.

Both Bactria and Turkestan were conquered by the Arabs—or by the Muslim host, the nucleus of which was still Arab—during the eighth century. Arab travellers provide a rich source of information about Central Asian conditions at that time, and incidentally about the Turanian horse. At that time it enjoyed a great reputation, not only in the Far East but also in the West. Arabian journals of travel in the ninth and tenth centuries always emphasize the importance of the export of Bactrian horses from Kotal.

After the Seljuk Turks had advanced as far as Asia Minor—which led to the collapse of Arab power in Central Asia—the world was shaken by the ravages of Jenghis Khan's Mongol armies. This also struck a blow at Turanian horse-breeding, because all the most valuable stock in the conquered territories was haled off to Mongolia. Timur-i-leng or Tamerlane (1336-1405), founder of a new nomad dynasty, attempted to revive Turanian breeding by distributing five thousand brood mares among the Turkoman tribes.

That famous Venetian Marco Polo, who travelled through these countries in the late thirteenth century, says of horse-breeding there:

> They breed a great many excellent horses, very swift. They are never shod, though they run on the mountains and on stony ground, very bad roads, for their legs are superb and their hoofs very hard. They can carry their rider down slopes so steep that other horses will not face them or can only be got to do so with difficulty; but this they do at speed.

Marco Polo describes the extinction of the breed thus:

> It was told Messere Marco that in the province of Badasan [in Northern Afghanistan] there was until recently a breed of horses that were descended from Bucephalus, Alexander the Great's horse, and among them the foals were born with a star and a crescent moon on their foreheads, as if Bucephalus himself had covered the mares. Only the king's uncle possessed this strain. But as he refused even to let the king have some of them, the latter condemned him to death, and in revenge his widow destroyed the entire stud.

Contact was lost during the three hundred years of the Turkish menace, between Europe and Central Asia. The only news of it that reached Europe did so via Persian and thence Ottoman intermediaries, and only occasionally did a Turanian-bred horse reach a European stud (and then often under another name), as for example some foundation sires from Turkestan used at Trakehnen in the eighteenth and nineteenth centuries; but it is to them that that famous breed owes its reputation.

Reports from the nineteenth century, or the second half of it, give a more comprehensive picture of horse-breeding among the Turkomans. The pure Turanian breed had by then long been a thing of the past; and the 'heavenly heritage' of the blood-sweating golden horses of old Taiyuan only gleamed faintly here and there among Turkoman tribesmen and in some princely private studs in South Russia. But many attempts were made at a conscious revival of the old breed. For instance, Nasreddin, Shah of Persia, gave the Turkoman breeders six hundred mares. About the beginning of this century private studs in the Khanate of Karabakh tried to 'reconstruct' the ancient breed, which was near extinction, by a cross of Arab stallions on Turanian mares. Count G. Wrangel described the survivors of the old breed thus: "It is a peculiar feature of the Karabakh breed that it is very shortsighted and consequently uncommonly nervous. If it even suspects danger, it trembles all over and stands stock still, instead of taking to flight as other steppe horses do." [One might better say 'as all normal horses do'; this sounds like a typical manifestation of decadence, probably caused by inbreeding among the last representatives of a dying race. *Tr.*] A. Born said that on his journey to Bokhara in 1850 he observed something he would not have believed credible—that the neck arteries of Turkoman horses did in fact exude blood after severe exertion or when they were heated.

The horse-stock of Turania in the second half of the last century were known collectively as 'Turkoman' horses, but comprised many strains, which, however, differed little from each other: Jomud and Akhal-Tekke and Jomali horses, which to judge by their exceptional performances must have had the blood of the 'heavenly horses' in their veins. H. Moser, the Swiss traveller who journeyed in these parts in 1883, emphasizes the excellent qualities of the Akhal-Tekke race. According to him, the best of these were comparable with the English Thoroughbred. The clans living round the oasis of Akhal-Tekke who bred these horses lived by stock-raising and cattle-stealing. The outstanding performance of their horses on these raids, which they called 'Alaman', is well known. They could ride for twenty hours at a stretch, 200 versts. The very fine golden-dun coats of the horses looked magnificent, especially in bright sunshine.

Nineteenth-century Turkoman Horseman
Drawing by Evert van Muyden, 1886

In our day the breeding of the Turanian horse, once more on the verge of extinction, has been revived. Marshal Budenny took the initiative in establishing State farms, where a horse about 15½ hands of a uniform riding type has been bred. Today the coat varies considerably from the formerly universal golden colour, and includes silver-dun, dapple-grey, and even black. But reliable figures of performance are available. Times are recorded of 3400 km in 84 days (Askhabad to Moscow, 1935), and in 1949 one of their sprinters did 1000 metres in 66 seconds, which is on a par with the speeds attained by Thoroughbreds.

Origin of Hot-blooded Light-horse Breeding

All the available information about this breed of horse leads us to the evidence that Turania or Turkestan was for thousands of years the home of a fast horse of great quality and staying power. The question is, where did it come from, and when and under what circumstances was it first deliberately and systematically bred?

The specialist literature presents conflicting views. Hančar, it is true, adopts no decided position, but does point out the fact that the beginnings of Turanian horse-breeding lie further back in the past than the Pazyryk burials, and is inclined to think that tall horses of 'quality' appearance originated in this region. According to his view, this strain was represented in the horse-stock of antiquity in Central Asia, China, the Near East, and everywhere in the Roman Empire. V. O. Vitt considers the Pazyryk horses were a local product. He holds that in equines length of limb is inseparable from its thickness. Longer legs are always proportionately more slender, and short ones proportionately thicker. Thus he thinks of 'grading up' as a literal process of drawing the whole stature upward, at the same time drawing out the legs much finer, and holds that Groups 2 and 3 of the Pazyryk horses show different degrees of this development. [It is difficult to see how this concept could be applied to such breeds as the Clydesdale, whose legs are both long and thick. Tr.]

But this argument cannot be generalized. In comparing, say an Arab and a pony of Ebhardt's Type II or a Mongolian Wild Horse (Taki), it is impossible to speak of variant forms or of relative correspondence of proportions and dimensions. The Arab, with its small head, short back, and long legs, and the 'Forest' pony, with its big head, long back, and short legs, are original types in their own right, and they are as little amenable to the theory mentioned above as are animals derived from a cross of these types.

To make any progress at all we must check back on the available data about original wild stock, for it seems most unlikely that simply by means of crossing all or any two of the Taki, the Tarpan, and the European Pony together a hybrid could be produced which would so excel its wild congeners in speed and endurance. We have only to think of the riding exploits of the nomad breeders in their perpetual wars, with their forced marches and surprise attacks. This could hardly have been done on donkey-sized ponies of either Taki or Tarpan stock, which hardly weighed more than did the rider with his saddle and equipment. It is much more likely that the horses of the more sophisticated nomads were like the riding-horses in the Pazyryk barrows, among which the genetic influence of a high-bred strain is clearly visible.

The existence of such a 'wild blood-horse' is conceivable in the light of pictures occurring in Palaeolithic cave art. In Europe these pictures present among a variety of equine types, including recognizable Northern Pony and Tarpan types, not only some markedly 'cold-blooded' specimens such as this ram-headed 'earth-horse' from Combarelles but also a stamp of horse full of quality, 'hot-blooded' in modern European parlance. Such are seen among others on the walls of caves at Altamira and Lascaux, and must imply that in the Cantabrian region long before domestication there was a stamp of wild horse that has vanished. One such variety, apparently about the size of Grévy's zebra among modern equines, and perhaps striped (since some European pony breeds show vestigial stripes on the legs and blurred marks on the shoulder, in combination with an eel-stripe), represents the unknown factor in the ancestry of our domestic horses.

Wild Horse of Heavy Type,
with Roman Nose.
Drawing in the cave of
Les Combarelles, Dordogne

This very possibility is confirmed by folklore traditions in Bactria and Turania. The Turkomans used to say that their forefathers came by the finest foals by turning out 'horsing' mares at night in the mountains, so that they would be covered by wild stallions full of quality that came out of the mountains.

A Hungarian expedition found horses living wild in the Mongolian mountains north of Tienshan. These were obviously the last surviving band of Przewalski's Horse. The place from which they were observed at long range is called Takhin Shar Nuru—i.e., "Yellow Horse Mountain". It is altogether possible that this place-name is a memorial of the golden-coated 'wild blood-horses'. The word *shar* means either 'yellow' or 'golden', and to this day the Turks call golden chestnut horses *sharylar* (in Hungarian *sarig*, or *sarga*). It cannot be a coincidence that this locality should also be the last refuge of the true wild (as opposed to feral) horses of our time, the brown-dun or sandy-bay Takis—a hilly, waterless wilderness, remote from all human settlement.

Chinese sources also speak of mysterious horses in Tienhansu, which lived wild on the mountains of Taiyuan. Persians travelling through this region in the ninth century said that these horses came 'out of the springs' [which brings us back to British folklore with its numerous Celtic legends, like that in the West of Ireland about the marvellously handsome horse that came up out of the sea and covered the poor man's mares, leaving magnificent foals. *Tr.*] The probability is that the rock-drawings from Ferghana (Aravan) which can be ascribed to the first millennium B.C., here reproduced, show such a coupling. It is accepted as part of the general history of domestication that at a certain stage, and especially with horses and cattle, herdsmen did not keep stallions—only mares and foals—and relied for the increase of their herds on this device of leaving the mare in season where the wild stallions could cover her, but so that she could not get away. [We have already explained why the reverse cross, that of tame stallion on wild mare, never happens. With this system of breeding the vigour of the wild sire, reimparted at every new generation, would do much to compensate for the debilitating effect of the first inefficient attempts at horsemastership by people with no long tradition of this branch of husbandry; but conversely there would be a steady loss of mares to the wild herds, despite all efforts to the contrary. *Tr.*]

All that we know of the origins of the Turanian horse tends to confirm the possibility that at the time of domestication such a 'wild blood-horse' did in fact still exist in Central Asia, with outstanding speed and endurance, high on the leg and with a 'dished face' and a highly developed nervous system quite different from other wild sub-varieties—as different as the modern Thoroughbred is from common horses. [Lady Wentworth believed implicitly in such a hypothesis, only her 'wild blood-horse' was domiciled in Central Arabia—specifically in the Nejd. *Tr.*]

The prepotency of such sires is the more credible in the light of modern biological knowledge. It is notorious that feral horses—the descendants of runaway domestic horses—after only a few generations lose the properties conferred by domestication and resume more and more those of their wild ancestors. Thus the mustang of the American plains, now itself on the road to extinction, lost no time in shedding the attributes of the pure-bred Andalusian, and acquired recognizably those of several different ancestral wild types. We may assume that its ancestors in the Old World had included Andalusian, Barb, and the *Asturión* or pacing pony of

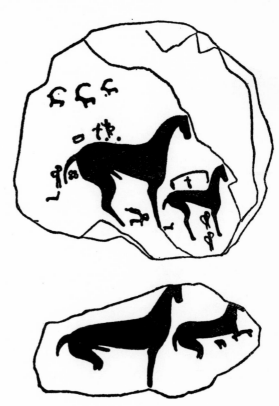

Rock Drawings from Aravan,
near Ferghana, late first
century B.C.
From Hančar, 1955

Northern Iberia. All three in their turn were of composite wild ancestry. As these types once again began to 'separate out' in the process of wild breeding, natural selection again came into play, and 'survival factors' were the only forces that determined the ultimate constitution of mustang herds. Among them a type was thrown up, about $14\frac{1}{2}$ hands high, with 'Thoroughbred' features, such as might be sought in vain among Pony Type II or the Taki. The long-range influence alone of the Turanian horse, imparted drop by drop in Spanish horse-breeding of the pre-Conquistador centuries, can account for this. This influence is still at work among all domestic horses, throwing up once in so many thousand foalings the Turanian type but more frequently, of course, among 'hot-blooded' light-horse breeds.

Part II The Day of the Horseman

Distribution of the Bactrian Horse in Early Times

Even before the Asiatic Huns attacked China and the Emperor Wu determined to import Heavenly Horses from Taiyuan, the Bactrian Horse had appeared beyond the Iranian mountains to the south of Bactria as the chariot horse of the Ancient East. The countries famed in classical antiquity as ancient centres of civilization—the Nile, the Euphrates, the Tigris, and the Indus valleys—are the home of our oldest written traditions.

Although in the Asiatic part of these regions the only wild equine was the onager, and in the Nile valley only (possibly) one of the two African races of wild ass, these records provide valuable data on the beginnings of the horseman's way of life, in its earliest stages. In the fifth millennium B.C. oxen were the sole draught animals, but a thousand years later there is evidence that the onager had been harnessed. We have abundant illustrations of it from the third millennium. Pottery from the city of Mari shows these animals (*Hemionus onager*) harnessed and muzzled; this speaks much for the viciousness of the species, for which captive onagers are renowned among zoo-keepers. It was replaced in the second millennium by the horse, brought in from Central Asia. The first mention of the use of the horse belongs to the reign of Hammurabi, king and lawgiver of Babylonia (1728–1686 B.C.).

The Ancient East, apart from the numerous inscriptions, can also show many pictorial representations of horses. These sculptures and ceramics with their highly artistic and life-like portrayal allow us to draw certain conclusions about the type of horse then in use. They show—from the Nile to the Indus—a horse of noble bearing and all the attributes of quality, with a dished face, deeper in the body than the Pazyryk horses, but with the characteristic features of the Bactrian horse.

The distribution of the Central Asian horse throughout the Middle East is often associated with the advance of Indo-European language groups such as the Hittites, Mitannians, and Kassites towards Mesopotamia. But it is more likely to be due to the rise of commercial contacts, and probably took place primarily through peaceful channels initiated in the first place by Medes and Persians (whose lands bordered on Bactria to the north) through the kingdom of Urartu.

The Silk Road

We mentioned above that the most famous trade route of antiquity, the Silk Road, passed through these districts. From end to end it was some 6250 miles long, its eastern terminus being the Chinese Pacific coast, and its western Alexandria, on the Mediterranean. The middle sector, from Chinese Turkestan to Ecbatana, successively the capital of the Medes, of the Parthians, and later of the Sassanid dynasty, crossed the 13,000 ft. Terek Pass to Ferghana, thence traversed Bactria, and led into the heart of Iran.

We owe to the Swedish explorer Sven Hedin (who discovered the remains of the

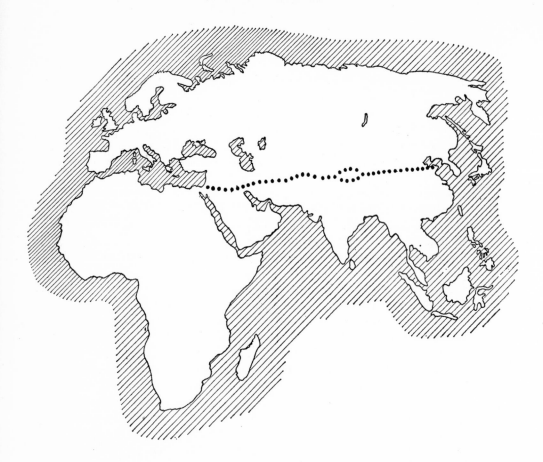

buried city of Lou-Lan near the dried up Lop-Nor lake in 1903) a clear picture of the importance of the Silk Road in economic history. Finds there indicated the kind of goods that had been traded along that road over the centuries. From the West came purple dye, spices, incense, precious metals, amber, and gold. The treasures of the East comprised principally silk, symbol of luxury and riches, sold in all the markets of the Ancient Orient and the Mediterranean. The caravans consisted of different animals on different stages of the route, according as the terrain and climate demanded. There were immeasurable difficulties to be overcome; the whirling sandstorms of the desert, icy snow-squalls in the Pamirs, attacks by robbers all along the way, took their toll of man and beast. The precious merchandise reached its destination only after years. Even in those days enterprise and the profit-motive were boundless. Caravan followed caravan, and according as the way lay through deserts, over mountains, or through the steppe, it demanded thousands of pack animals, be they camels, horses, asses, mules, or yaks. And despite prohibitions of export, a trade in draught animals sprang up along this route.

Having said all this, we may still wonder how the Bactrian Horse came to be distributed all along this route, when the trade between the Central Mediterranean and China was not developed until much later than the second millennium—not until the days of the Roman Empire.

Trade routes do not spring up from one day to the next, especially not when their exploitation depends on the collaboration between many nations and countries, and when not only natural obstacles but those of language and politics have to be overcome. It was centuries before the various sectors of the Silk Road, crossing many frontiers, could establish economic contact between innumerable states.

The connection between the Ancient Orient's many civilizations and those of Central Asia was of long standing. The finery recovered from the frozen tombs of Pazyryk includes objects of use and ornament from Persian as well as Chinese sources. Mesopotamian objects of art often have Central Asiatic motifs, and vice versa. A Kassite cylinder-seal shows a centaur shooting arrows backward, which is a further proof of the influence which the fighting technique of Asiatic mounted nomads had on decorative art.

Evidence of early contact along the Silk Road in its Persian-Bactrian sector is much older, and can be explained in the light of our knowledge of early stock-

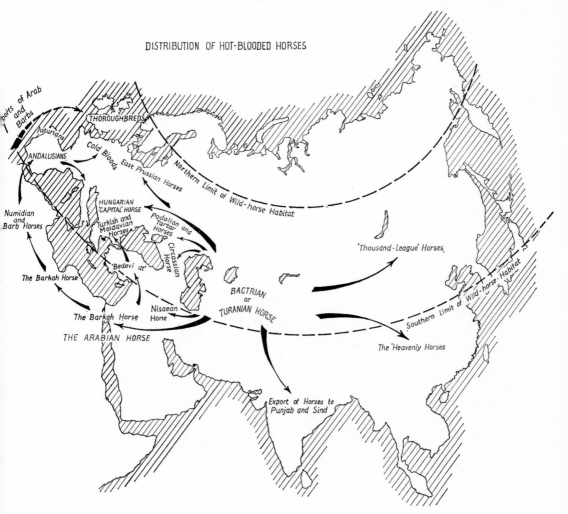

DISTRIBUTION OF HOT-BLOODED HORSES

breeding. We mentioned above that in the region of the Upper Indus, in Rana Gundai, remains of camp-sites from the fourth to the first millennium had proved the employment side by side of horses (Asiatic) and asses (African) as pack-animals. The difficulties of crossing the Afghan mountains between Bactra and the Indian Ocean could only be overcome by using them or their hybrid, the mule.

We may assume that exchange of tools, animals, and objects of value took place along single stretches of the Silk Road in early historical times between Central Asia and the Ancient Orient. So the ass came to be distributed in Asia and the horse in North Africa, the latter along with the camel, which is also of Asiatic origin, and the traditional caravan pack-carrier. Once both had reached Asia Minor, their further distribution was inevitable.

The War-chariot

Documents of Sumerian, Kassite, Mitannian, Persian, Egyptian, Sanskrit, and Hebrew origin are all very revealing about the status of the horse once it had become established in the countries of the Near East. In the city of Mari, on the Euphrates, clay tablets with cuneiform inscriptions have been found, as at Tell Halaf, Nuri, and Susa, and we also have the book by Kikkuli on the care and training of the chariot team, documents in Egyptian hieroglyphics, and the Hindu *Rig-vedas* with their chronicles of ancient wars, all telling the same story—that the peoples of the Near and Middle East used the horse exclusively in harness in the second millennium.

Letters from the kings of the Kassites and the Mitannians to their brother-ruler

War-chariot of Rameses II at the Battle of Kadesh, 1296 B.C.
Low relief in Thebes Museum

Pharaoh all end with the traditional salutation: "We wish you, your country, your house, your womenfolk, your high officers and your horses and chariots the best of health and prosperity." Those dynasties all fought and hunted from the chariot (though whether such hunting was really in open country or in a game-preserve with prepared tracks for the chariot must remain an open question), and all of them patronized chariot-racing. The ideal masculine type of the period is portrayed in art driving a two-wheeled chariot to a pair of horses or four-in-hand. For centuries this was the image of majesty. Archaeological evidence all points the same way; from Persia, 2000 B.C.; from India, 2000 B.C.; from Ethiopia, 1500 B.C.; from Egypt, 1570 B.C.; from Palestine, 1000 B.C., etc.

The late appearance of the horse in Palestine is striking, but it has its historical reasons. The Jews brought no horses with them out of the Egyptian captivity. Moses forbade the Hebrews to keep or breed horses at all (Deuteronomy xvii, 14–16), and for long they hamstrung or killed captured horses (Joshua xi, 2–9). David is the first recorded Israelite king to give up this practice, and even he only kept a select proportion of such spoils, and he kept them for his personal use, and that of his close following. Solomon his son had impressive stables, which have been excavated, and imported horses both from Asia Minor and from Egypt (1 Kings iv, 26).

It often happens that mistrust so far prevails over common sense that a reasonable code of conduct is no longer possible, and so it must have been in this instance of the Mosaic law. Contempt for the hated enemy made the horse, symbol of Pharaonic power, anathema, so that the lawgiver would rather lame or destroy captured chariot horses than turn them to his own use. We shall find instances of similar behaviour later. [But the question does arise, where would Moses and Joshua have found drivers among the Jewish army, who were all accustomed only to handling pack-donkeys? In the conditions of stress obtaining during the prolonged rearguard-action which we call the Exodus, there would be little opportunity to train drivers, or rather for drivers to train themselves, to the standard required for active service. If you do not know how to load or fire a captured gun, you blow out the breech-block. *Tr.*]

Riding became naturalized in the Near East relatively late. All we know is that at the end of the second millennium it was no longer totally unknown, and that the first step to the great revolution had taken place. For the first time, in Babylon, riding-horses are mentioned in the reign of Nebuchadnezzar I, 1200 B.C. Three centuries later a relief was put up in the palace of Assurnasipal (884–859 B.C.) showing mounted nomads in their characteristic warlike posture—shooting backward. They are dressed in trousers, cross-belted, and shod with soft-topped boots—all items which show a Central Asiatic influence. The employment of horses as riding-animals had been forced on the inhabitants of these regions by the advance of the Medes and Persians from the north, as it had been on those of Khorasan and China by the inroads of the Asiatic Huns. Besides this, the appearance of mounted armies was the stimulus to the building of fortified cities and citadels. (See also Habakkuk i, 8: "Their horses also are swifter than the leopards.")

The Spread of Riding

A short survey of historical events sets the scene for the expansion of riding among the peoples of the Ancient Orient. The Medes inhabited the mountainous country in the northern part of what is now Persia, south of the Caspian. The earliest historical sources state that their country was conquered in the tenth or ninth century B.C. by the Bactrians from Central Asia. From that time onward the population of the country was mixed, the Median element paying tribute to the Bactrian ruling class. At length they fused to form one ethnic unit, which was the first in the Ancient Orient to adopt the riding tradition brought in from Central Asia. Understandably, they exploited their superiority, pressing onward to the south and conquering new territory. For centuries they struggled with their dourest enemies, the Assyrians, and according to Herodotus it was they who, in alliance with the Babylonians, destroyed Nineveh, the most considerable city of the Near East, in 612 B.C. The fame of the Nisaean horses bears witness to the high level of their horse-breeding. When the Assyrians temporarily got the upper hand they demanded a tribute of Nisaean horses, annually.

Oppian in his *Cynegeticon* describes the breed as follows: "The horses of Nisaea are the handsomest, fit only for mighty rulers. They are splendid, running swiftly under the rider, obeying the bridle willingly, with ram-nosed heads carried high, and streaming golden manes." Of the horses of the neighbouring Parthians he says: "These have great quality, with bright coats of splendid colours, having great courage". There can be little doubt that these horses were also of Bactrian origin, derived from Types III and IV in Ebhardt's classification.

The dominion of the Medes, which lasted more than three centuries, was broken by Cyrus, the ruler of the neighbouring Persians. He had once been a vassal of the Medes, but came to power as leader of a rebellion against them. According to Xenophon, up to that time the Persians had fought only from chariots, so that Cyrus must be regarded as the founder of the Persian cavalry.

On coming to power, Cyrus laid claim to the overlordship of the neighbouring principality of Bactria, but had no success. However, what rulers could not achieve by force of arms they often managed, then as now, by clever diplomacy or alliance. In this case, dynastic alliance; Cyrus married the daughter of the defeated Median king, Astyages, and as soon as this princess, Amythis, became his wife the Bactrians acknowledged his suzerainty.

The dowry which this lady with the euphonious name brought with her proved one of the most valuable acquisitions ever made by any ruler in antiquity; Cyrus having become master of the Bactrian cavalry, auxiliaries who helped him to the fruition of his ambitious plans for world dominion. His first campaign against the fabulously rich Croesus, ruler of Lydia, was won, according to Herodotus, because he placed camels in the forefront of his army and the Lydian horses panicked at the sight and smell of these unfamiliar creatures, throwing the host into disarray so that it could easily be overcome. After that Cyrus overran Mesopotamia and stormed Babylon. He expanded his empire in the east as far as the Oxus (Amu-Darya) and the Indus, and in the west to the Bosporus. His successor Cambyses conquered Egypt, thus bringing the whole of the Ancient Orient under Persian sway.

The horse even decided the enthronement of Darius I, great-nephew and son-in-law to Cyrus. Not that he seized the throne with the help of his cavalry—in this case his charger and his Master of the Horse sufficed of themselves.

When the candidates for the throne could not agree to elect a successor, they determined to leave the choice to their horses. The prince whose horse was first to

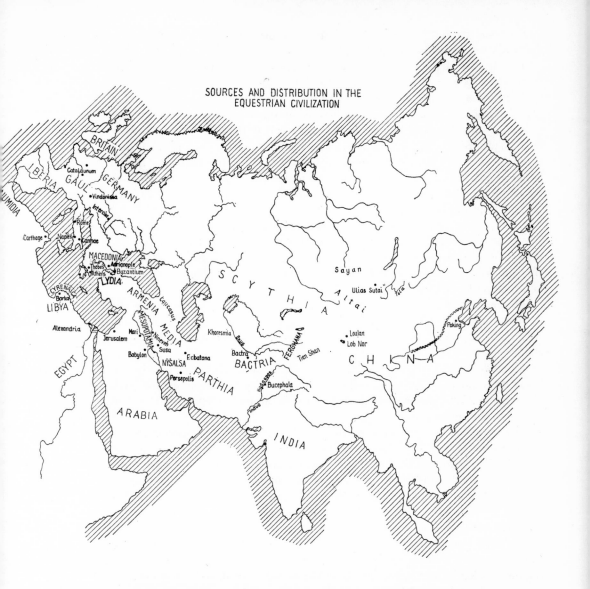

neigh as they rode out of the city gates at dawn should be King of Kings. Oibares, Master of the Horse to Darius, was determined that his master should win the election, and thought of a trick; he touched a horsing mare and carefully kept that hand in a fold of his garment until the candidates rode up. Then he stepped forward to the horse of Darius, and held his hand under its nostrils, whereupon the stallion uttered a loud neigh. Herodotus says that in gratitude Darius had a statue erected to his horse and to his Master of the Horse.

The Persian kings throw some light on horsemastership and the techniques of warfare and commerce associated with it in the Ancient East. In his account of the Grecian campaigns of King Xerxes, Herodotus describes the Persian troopers in their bronze helmets and infantry weapons, the Sagartians, who were a race of herdsmen armed with lassos and daggers, the Medes, Bactrians, Caspians, and so on, also armed with infantry weapons. The Libyans of North Africa and the Indians fought from horse-drawn chariots, but some of the Indian chariots were drawn by onagers; so the onager was still being used in draught at that time.

The Arabian contingent was mounted on camels; and since these made the horses shy, they were drawn up in rear of the main body.

The Persian hegemony of the Near East was brought to an end by Alexander of Macedon (336–323 B.C.), the immortal hero of antiquity and one of the great captains of all time. He owed his military success largely to the newly created cavalry force bequeathed to him by his father, King Philip. When he came to the throne at the age of twenty he won his first cavalry victory, against the Thebans. Then he began to desire possession of the Ancient East; first he wrested from the Persians the satrapies of Asia Minor, then he turned southward to conquer Egypt. Not until then did he proceed to attack Darius himself.

But in any case by that time the power of the Persian monarchs was on the wane. The subject provinces of their empire, and primarily Bactria, at first delayed and then refused to support the King of Kings. But the open breach did not come until after the defeat of Darius by the Macedonians and his flight into Bactria, where the satrap turned on him and had him murdered.

Alexander followed the example of Cyrus. He consolidated his power in Bactria by marrying the daughter of the Bactrian king Oxyartes, Roxana. According to Arianes, the main body of his army already at this time contained mounted lancers and horse-archers, who took part in his Indian campaign.

Alexander's career mounted steeply to its climax, with his early death in 323. His army commanders partitioned the empire, founding new dynasties, but parts of it regained their independence. In 256 Bactria became an independent kingdom again, but now under a Greek dynasty.

Alexander was not only a famous commander but a genuine horseman, in the modern sense of the word, who knew the strategic worth of cavalry, and was an enthusiastic admirer of the true-bred Oriental horse. When his charger Bucephalus was killed at the battle of Hydaspes, he founded a city called Bucephala in memory of him. Bucephalus means 'ox-head', presumably because to European eyes the broad forehead, large round eyes, and concave profile of the 'Arab' type suggested bovine rather than equine features.

The horse was also highly esteemed by other nations of the Ancient Orient who had reached a high stage of equestrian culture. When Xerxes went to war the column was led by ten 'sacred' horses of the Nisaean breed, and a team of such horses also drew the royal chariot.

In the traditional literature of the Hebrews, a well-known passage from the Book of Job describes the horse thus, in praise of God's majesty:

Hast Thou given the horse strength? hast Thou clothed his neck with thunder?
Canst Thou make him afraid as a grasshopper? The glory of his nostrils is terrible.
He paweth in the valley, and rejoiceth in his strength. He goeth on to meet the armed men.
He mocketh at fear, and is not affrighted; neither turneth he back from the sword.
The quiver rattleth against him, the glittering spear and the shield.
He swalloweth the ground with fierceness and rage. (Auth. Version.)
Triumphantly he echoes the bugle's note. (Mgr. Knox.)

Now, this was the very people whose leaders had once held the horse in such abhorrence that they had forbidden Jews to keep them, and ordered the destruction of all captured stock. [But it is relevant to add that Job was not an Israelite; he dwelt in the land of Uz—that is, Edom, the modern Jordan—and his Book was originally a Bedouin saga, taken over by Hebrew literature on the strength of its high literary and religious merit. *Tr.*]

Horsemanship and Equitation in Classical Antiquity

As the art of riding began to spread through the Middle East, a new chapter was beginning in the history (partly in the prehistory) of the European peoples. In the Mediterranean the literate Classical Age is dawning, while north of the Alps the Age of Iron is succeeding the Age of Bronze. In both regions new possibilities in the fields of transport, of communications, and of warfare open up. Political life comes to be dominated by the mounted warrior rather than the charioteer. Mediterranean

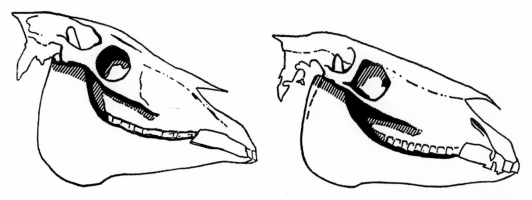

Skulls of Arab (Kehailan) Horse and Shetland Pony compared
From J. E. Flade 1962

lands first felt the influence of fashions from the Near East, and thus the Mediterranean was the cradle of European equitation.

The wild-horse stock of Europe, the pony of the north-west and the Tarpan of the south-east, were both of low stature, which the early stages of domestication did nothing to increase. Indeed, rather the contrary. The height at the withers of horses in Gaul and Switzerland, to judge by skeletal remains dating from the La Tène period (beginning about 400 B.C.), was under 13 hands, and the average in Britain at that time lower still. The domesticated Tarpan of the Black Sea region was no bigger, and the horses of the Western Scythians were none of them as tall as the smallest horses buried in the frozen tombs of Pazyryk at that period.

The spread of riding is to be attributed to two events widely separated in space and time: the introduction of the Bactrian Horse from the Near East by the Greeks and the Romans, and the incursions of mounted nomads from Asia.

There is written evidence that about 630 B.C. some hundreds of Greek settlers established themselves on the African shore at the mouth of the river Cyre, where they founded the city of Cyrene, the nucleus of what is still called Cyrenaica, in Libya. This rapidly expanding colony became a great cultural and commercial centre in ancient Africa.

Herodotus says of the Cyrenian Greeks that the neighbouring Libyans took over from them the mode of harnessing four horses to a chariot (quadriga), and that they were principally occupied in breeding and breaking horses.

In the veins of the Cyrenaican horses coursed the blood of the Bactrian Horse, already naturalized in the Near East, as is abundantly shown by North African and Greek equestrian art, as well as by documentary evidence.

North Africa played a vital intermediary part in the further development of equestrian culture, though it did not come into its own as a land of horsemen until the westward expansion of Islam under the leadership of the Arabs, at a time when Arab enterprise in horse-breeding was profoundly affecting the material culture of the Near Eastern peoples.

So the Cyrenian colony played the same part in Greek history as had Bactria in the Persian. Its influence on horse-breeding in the Greek homeland persisted for centuries. Cyrenaica and Bactria had been connected, by way of the Silk Road, for centuries, so that it will have been possible at any time to reinforce the breeding-stock by a refreshing draught from the original source. When Darius of Persia conquered the town of Barka, in Cyrenaica, during his Egyptian campaign he transferred the population to Bactria. There those Greeks founded a city, likewise called Barka. The maintenance of their connections with the previous African settlement is very probable, even before the further settlement of Greeks in Bactria by Alexander the Great.

Hellenic horse-breeding soon became world-famous due to the importation of stock, both from Cyrenaica and from Asia Minor. When the Persian king Xerxes invaded Greece in 480, reaching Thessaly with his vast land army, he instituted a race between local horses and his own, in order to maintain the reputation of his own breed. In fact the 'sacred' Persian horses did win, which perhaps is not surprising in the light of breeding conditions of that day.

Many traditions bear witness to the high standard of horsemanship in Greece. The horse plays a prominent part in the mythology of Hellas. Thus the chariot of Ares, god of war, was drawn by four grey horses, as he went before the rising sun to announce daybreak. Heracles usually travelled in a two-wheeled chariot. The horse also figures largely in epics of the heroic age of Greece; the leading personalities in the Homeric poems drive chariots, but occasionally ride also. Beginning with the 25th Olympiad in 676 B.C., races between four-in-hand chariots were instituted, and from that time onward equestrian events were included in the Olympic programme, eventually also ridden events. Harness teams were driven only from the chariot; there were no outriders.

There is a striking Greek legend about riding: herds of wild cattle came down from Mount Pelion in the reign of King Ixion and laid waste the fields of Thessaly, spoiling the corn-lands of the whole plain. The King offered a great reward for the elimination of this plague, whereupon some bold youths took chariot horses

22 War-chariot and Four, from the Crater of Vix (Burgundy), made in Sicily or
Apulia
5th century B.C.

23 Assurbanipal of Assyria's Campaign against the Elamites
Relief from the palace of Nineveh, about 639 B.C.
British Museum

24
Detail from Parthenon Frieze, about 432 B.C., by Pheidias or his School

25
Roman Triumphal Car

26 Roman Tombstone from Pannonia, showing Saddle Horse and Draft Horses
Pannonia is approximately the modern Hungary.
National Museum, Budapest

27
Tombstone of a Trooper
from a Roman Auxiliary
Cavalry Regiment
recruited in Noricum
(approximately the
modern Austria)
Altertumsmuseum, Mainz

28 The Stone of Hornhausen
    Seventh-century Carvings of a
    Saxon Horseman

29 West European ("Frankish")
    Mounted Warriors of the
    Ninth Century, without
    Stirrups
    The saddle is virtually
    identical with the late Roman
    pattern.

which had never been ridden before from under the yoke and drove off the dangerous herd of aurochs. The same youths then perceived the military value of the ridden horse, turned bandits, and attacked the King himself. The tradition of the mythological centaurs is connected with these early horsemen. The Thessalians, who had never before seen a man riding, took them for monsters with human trunks growing out of a horse's body.

Centaur with Nomad
Bow
Relief in Church of
Panagia Gorgopico,
Athens

Herodotus says that Greek armies in the days of the Persian wars consisted exclusively of infantry; there were only some mounted messengers. Riding did not become general until later. This is confirmed by Xenophon (434–359 B.C.) in his *Hippike*, which shows an extraordinary degree of technical knowledge, and is remarkable for its advice to the reader to deal gently with the horse—a principle still obtaining today, quietness and an absence of violence being the basis of successful horsemanship. Xenophon was himself a cavalry leader who conducted the retreat of the Greek auxiliaries from Mesopotamia after the battle of Cunaxa in 401 B.C. He describes this prolonged rearguard action in his *Anabasis*; a soldier of wide experience in the service of more than one state, the Mesopotamian campaign alone must have brought him into contact with mercenary cavalrymen of many Asiatic nations.

The Romans

Whereas in Greece the Bactrian horse was primarily responsible for the rise of equitation as an art, in Italy it served more utilitarian purposes, in both the commercial and the military field. The reason is that the main striking force of most Greek states was the navy, whereas in Rome armed force meant primarily the land army. In any case, cavalry was of no great military significance to the Romans until they came into conflict with the Carthaginians from Africa, by which time they were already a Great Power.

In the three Carthaginian campaigns in Italy, Sicily, and Spain which the Romans fought, the cavalry, including the African cavalry, swayed the balance. The fortunes of war favoured always that side on which the Numidian squadrons of light horse could be bribed or otherwise persuaded to fight. Hannibal triumphed over the Roman legions only until the day when the fickle Numidians turned against him—which was probably a triumph for Roman diplomacy. Once the scene of operations shifted to the African theatre this factor became more decisive, since more Numidians could be brought into action on the Roman side.

Naturally, the Punic wars had their influence on Roman military and transport technique, as is best shown by contemporary descriptions of Roman horsemanship during and before those wars.

The Romans had been a nation of charioteers, and were reluctant to mount the horse, especially for military purposes. This role they delegated to auxiliaries, drawn from the non-Roman inhabitants of the provinces. Polybius says that they engaged Hannibal's auxiliary Celtiberian cavalry at Cannae, both sides being dismounted. They tethered their horses to stakes to prevent them running away. At that time the Roman cavalry were equipped only with cuirasses of leather straps, thin leather shields, and light spears, in order not to be hindered in mounting. This was still very different from the arms and accoutrement of equestrian peoples. They had neither saddles nor stirrups, only a felt pad made fast with girth and breastplate. The lance was added to the javelin in time, and later armour, as a protection against arrows, was adopted.

The earliest Roman vehicle was the two-wheeled cart, in which the drivers sat. To begin with they employed a type of wagon of Near-Eastern pattern. It was very primitive, consisting essentially of two carts lashed one behind the other, having only the bed in common. Thus all its four wheels were of the same diameter, and consequently the vehicle did not turn easily, while as its loading surface was high above the wheel-base it was also unstable. The first Roman wagons were unmanœuvrable, and their cross-country performance negligible.

The expansion of economic contacts and of traffic enhanced the importance of road-building. The cities of the Empire were connected by carefully paved roads, skilfully laid out, crossing rivers and ravines by bridges, in the construction of which the Romans soon reached a high degree of skill. Roads were also built behind the frontiers to provide lateral communication for the garrisons, as well as for trade purposes.

After the Punic Wars Roman horse-breeding received a great impetus. The appearance of the Numidian horse in Spain led to the production there of a more massive European type, Bactrian in origin. From then onward Iberia became the most important province as a source of remounts for the Roman cavalry arm, and also for the dissemination of good-quality horses throughout the western part of the Empire.

According to Tacitus, Rome provided all the new auxiliary cavalry regiments of European origin with Spanish horses. As Arrian, Strabo, and Caesar tell us, Gallic, British, and German horses were small, and Tacitus adds that the German horses were slow and ugly. These strains were primarily used as pack-animals and in harness, rather than for riding, but archaeological evidence confirms the greater stature of the Iberian horse. The finds in the Roman ampitheatre at Vindonissa (Switzerland) includes bones of horses up to 15 hands high, and horses of the same size are seen on a carved relief from Intercisa in Pannonia, which shows saddle-horses and harness-horses on the same register. This explains why the Romans called the riding-horse *materia generosa* ('quality') and the harness-horse *materia vulgaris* ('common'). The term 'quality' might well be applied to the Bactrian horse. About 70–60 B.C. the Roman forces on the eastern frontier made contact with a nation of horsemen whose mode of fighting they had not so far encountered. These Parthians, having left Khorasan, overran Persia and pressed on into the Roman province of Mesopotamia.

Pompeius Trogus, writing in the time of the Emperor Augustus, says of these people in his *Historiae Philippicae* (lost, but quoted by Justinus) that they were dressed like Medes and spoke a mixture of Median and Scythian. Their army consisted of slaves, whom they trained in the arts of riding and archery with the same care as they trained their own sons. The richer a man was, the more mounted archers he led under the banners of the king. Their method of fighting was novel. Often after an attack they turned about and feigned flight. Both they and their horses wore scale-armour.

According to the Greek geographer Strabo (63 B.C.–20 A.D.), the Parthians came from Bactria, and their rulers bore the proud title of Pahlavi, which means Bactrian.

The Roman consul Crassus was sent against the Parthians and in 53 B.C. he tried to bring them to a pitched battle in Mesopotamia. But they kept on drawing back into the desert, and did not begin fighting until the Romans were wearied by the pursuit, and thinking of retracing their steps.

Crassus, ignorant of Oriental tactics, insisted on forming a close hollow square, and this was his downfall. The Parthians charged, shot off their arrows, turned about, only to charge again, but never charged home; at last Crassus committed his own cavalry, which was outnumbered and worse-armed. They were destroyed, and once they were gone the Roman infantry was doomed; they took to flight, and the two legions were destroyed almost to a man.

Though Rome lamented the shame of this defeat and the loss of so many fine troops, no useful lessons were learned for a long time. In the days of Augustus, fifty years after the Parthian disaster, the Roman establishment consisted of twenty-five legions stationed in various provinces, each 5300 men strong, and each containing only one squadron of 120 mounted troops. Rome attempted to match the Parthian superiority in cavalry by groups of auxiliary cavalry in the provinces of Asia Minor, and along the Parthian frontier a defensive zone was created with fortified camps and systems of watch-towers. [But for two centuries an effective cavalry army, or one in which cavalry was the prevailing arm, could not be erected because the machinery of command did not exist. Only the legions had a staff and a hierarchy of officers through which orders could be quickly and effectively transmitted in action. The largest cavalry unit of the Roman army was the *ala millaria*, a regiment a thousand strong; but most of the cavalry units were only five hundred strong. Since convention demanded that auxiliaries be attached to and under command of a legion, even if a force were organized in which the number of cavalry equalled the number of legionary infantry, its commander would have to issue orders simultaneously to the officers commanding the infantry cohorts comprising the legion and the Tribunes or *praefecti* of up to ten *alae* of cavalry, without any intermediate echelon. An 'orders group' of this size is not a practical proposition, in any army in any age. *Tr.*]

This was so until the reforms of the Emperor Gallienus (A.D. 260–268). The pressure of Germanic tribes on the *Limes*, as well as a series of internal conflicts, brought the problem of an effective cavalry arm to a head. It had been conclusively proven that the striking power of the army could only be assured by a cavalry arm permanently organized and instantly ready for action, and capable of being brought into action tactically *en masse*. Gallienus provided the solution with the establishment of an independent corps of cavalry with its own chain of command, recruited and mounted by provinces. His successors Diocletian and Constantine continued the development of the cavalry, until Rome was on equal terms with her opponents, the mounted warriors of the East. The second-century Roman cavalry general Arrianus (a Greek by birth) shows in his tactical work *Acies contra Alanos* the limitations imposed on a Roman commander before the Gallienian reforms. He also says that the enemy (the Alani were not Germans, but spoke an Indo-European language allied to Persian) were all mounted, but armed only with throwing-spears, and thus more to be regarded as mounted infantry. According to Procopius, they did not adopt the essential tactic of mobile missile warfare—archery from the saddle at the gallop—until the sixth century.

Apart from this, the question arises, who were the mounted enemy on the eastern frontiers of Rome, since at this time the East Germanic tribes in general only drove horses in harness, without riding? When the Age of Migration entered its final stage the appearance of the Huns in Eastern Europe had become a reality. Now the process which had begun centuries before in Central Asia among peoples displaced by the nomads was repeated, or rather continued. Those Germanic tribes who were threatened by the Huns were already fighting on horseback, just as the Bactrians, Medes, Khoresmians, and Parthians had done at the time of their début on the stage of history. Their immediate contact with the Huns, which was more often peaceful than hostile, led to their adopting many Hunnish customs, and in the end the Hunnish method of warfare. (Note 4.)

The Huns

After the reform of army organization the Romans were quite capable of dealing with mounted Germanic hosts. At the battle of Strasbourg in 357 the Alemannic war-bands were shattered by the impact of the mail-clad Roman cavalry. But when the Huns appeared not much later, the tide turned again.

The Huns had caused the most recent and considerable migration on the part of the Goths, and in 376 they began to trespass on the Roman sphere of interest. They were conspicuous in the ranks of the Gothic host. In his summary of sources dealing with this equestrian people, Peter Váczy writes:

> Western authors are full of admiration for the skill of the Huns in horsemanship. Thus Claudianus says that nature herself has not welded the two parts of the centaur more firmly together than the Hun sits his horse. Sidonius points out that the children of the Huns, at an age when they cannot walk without the aid of their mothers, each have a horse to ride. It is as if they grew out of their horses. Other nations sit on horseback; the Hun lives there. *Equis prope adfixi*, as Ammianus puts it, adding: the Huns do not even dismount to perform their natural functions, and they transact all their affairs in the saddle, even eating and drinking there; they even sleep stretched out on the slender necks of their horses. They also hold important conferences on horseback. Ammianus Mar-

cellinus reported, credibly enough, that the Byzantine ambassadors negotiating a truce with the 'king of the Scyths' at Margus on the Danube, had to remain on their horses since the Huns would not dismount. Jordanes describes them as riders swift as the wind, who came up like a tornado and disappeared like a flock of birds. Their skill at archery commanded admiration everywhere, as Olympiodorus, Sidonius and Jordanes all affirm.

Chinese Brush-drawing
of Mounted Hun

The first direct confrontation between the Romans on one side and the Goths and Huns on the other was at Adrianople in 378. Both sides had drawn up their array in depth, in the formation called *pugna stataria* in Roman tactical manuals. But the novelty consisted in the Hunnish tactics of repeated feint attacks which brought the ranks of their adversaries into such disorder that the battle ended in a devastating defeat for the Romans. This was regarded by contemporaries as the beginning of the end of Roman rule. And indeed from that time onward the Empire was no longer in a position to put in hand the necessary army reorganization.

The fate of Europe was finally decided in 451 at the battle of the Catalaunian Fields, the most gigantic cavalry engagement of all antiquity. Although the Romans had made some attempt to adapt their mounted troops to the demands of new conditions, it was in vain. They had, for instance, followed the example of the Huns and Alani by ceasing to wear armour on horseback, in the interests of mobility, according to sources of the late Empire quoted by Várady (1961).

It is said of the Catalaunian Fields that before the battle opened Attila had all the saddles collected and burnt. In the light of Western ideas this order is scarcely comprehensible. But perhaps it can be explained as follows: by doing this Attila would effectively dismount the non-Hunnish part of his force, who by their lack of skill might have endangered the success of the nomad riders who carried out their accustomed manoeuvres like clockwork; at the same time he prevented the possibility of these less disciplined contingents spreading panic and perhaps flight throughout the host.

The battle began in the early afternoon and ended after dusk without any clear advantage to either side. Attila, disappointed after having been so confident of victory, withdrew his entire force from the battlefield, and although he was undefeated this withdrawal diminished his prestige, and the reputation for invincibility possessed by the Huns, as soon became apparent. The result, being seen as indecisive, encouraged the tributary peoples to try to regain their independence, and led to the rapid dissolution of the Hun empire after Attila's death in 453.

But on the Roman side too, this indecisive engagement had its effect on the attitude of subject peoples, and on the allies of the Romans. In practice, all that was left of the once mighty Roman empire was the name, and as for a long time the senior officers of the Praetorian Guard, and sometimes generals of the field army, had decided who should be the next Emperor, the consequence of those high offices being increasingly filled by German soldiers could be foreseen. At last, in 476, one of them, a Rugian officer called Odoacer, was elected King by the German mercenaries, and the Emperor Romulus Augustulus, the last actor in a charade presented on the Roman stage by managers who were anything but Roman, was deposed. The Roman Empire of the West had ceased to exist.

Now for a time the march of historical events came to a halt with the confrontation on equal terms of horsemen of the East and of the West. Now the past was buried and a new era was to begin, because a balance had been struck with the collision of two world Powers, each with a huge army of cavalry. The result was on the one hand the final fall of the Roman Empire and on the other a retreat by the forces from the steppe.

Decline and Renaissance of European Horsemanship

In the years after the fall of Rome, the focal point of equestrian affairs shifted to Eastern Europe. Once Attila was dead the Huns left their temporary home in the Carpathians and settled on the East European plains, living in a chronic state of warfare which had already been their lot for centuries, due to internal dissension and quarrels with neighbours which weakened the tribes. They now took part in the wars between Byzantium and Persia, sometimes on one side, sometimes on the other, according as their temporary advantage dictated.

The Byzantines mastered the art of employing these formidable horsemen in the most distant theatres of war, often overseas. Thus in 534–535 Count Belisarius broke the power of the Vandals in Africa with the aid of Hunnish mercenaries, and in 553 they helped to defeat the Ostrogoths before the walls of the now unimportant city of Rome. For a century after the collapse of the short-lived Hun empire their warriors, in foreign pay, still often dominated the battlefields of Europe.

The Avars

Eastern Europe, perpetually the scene of cavalry wars, presented in the sixth century signs of exhaustion, impoverishment, and decadence, just as Western Europe had done in the fifth. About the year 570 a nation of horsemen—the Avars—appeared on the scene, and were joined by some of the tribes of the Huns, such as the Utigures and Kutrigures; other Hun tribes became merged in the Bulgarians and Khazars. The Slavs began to settle wide tracts of Eastern Europe. The Arabs conquered Asia Minor and the Byzantine provinces of Africa, together with Persia. Only Constantinople itself withstood the alternate onslaughts of Slavs, Avars, Arabs, and Bulgars.

As the ethnic composition of Eastern Europe changed, so too did its civilization. New influences made themselves felt; the Avars were just one more wave of mounted nomads making their way into the heart of Europe. They had come originally from Mongolia, the homeland of wandering stock-breeders. Their Chinese neighbours mention them in the written sources under the name of Shwan-Shwan, describing at some length animal husbandry as practised in the Avar economy. The Chinese ruler T'ai-wu-Ti (of the T'o-pa dynasty from Sion-pi) declared during a council of war that the best time to launch a campaign against these northern barbarians was the summer, because then they would be grazing their herds in the north, around Lake Baikal. At this time their horses were not available for warfare, since the stallions were covering mares, and the mares were suckling foals. But in the autumn the barbarians drove their herds south, and spent the winter in harrying the Chinese border provinces. This description agrees with the account written five hundred years earlier of the Huns "migrating annually in search of water and grazing". (The northward movement of the nomads in summer—as is generally known—is done to avoid the plagues of midges, which also makes raiding difficult.)

The Avar dominion in Eastern Europe was short-lived, weakened as it was by the chronic feuding which was the curse of the mounted nomads, and inseparable from their way of life. Added to that was perpetual friction with the Slavs. The first of these to throw off the Avar yoke were the Czechs and Moravians in 623;

Mounted Archer
Illustration from a Chinese encyclopaedia of the sixteenth century

then it became the turn of the Croats. Charlemagne dealt the Avars the final blow in the years 791–796. The Avar nation disappeared without trace, and their territory was divided among the Slavonic tribes, under petty princes. The only traces remaining today of their rule in Central Europe (which lasted two and a half centuries) are the graves of their horsemen, from which stirrups—perhaps among the first seen in Europe—are often found. The saddle and the stirrup are what they bequeathed to European horsemanship.

The Byzantine army also learned much from them in the way of mounted tactics and skill at arms, being constantly threatened by Avar incursions. The Emperor Heraclius (610–641), who was perpetually having to contend on the one hand with the Avars, Slavs, and Persians, and on the other with the Arabs, wrote a tactical manual which was the basis of the later and better-known work by Leo the Wise, dealing mainly with the reorganization of cavalry units, in which he exploited experience gained in fighting the Avars as well as the Huns, and studying their methods. His cavalry were armed with Avar weapons, together with bows and arrows and swords, and his battle formations were based on the practice of the mounted nomads. These reforms proved so effective that the Byzantines were at last able to vanquish and destroy the Persians who had been a standing threat to their eastern frontier. This success was consolidated, according to the time-honoured practice, by diplomacy, alliances with the Khazars against the Persians and with the Bulgars against the Arabs being made.

The Advance of the Arabs

The half-nomadic Arabs had originally been anything but horsemen. In the army of Alexander the Great there had been Arab cameliers, and the Roman commander Gallus found no horsemen among them in 26 B.C. Some of them lived in towns, some of them were seafarers, trading in the Mediterranean, the Red Sea, the Persian Gulf. But the core of them, the Bedouin, to whom the generic term A'arab originally applied, were wandering stock-breeders in the desert, keeping a few cattle but more camels, sheep, and goats. In the time of Mahomet they still bred a lot of asses. Horses, like cattle, really require more water than the Bedouin grazing-grounds can provide, but in the days of the Prophet they did breed a few horses, and he himself kept some.

The tribes were by no means at one among themselves, either in politics or in religion, until the teaching of Mahomet united them in a brotherhood as the servants of the One God, in whose service they were inspired to fight by the promise of eternal life among the delights of Paradise for all those killed in action. The expansion of Islam, the concept of *jihad*—the Holy War—was not a mere excursion in search of plunder; its aim was the conversion of the world to the cult of the One True God.

In the beginning, the Arab armies were very different from those of the steppe nomads. At the battle of Mount Ohod between Mecca and Medina in 625 the victorious Meccan cavalry comprised only one-tenth of the army. The main body of the hosts of Islam still consisted of infantry, though on the march many of them rode pillion behind the horsemen and cameliers. But the mounted arm was of high quality, due to the excellence of their horses.

The Arab campaigns met with unparalleled success. One after another they conquered the most valuable provinces of the Byzantine Empire, Syria, Palestine, Mesopotamia, Armenia, and, between 639 and 643, North Africa. Once they had conquered the islands of the Mediterranean their fleet menaced Constantinople.

The campaigns waged simultaneously against Persia had quick success also. In 642 the main Persian army was destroyed, and that whole empire overcome. In their advance eastward, the Muslims reached the Indus valley in 664, and between 706 and 716 Khorasan, Bokhara, Samarkand, and Ferghana in Central Asia. Further progress was checked by the military might of the Chinese Empire.

ARAB CONQUESTS
632-827

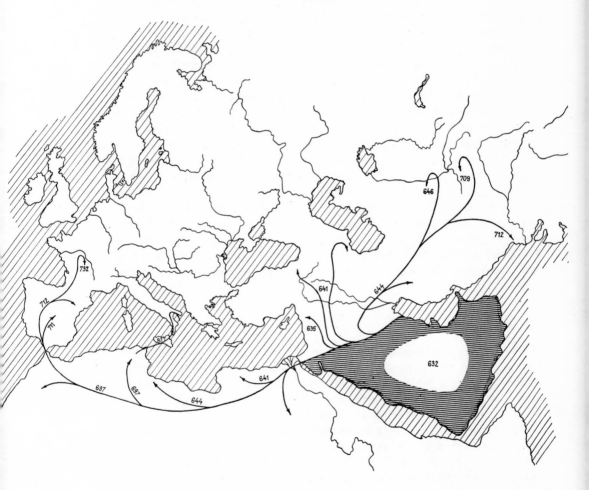

The connection first brought about by Cyrus the Persian between the civilization of distant Bactria and the lands of the Mediterranean a thousand years earlier was revived by the Muslim advance. Traffic along the Silk Road, which had always depended on the balance of power, gained a new impetus. The steady importation of Turanian horses from Ferghana is now confirmed by written evidence. This strain thus reappears in the area from which more than a thousand years ago the horses of Cyrenaica, of Barka, Numidia, and Spain, had come to influence the destiny of Western peoples. Now this happened in the case of the Arabs. In a unique series of victories they conquered North Africa and crossed the Strait of Gibraltar to Spain. In 711 the kingdom of the Visigoths, weakened by internal discord, fell easily before them. After taking firm possession of the Iberian peninsula, they crossed the Pyrenees and pressed onward into Gaul.

The Frankish kingdom in Gaul was then ruled by the Merovingian dynasty. Eginhardus, contemporary and biographer of Charlemagne, says of the last Merovingian king that he used to travel in an ox-wagon. This is just one example of the retrograde development that had taken place in Gaul, the decay of the equestrian civilization, since the fall of Rome. When the Franks had invaded Italy, fighting against the Goths in 539 and 552, they had fought on foot, only the King's personal escort being mounted. (Note 4.) Repeated attacks by the Muslims at last caused Charles Martel, Mayor of the Palace to the Merovingian kings, to raise a force of cavalry. He rewarded his vassals for service on horseback with grants of land.

Meanwhile in neighbouring Spain the Muslims, known as Moors or Saracens, had taken a firm foothold. The Caliphate of Cordoba became the advanced bulwark of Islam as it pressed forward with fire and sword, but at the same time it was the centre of a new civilization. In Europe the turmoil of the Migration Period had left only ruins in its wake; the cultural riches of the antique world had been succeeded only by the foggy and clumsy speculations of the Nordic peoples. As the Arabs gained a footing in Europe—in Spain and Sicily—the fertilizing influence of the Near East was again felt; after all, it had been the source of the classical art and thought of antiquity. And so once more the clear light of the Mediterranean day was let in on the inhospitable castles and manor-houses of the West; comfort and elegance in dress and appurtenances, a more sophisticated style of living, became general in Iberia, and thence in Gaul. To this new way of life, for the upper classes at least, better communications were essential, and that meant faster horses—Oriental horses.

The Battle of Poitiers

Charles Martel ("the Hammer")'s efforts to improve his army were soon crowned with success. In 732 the Frankish armoured horsemen clashed with the Saracens for the first time, at Poitiers. After repulsing repeated attacks by the Muslims, the counter-attack by the Frankish armour was decisive. But it could not be fully exploited because the pursuit could not follow the fleeing Saracens fast enough.

This battle was a turning-point in the reawakening of Europe, and may be compared in importance with the battle of the Catalaunian Fields.

As to horse-breeding in Western Europe at that time, it has been established archaeologically that most of the stock was a pony type with strong bone and a height at the withers of 13 hands 2 in. or 14 hands. [In British terms, like the Fell or Highland pony of today. Tr.] Little is known of its origin. It is held that it had its origin in Flanders, whose heavy soil is conducive to the breeding of heavy horses. This theory is not entirely convincing, though often repeated, for the constitution of the soil is not the decisive factor in the development of a new breed of horses. It is also widely assumed that this ancestor of the heavy horse breeds such as the Belgian

Ardennais was itself descended from a wild type which early became extinct, and is known as *Equus robustus*.

Undoubtedly the heavy breeds of today do trace back to this ancestry, but it may also be assumed that many more early types figure in their pedigree, and primarily the Turanian horse, though not by the medium of direct introduction but as a cross among the horses bred in this region (Gallica Belgica, Germania Inferior) in antiquity. Nevertheless, we can perceive the influence of a third type, probably derived from the Central Asiatic Taki (*Equus Przewalskii* Poliakoff) brought in by the Huns, and corresponding to Ebhardt's Pony Type II.

Historical analogies point to this. Cold-blooded horses were not only bred in Western Europe. Long before the Central Asiatic nomads reached Europe, and with them these horses of Taki blood, both in the Far East and the Middle East larger horses with more bone had been bred, especially in China and in Persia. The latter country was particularly well situated, geographically, for horse-breeding. Breeding of cold-bloods began there in the last few centuries before our era; thus, after the appearance of the Huns. This fact of itself shows the connection between the breeding of cold-blooded types and the Hun horses. The horses of these nations who came swarming out of the homeland of nomadic stock-keeping are described even in late sources—such as Ammianus Marcellinus in the case of the Huns—as ugly and clumsy. This type is still widely distributed in Mongolia. The stocky build and the low-set massive head both show characteristic cold-blooded features. In the breeding of the West European heavy horse the crossing of the above wild types must have been the basis, but the decisive factor in their development was a fixed objective, aimed at through selection and refinement.

The Oriental horse, naturalized in Spain by the Saracens, was now brought into contact with the West European horse mentioned above, and interbred. The battle of Poitiers—together with many other and more recent proofs—had shown that armoured cavalry fighting in close order was an effective counter to Arab mounted attack. The proper horse to carry this 'wall of armour' was the cold-blood enlivened by some characteristics of Oriental origin. The strategic equilibrium which obtained for a time in Europe with the victories over the Avars and the Arabs was in part due to the employment of such horses.

The Battle on the Lech

But this equilibrium was maintained only until 887, when a new wave of mounted invaders hit Europe in the form of the Magyars. For half a century they were able to put Europe to the sword and the flames without let or hindrance, raising the dreaded ghost of Attila's hordes all over again. Where was the armoured host of the Franks, which had vanquished the Avars and the Arabs? In spite of these successes, Western chivalry was no match for the Magyars, in either numbers, armament, or horseflesh. In particular, the lack of remounts was probably the reason for the failure to raise adequate mounted forces, as witness a decree by Charles the Bald in 864, almost 150 years after the battle of Poitiers, obliging his vassals to take the field on horseback.

For all that, Western chivalry was not useless, even though it had no success against the Magyars within the Frankish frontiers. Other nations who were threatened by the same enemy took the Frankish knight as their model. Saxons, Swabians,

RAIDS OF THE MAGYARS
898-961

and Bavarians had been, so to speak, taken unawares by the Magyar incursion. These nations still hardly ever fought on horseback; the army of Louis the Child, destroyed by the Hungarians at Bratislava in 907, was composed predominantly of infantry.

Now a remodelling along Frankish lines became urgent, and this did occur in a comparatively short time. At the battle of Riade on the Unstrut (near Merseburg) King Henry gained his first success by employing cavalry against the Hungarians in 933. According to the old Saxon chronicler Widukind, his army had been preparing for this battle for nine years. His son Otto I developed this plan further, and had at his disposal a considerable body of cavalry, with which he defeated the Hungarians decisively at the battle of the Lechfeld in 955, after the latter had ceased to reckon with any serious resistance.

Not that this victory broke the military power of the Hungarians. Nevertheless, this battle must rank with those of the Catalaunian Fields and Poitiers in the story of the newly awakening Europe. It was another victory of heavily armed cavalry restoring a parity of strength between East and West.

Its immediate effect was apparent, in that the Hungarians ceased from their raids and began to adapt themselves to the community of European nations. There was a further gain for the West, in that from now on Europe constituted a firmly united entity against Oriental aggression, with Hungary as its advanced guard. Against this united Europe the assaults of the Petchenegs, Uzes, Kumans, Mongols, and Osmanli Turks beat in vain.

Along the road which the mounted nomads had trod for centuries, wandering ever westward in the search for water and grazing for their herds, and more portable booty for themselves, there rode also the four apocalyptic horsemen—War, Famine, Pestilence, and Death—and yet this lamentable darkness was not unilluminated by flashes of light: Europe would never have been able to play so great a part in the history of mankind if it had remained in isolation. By its contacts with the peoples of the East, it became familiar with distant civilizations, from which it adopted many things; often these were quite mundane, of no more aesthetic significance than the wheelbarrow, borrowed from China; but tools, weapons, customs—even words—taken together all added to the fullness of life in Europe. What we call 'European culture' as it has developed over thousands of years is the sum of such borrowings from many different quarters.

These peoples who have been famous in Europe for their horsemanship have contributed much to the solution of humanity's perennial problem: the perfection of transport and communications. The last phase of this solution falls within our own century; its equestrian stages began with the appearance of the Magyars and ended in the first decades of the 1900's.

Europe at the Time of the Last Eastern Mounted Invasions

A study of Chinese history cannot but emphasize the historical significance of communications technique, with the trenchant phrase "The state is founded on the horse's back". We might adapt it to apply to equestrian history in Eurasia, by saying that history itself takes shape from the back of a horse. Since the earliest appearance of the mounted nomads from Asia the course of history flowed always in the same direction; it followed the tracks of the high-bred horse. This theme can also be expressed in terms of European progress. Just as the historical centre of gravity shifted eastward with the departure of the Huns and the fall of the Western Empire, with the onset of the 'Dark Ages', so with the arrival of new peoples riding out of the East a new historical development began.

It also became apparent that a certain pattern or rhythm of events obtained. The avenues of invasion were determined by geographical limitations. The Black Sea and the Mediterranean, which divide the temperate zones of Europe and Africa, left two alternative routes open to westward migrants; one through the 'gateway of the East' between the Urals and the Caspian, the other south of the Caspian to the Mediterranean coasts and via North Africa to the Strait of Gibraltar, entering Europe via Spain. These highways were also the approach routes of the hot-blooded strains of horse. At this time the amount of traffic by other routes over the Bosporus or by other seaways was negligible.

Along these two approaches different equestrian traditions entered Europe, and they have played a decisive part in the evolution of military and economic techniques there. The line of demarcation between the two equestrian cultures has by and large coincided with the western boundaries of Hungary and Poland, and only varied as these frontiers have themselves varied over the centuries. (Note 5.) West of the line was the domain of the heavily armoured, heavily armed knight, while east of it the domain of the mounted archer stretched away to the borders of China. The only exception was in the lands of the Middle East. Here a third tradition, that of the Arabian horsemen, replaces the two aforesaid; this was a late development, but a highly characteristic one.

In the Polish sector the line of demarcation between East and West was at times blurred, but very clear-cut in the Hungarian sector. Here the frontier between the two cultures represented not merely an ethnic and economic break but also a political one, marked by obstacles and hedges which were great impediments to cultural exchange, either way. Isolation was also often artificially increased by the ban on exports which is characteristic of the hippocentric political structure. A state which enjoyed a superiority, real or fancied, in matters concerning the horse would make of the sale of horses across the frontier an indictable offence. [For centuries this rule obtained within the British Isles. Not only are there laws by the Anglo-Saxon kings forbidding the export of horses except by way of gift (which for practical purposes meant royal gift with a political motive), but the last of the statutes forbidding the sale of horses by Englishmen to Scots was not repealed until 1603. Tr.] One of the earliest Continental decrees on this subject was that of St Ladislaus, King of Hungary 1077–95. The motive in this as in all cases was primarily military; such laws remained in Hungary until the end of the Middle Ages.

The essential differences between the two equestrian traditions arose out of a different way of life in East and West. While in the East everybody, including women and children, was accustomed to handle and ride horses, in the West riding was for centuries the prerogative of the ruling class, and in some instances of the male sex. (Note 6.)

The Western Counter-attack

When the mounted warrior became the armoured knight this implied a uniform Western technique of riding. But the chivalrous way of life did not only represent a personification of the military virtues, it also embodied the highest ideals of the age.

The origin of this development, which had its religious components and can be broadly termed Franco-Norman, is also Oriental. The mounted archer of the Migration Period, who projected the life he had enjoyed beyond the frontier of death, and therefore took with him into the grave either a horse or something (a skull, a bit, a stirrup) to symbolize a horse, or the Roman for whom the equestrian statue stood for the memorial of courage and the military virtues, are all—together with the medieval knight—phenomena characteristic of the equestrian culture. The Man on Horseback, properly the knight, cavalier, chevalier, caballero, represents for that era the ideal superior human type, just as the technician does in popular esteem today.

The chivalrous social system became a source of expansive power. The West modified its tactics vis-à-vis the East, and passed to the offensive. Thus in Spain the era of the Reconquista dawned, with a general rising against the Moors. The Cid, national hero of Spain, took Valencia in 1094 and founded an order of chivalry whose task it was to protect the Christian faith. The most significant event of the two-hundred-year struggle was the joint triumph of the Kings of Castile and Aragon at Las Navas de Tolosa in 1212, which initiated the gradual decline of Saracen rule in Spain, and led eventually to the liberation of the whole peninsula.

At the Synod of Clermont in 1095 Pope Urban II called for the liberation of the Holy Land from the infidel, who, in the person of the Seljuk Turks, had conquered

Palestine in 1071. In 1097 the first Crusading army reached Asia Minor under Godfrey of Bouillon. The impetuous tactics of Western chivalry, hitherto unfamiliar to the Seljuks, led to the storming of Jerusalem in 1099.

The liberated Holy Land became the Kingdom of Jerusalem, which the newly founded orders of the Templars, the Knights Hospitalers, and the Teutonic Knights defended against repeated Turkish attacks. All these orders were founded in the

The Emperor Frederick I on Crusade
From a MS by Peter de Ebule

twelfth century. This was the furthest outpost of the Franco-Norman civilization, whose boundaries can be roughly equated with those of Romanesque architecture. But it had to struggle for existence, with shallow roots in an alien soil; it was scarcely viable without repeated subventions from the West, and had to endure the hostility or at best the indifference of the neighbouring Christian Great Power, Byzantium. As the relations of this eastern Rome became more and more exacerbated in regard to the 'Franks', zeal for the holy cause was drowned in a flood of jealousy and suspicion, and the Holy Land in whose defence the West had expended so much treasure, blood, and sweat fell again to the Muslims in 1187.

The expansion of the West, after the fire had gone out of the Crusading idea and its forces had been disengaged from the Levant, redirected itself to the north-east. The knights of the Teutonic Order, under pretext of spreading Christianity among the Slavonic and Baltic tribes, took possession of East Prussia, and later conquered Lithuania, Livonia, and Kurland (Esthonia), often overrunning these boundaries on the Polish side. This was the heyday of European chivalry. A martial spirit, new methods of warfare, and the means to practise it in the form of adequate horses of the right sort, weighed the scales in favour of the West. Thereby the equilibrium of forces between Western and Eastern Europe was jeopardized.

Jenghis Khan

This was the moment when yet again a swarm of horsemen came out of Mongolia. The mounted Mongol hordes under Jenghis Khan raged like a destructive thunder-

63

storm right through Asia, reaching the Carpathians in 1240. Once more, as so often, the terror of the Four Deadly Horsemen paralysed Europe.

By all accounts the Mongolian horse of those days was not identical with the Tarpan-derived horse of Eastern Europe. Rogerius, Canon of Nagyvárad, was an eye-witness of the Tartar onslaught, and a chronicler of Hungarian events. He mentions that many Mongol horses came into possession of the Hungarians. Later documents also particularize 'Tartar' horses. This all goes to show that the horses of the Mongols could be easily distinguished from our own, probably because of their pronounced Przewalski features.

But the Mongols were also familiar with horses of Tarpan type with a dark eel-stripe. The unique source for the reign of Jenghis Khan, the *Secret History of the Mongols*, emphasizes every instance where this type is mentioned, as if it were something unusual. They also knew the Turanian horse. Ogedai Khan, when his people had forced Bagdad to surrender, demanded as ransom for the city not only jewels but also camels, pack-mules, and 'tall horses with long necks of western breed'. This means 'western' in relation to Mongolia, which lies east of Turania.

During the conquest of the Turkic tribes dwelling west of the Mongols the breeding of these Turanian or Turkestan horses had almost totally stopped, as was implied in the account of the Bactrian horse earlier. A more or less mixed blood-line of this race has since then been perceptible in the horse-stock of Asia Minor and North Africa.

It is worth noting that the *Secret History* also mentions the wild horses of Mongolia. They were hunted, like other game, on horseback. Jenghis Khan had a fatal accident out hunting, when a herd of these wild horses was unexpectedly put up. On sight of them his horse started and threw him on his back, and he died from spinal damage caused by this fall, in 1227.

The riding technique of the Mongols seems to be of Turkic origin; their horse-breeding, trading habits, and manner of warfare are also very similar to those of the Central Asiatic Turks. But other Turkish influences are also common among them, for instance in writing and vocabulary. These traditions too are mentioned in the *Secret History*, which traces the ancestry of Jenghis Khan to ancestors from the Uryanchai tribe among others.

Their ruthless attitude to horses is also reminiscent of Turkish practice. Whereas Western sources describe the Mongols as a savage mounted horde, they figure in Oriental writings as a disciplined army. According to Thomas, Archdeacon of Spalato (1268), the Mongols ride their tough little horses 'peasant-fashion', by which, apparently, he means in the Oriental manner, galloping them unshod over rocky, stony ground, as if they were chamois; and after three days on the march give them only a handful of inferior herbage. But the *Secret History* tells a very different story. It quotes a few lines from an order of the day by Jenghis Khan:

> Take care of the led horses in your troop, before they lose condition. For once they have lost it, you may spare them as much as you will, they will never recover it on campaign. . . . You will encounter much game on the march. Do not let the men go after it. . . . Do not let the men tie anything to the back of the saddle. Bridles will not be worn on the march—the horses are to have their mouths free. If this is done, the men cannot march at a gallop. If an order has been given, then those who disobey it must be beaten and put under arrest. But as for those who have disobeyed my personal orders, send those who are

30 Contemporary Statuette of Charlemagne. Damaged, and restored in the sixteenth century, but it seems fair to assume that if the original had shown stirrups the reproduction would have had them also

64

31   Persian Frieze showing Heavy Horses ridden by a King and a Deity

32   Asiatic Warrior extract-
ing Arrow from his
Horse
Note the method of
dressing mane. Hogged
short, so as not to
hamper the bow's use,
but locks left to assist
mounting. Tomb of the
Chinese Emperor
Tai-Tsong.
Musée Guimet

33 Magyar Marauders. Miniature from the Illuminated Vienna Chronicle.

34 King Béla IV of Hungary pursued by Mongols.
Miniature from Vienna Chronicle.

35
Kuman Archer.
Potsherd of the
thirteenth century.
*National Museum,
Budapest*

worth serious consideration to me. The rest, the unimportant ones, are to be beheaded on the spot. . . .

Was there ever a Western commander who ordered his troopers to take the bits off their horses on the march and reinforced his orders with such draconic sanctions? Scarcely; but then there was never a Western army that could point to such enormous feats of strategic marching on horseback.

Left Jenghis Khan, *right* Batu Khan. Chinese Portraits of the Manchu Era.
From a Hungarian edition of Secret History of the Mongols, 1962

Jenghis Khan's order is somewhat reminiscent of what the Emperor Leo the Wise says about the Magyars: "These people . . . suffer their superiors to punish them very severely for all transgressions, and they are held together not by affection but by fear". Old accounts of the Huns are similar; in their ranks were found many deserters. The art of war and the unsurpassed feats of long-distance horsemanship practised by the Oriental equestrian tribes had their roots, then, in the way of life of a warrior nation, who, hardened by centuries of fighting, had become accustomed to organization and iron discipline, and had made war their trade. What made the inexorable discipline bearable for the common trooper was the hope of rich booty, quickly won.

The observations of Archdeacon Thomas about the Mongol reserve horses are worth noting: "However many horses a man possesses, they are so trained that they follow him like dogs". A Hungarian bishop confirmed this on the evidence of Tartar prisoners: "They are followed by many riderless horses. One man riding in front and twenty or thirty horses after him". Now, this behaviour by the horses is not the result of training, as Thomas thought, but is the effect of the herd instinct which is the basis of nomadic horse-keeping, where horses are not driven but led to pasture in herds. Thus Leo the Wise writes of the Magyars: "Behind them follows a great troop of horses, both stallions and mares,[1] partly so that the horsemen can drink the mares' milk, partly to give the impression of a great host". The Pseudo-Maurikos had written almost exactly the same thing about the Avars nearly three hundred years earlier, and here we see how the supply system of the nomad armies worked, and this is the explanation of some of their marching feats: the spare horses followed the bell-mare, who was either ridden or led in hand, and were intended to be ridden in relays, and eventually eaten. The armies could thus move at a great pace over long stages, and supply was not the business of the army command, but of the individual soldier.

[As late as 1591 Giles Fletcher said of the Tartars in his *Of the Russe Commonwealth*: "... their souldiers to a certaine nomber, euery man with his two horse at the least, the one to ride on, the other to kill, when it commeth to his turne to haue his horse eaten. For their chiefe vittaile is horse flesh, which they eate without breade ..." *Tr.*]

Thus the nomad's life presented no great contrast as between war and peace. In either case all their possessions and all their 'vittaile', as Fletcher says, was of animal origin, the only difference being that when on the warpath their customary food—milk, meat, and blood—was all derived from the horse, and no other animal. The blood was drawn by turns from the veins of living horses, kept in gut bags, thickened over the fire, and finally fried like a 'black pudding'. The number of horses involved seems to imply that several troopers would belong to a 'mess', the basis of which was twenty or thirty spare horses: and all the time the picture is the same, horses running after the man on the lead horse.

But the spare horses also had their tactical uses. According to Leo the Wise, the Magyars tethered their spare horses to each other before battle, and put them immediately in rear of the fighting-line so that their men could not be directly attacked from behind. Rogerius says that the Mongols used to mount dummy soldiers on the spare horses to give the impression of greater numbers. [Just as in the desert campaigns of the early 1940s the 1st British Cavalry Division—which no longer had any horses, and had not yet any tanks—was employed in simulating vast masses of armour by means of disguised vehicles. *Tr.*]

The organization of Oriental mounted forces can really only be understood in the light of the use made of spare horses. That is how the advance guard of Subotai's army in 1241 managed to cover the ground between the Verecke Pass on the Hungarian frontier to the walls of Pest in only three days, a distance of 300 miles.

When the Great Khan died in 1241, Europe was saved from further devastation. Since the new Great Khan would have to be elected by all the Mongol chiefs, the hordes turned about, after laying waste the lands of the Kumans, Russians, Poles, Hungarians, and some Balkan countries, and after their scouts had penetrated Silesia, and took the road to their distant home in the East, taking with them thousands of prisoners from Christendom. Hungary was hardest hit by the Mongol scourge, although it would appear from the foregoing that the Magyars stood the best chance of survival against such an enemy.

The rout of the Hungarian forces at the river Sajó, a tributary of the Tisza, in

---

[1] Curious that he does not mention geldings.

1241, is explained by many contemporaries as due to internal confusion, the under-mining of the royal prestige and mistakes in the command of the army. Even so, Chinese authorities state that the Mongols suffered the heaviest losses of their European campaign at the hands of the Magyars, in a night engagement on the eve of the Sajó battle. When the next incursion took place forty-four years later the Magyars had no difficulty in defeating the Golden Horde.

The battle at the Sajó was at the same time the scene of an equestrian feat of historic importance. King Béla IV broke out of his laager of wagons, which was surrounded by the Mongols, and was able by means of repeated changes of horse (which his self-sacrificing entourage put at his disposal) to outdistance his pursuers, though these were full of endurance and determined to capture him. Bearing in mind that this horse-race for life and death was run between scions of the two races who were the most accomplished horsemen in the world, and that all was at stake, then the escape of the King must rank as the most significant equestrian event the world has ever seen.

In the century of these last mounted incursions Europe underwent far-reaching changes based on the experience of the Mongolian inroads, castles and fortifications were reconstructed, just as they had been earlier in the history of cavalry raids, all along the line between the Wall of China and the headwaters of the Danube and the Rhine. This was combined with the organization of armed 'train-bands' of citizens to defend the fortified towns. But this drastic phlebotomy in Eastern Europe gave a new drive to Western expansion.

With the expansion of the Teutonic Order the Western way of life became cur-rent over more ground, and the frontier between the two Europes receded east-ward in the Polish sector. Hungary continued to fulfil her historic role as before, both politically and economically, by means of a closed frontier lined with fortifi-cations and a ban on certain exports, yet cultural influences were unmistakably at work, in two directions. These elements of the Eastern way of life which had become naturalized only under the stress of compulsion were now voluntarily adopted and imitated.

If the onslaught of the Mongols was the last recognizable wave of the Migration of Peoples, the undertow and the eddies took the form of much displacement, much resettlement. So long as all the populations of the Eastern region were not finally sedentary, some nations in Europe would be subject to pressure of westward-moving elements. New storm-clouds blew up in the form of settlement by the Tartars, on the steppes of eastern Europe, and then in the Ottoman Empire, where the revived fanaticism of Islam led to expansion by violence in Asia Minor.

The Turkish Peril

The Osmanlis belonged, as the Seljuks and Kumans had done, to the family of Oguz Turks who had left their homes under pressure from the Mongols in the thirteenth century. In all some thousands of them entered the service of the Seljuk Turkish sultan in Asia Minor. The Seljuk kingdom shortly became the scene of events that were to be repeated many times over among the splintered survivors of once united Turkish tribes: the prince of the small Osmanli minority, Osman I (1282–1326), became the founder of a dynasty, and ultimately ruler of an empire, and the Seljuk population, which had become more or less Persianized, adopted the name of Osmanli under his rule. This was the Turkish syndrome. Under the slogan of the spread of Islam, their first aim was the mastery of Constantinople.

The appearance of the Turks in Europe meant, for the Hungarians, the beginning of three hundred years of defensive warfare. In the whole eastern region the duel between two mounted antagonists began all over again. But now it was no longer a quarrel about pasture and waterholes: the Turks were interested only in power, the Hungarians in self-preservation. Besides these cardinal objectives, however, the counters were booty and prisoners, and it was the hope of these that brought recruits to the colours on both sides. On every campaign the Turks brought away thousands of peaceful inhabitants, to be sold as slaves to landowners in Anatolia, or in order to bring up the boys as mercenaries in the Janissary schools. In the hope of ransom, soldiers captured noblemen and their families. This happened also on the Hungarian side, though in a lesser degree, but apparently with the same financial success. The ransom of a Turkish soldier came to a respectable sum in cash, or the equivalent in Turkish horses. Volunteers marched with the armies, in the Hungarian ranks known as Heiducks, corresponding to the freebooters among the Turks. To such men every campaign was what the Turanian warriors called an *alaman*—an excursion in search of plunder.

The combat raged over Hungarian soil for nearly a hundred and fifty years, and finally led to exhaustion on both sides. At a time when the population of Western Europe was doubling itself, the four and a half million Magyars lost half their total strength. Loss of manpower in the Turkish Empire led to decadence at the end of these wars. All this served as a pretext for the house of Habsburg to expel the Turks at the end of the seventeenth century and establish their power in Hungary.

The Turkish wars had brought new experiences to the art of warfare on horseback; they led to the final abandonment of armour in Europe, so bringing Western practice nearer to the Asiatic norm. The greater emphasis on light cavalry led to the preponderance on the battlefield of the hot-blooded horse, and the breeding of half-blood horses, which in turn had beneficial effects on transport in general.

Apocalyptic Horsemen in the New World

While in Europe the Turkish wars saw the cavalry of East and West measured against each other, the European horseman in the Americas spread the same terror as his predecessors had once done in the Old World, as they swarmed out of Asia. Only the numbers were on a quite different scale.

The report by Hernán Cortez to the Emperor Charles V on the conquest of Mexico in 1519–21 tells an unvarnished tale of inhuman massacres perpetrated on the native population under the pretext of conversion to the True Faith, but actually inspired by immeasurable greed for wealth and power. Consciousness of their military superiority awakened in the Spaniards primarily the baser human passions.

The New World offered a re-enactment of previous historical events. The appearance of the mounted hidalgo paralysed the proven valour of the native population, as once the appearance of the 'centaurs' had robbed the astounded Europeans of their natural courage. The astonished aborigines lost their heads and fled, again and again, during the triumphal progress of the conquistadores. And yet the Mexican warriors were not really so defenceless. They had arrows and other missile weapons tipped with various metals (though no iron), and also obsidian and bone;

Aztec Temple stormed by Spanish Soldiers
From a sixteenth-century MS

but for the moral effect, they could easily have overwhelmed the handful of Spanish lancers.

The Mexican defensive measures showed themselves repeatedly in the same pattern: they dug deep pits as obstacles for the opposing cavalry, and these were effective, in so far as Cortez reports: "I continually admonished my men to make every handsbreadth of ground we won passable for the horses, for our cavalry were the decisive factor in the campaign". Whenever possible, these pits were filled in before the attack, even though it meant an embittered skirmish on foot, an escort fighting to protect the pioneers.

The horse, now an indispensable factor in the military and commercial life of Europe, played a decisive part in the further development of the fate of nations on the American continent, exactly as it had done in the Migration period. Wherever the White Man as soldier, hunter, pioneer, or farmer appeared with his horse, then it was time for the aborigine to fade away. The bounds of this new Migration of Peoples were set by climatic conditions. The icy North and the Tropic Zone—in neither of which can the horse flourish—were the last refuge of the autochthonous peoples. The same is true of Africa and Australia, except that one of these extremes is missing from both these continents.

Meanwhile in Europe that tract of the human story which had begun with the horsemen swarming out of Asia was drawing to its close, and as the Ottoman crescent waned the balance of power in East and Central Europe shifted once again, and in the new equilibrium the interests of the house of Habsburg and of the house of Romanov formed the counterweights. Gradually the line of demarcation between the two sectors of Europe, the two contrasting ways of life, was fading. And all this hastened the amalgamation of European horsemanship into a uniform standard.

Part III The Equestrian Civilization

The Threefold Turanian Legacy

The development of a uniform European standard of horsemanship was delayed, during the Middle Ages, by the same forces which had set bounds to it in the past. Custom, prejudice, and religious taboos and encumbrances put obstacle after obstacle in the way of people who were trying to make progress in various respects. It was not until the beginning of the nineteenth century that European horsemanship achieved its fullest development, even though the earliest traces of its development under various external influences were already evident in the Middle Ages.

But in order to treat of this historical process we must define what is meant by the 'equestrian civilization'.

It is determined by three factors: the man, the horse he rides, and the way he rides it. Yet all these together do not add up to an 'equestrian civilization'. Each of them must attain a certain standard, individually and collectively. So far as the man is concerned this standard is determined by the equestrian way of life, in the physical and mental sense. Of course, there are no hard-and-fast patterns. Different types of horsemen of different periods, different schools of riding and driving, can all be regarded as positively contributing to the equestrian civilization, presuming they are not only outwardly concerned, from motives of pleasure or display, but also inwardly committed, having the psychological attitude characteristic of the true horseman. Such a man sees in his horse not merely an animal that is of use to him, just some quadruped subject to his dominion, but regards it rather as a companion by whose help he can attain a higher way of life.

The second and passive partner is the horse, but not just any horse. The Good Horse, as such, stands out from the mass of *Equus caballus*, bearing in mind the special meaning which the word Good has in this context.

I am sure that many of my readers will have experienced that feeling which is so typical of the hippophile, at the moment when, after some strenuous journey, some dangerous ride, or the passing of some perilous obstacle, he gets down from the saddle or the driver's box and gratefully pats the neck of his horse, which has once again proved itself a reliable partner. Such gratitude has its roots in the reliance we place on the extraordinary capacities and high qualities associated with the 'good horse'.

In the past, and in part also today, that sort of horse embodied everything that went to make up the horseman's ideal.

But the outstanding qualities of a good horse depend not on its individual capabilities alone, but primarily on its breeding and pedigree. The part which the horse has been able to play, therefore, has been sustained thanks to its inheritance from Bactrian, Turanian, and Arabian ancestors, the *materia generosa* of the ancients. For thousands of years men have been trying to beg, borrow, buy, plunder, or steal horses of this kind, just because the attributes of the 'blood' horse are so highly prized. And this points to the real prerequisite of the equestrian civilization, which is a purposeful breeding policy whereby an adequate supply of the right sort of horse is ensured; and this demands much technical knowledge, and a heavy sacrifice of time, money, and patience.

As to the third and no less important factor—the actual techniques of riding and driving—one may regard this as part of the history of transport and communications, of war, or of sport, but in any case it does not require further elucidation at this stage.

In the art of horsemanship, as it had evolved in Europe by say 1800, the influence of three separate traditions was perceptible, all ultimately going back to Turania. The oldest of these was that of Central Asia, going back to the mounted nomads of that region, and it proved to be the one which exerted its influence latest on Western Europe. The second was the Arabian influence, exerted primarily during the campaigns of Moslem expansion through North Africa and against all the major peninsulas on the north shore of the Mediterranean. The third influence was internal, arising in Europe itself; here the West European institution of 'chivalry' (which originally had the same meaning as 'cavalry') grew up around the nucleus of a school of horsemanship that owed something to Near Eastern and much to Scandinavian influence. The knight of France-Norman pattern becomes the typical figure of Western Christendom in the Middle Ages.

We shall explore the history and achievements of these three equestrian civilizations in the following chapters, beginning with Western Europe and working backward via the world of the Arab horseman to Central Asia.

The West European Tradition

A deliberate horse-breeding policy became necessary, at the very latest, at the moment when German and French knights found it imperative to protect themselves and their horses from the hail of arrows discharged by the mounted bowmen of Central Asia; the horse must be able to carry the weight of armour over and above that of the rider and his weapons, and according to their ideas only a heavily built horse could carry heavy weights. (Note 7.) The Arabs, on the other hand, did not at this period shoot from the saddle, and indeed they did not adopt the stirrup until about 1150. They rode light horses, and the Christian knights of Mediterranean lands were able to oppose them on equally light horses.

France was the country in which the influence of Oriental stock brought home by the Crusaders, and used as sires to cover mares of local breeds such as the Ardennais and the Limousin, was important. Like all the North French breeds derived mostly from the mixture of Pony Type II, Horse Type III and Horse Type IV, (see p. 14) such races as the Percheron and the Boulonnais were big and slow and powerful, but after the twelfth century they acquired even more qualities of Oriental origin. They also began to be bred far outside the confines of France itself; not only in England (since 1066) but in Northern Italy and beyond the Rhine as far as Bohemia and Austria, in Denmark, and perhaps even in Sweden. The striking power of every Western army consisted of armoured knights on cold-blooded horses which had to be bred at home because all Western monarchs forbade the export of such horses on principle.

36 Mongolian Horses of Taki
Strain

37
Mongolian Horse,
hobbled by Leading
Rein on Treeless Steppe

38 Sultan Soleiman's Army crossing the Drava.
Contemporary miniature.
Chester Beatty Library, Dublin

39 (above)
The 'Steel Wall' of Western Chivalry
From the *Roman de Tristan*, 1468

40 (left)
St George.
Engraving by Albrecht Dürer

ANO · DNI · MCCCXXVIII

The breeding of heavy horses in the West was intended to produce the armour-carrying destrier (to adopt the Norman term; indeed, the word only occurs in Western languages). Derived from the Latin *dextrarius*, which means right-handed, this expression has been interpreted in different ways ever since medieval times; either it means that the groom or squire led it off the right hand, or the right hand is conceived of as being more powerful than the left (as it is in most people, but not in most horses). Thus a thirteenth-century chronicle compares the destrier as a type with Bucephalus as an individual, excelling all others in strength. It is significantly still the custom in Eastern Europe to harness the stronger horse on the right side of the pole—the dexter side, in terms of heraldry. There is documentary evidence that the destrier was exclusively an entire and specially trained stallion. It was accounted scandalous to use mares for military purposes. The dextrarius was in fact just the horse for the chosen method of fighting—charging in close order over comparatively short distances. It was not capable of a sustained gallop, but its very mass added weight to the impact. The aggressive instincts of the stallion were also exploited, but not always to the advantage of the rider, because horses which had been trained to be aggressive could only with difficulty be induced to go over to the defensive, or even to retreat. The care of destriers in camp was rendered more difficult by the fact that they could not be turned out to graze with other horses. (Note 8.)

They are first mentioned in connection with the struggle against the Moors or Saracens. It is recorded of the Emperor Otto II (973–983) that at the battle of Cotrone in Calabria (982), he was pursuing the Saracens after an initial success, but they lured him into an ambush and defeated him with crippling losses. The Emperor himself was barely able to escape capture on his marching-palfrey, after his destrier had been killed under him.

A Hungarian chronicle of about the same period tells us that Prince Béla of the Arpad dynasty, fighting in alliance with the Polish Prince Micislav, knocked his Pomeranian enemy out of the saddle of the destrier. Twelfth- and thirteenth-century documents often mention such chargers, notably in the records of the Hungarian King Béla IV for 1251, where this type of horse is described as the characteristic mount of the Western chivalry.

Detailed information about the breeding and care of horses in the West is available from the administrative accounts of the Teutonic Knights. In the archives of their headquarters at Marienburg a clear picture of the care and use of heavy horses is given. There are accounts of how horses were racked up in their stalls, about the building of stables and the fencing of paddocks, about rations of fodder and forage, about farriery, and so on. The general impression is one of similarity with modern practice. So also with breeding—the mares were put only to particular stallions, and we actually have a covering calendar with accurate entries of dates.

All of which goes to show that already there was a profound difference between stud practice East and West. The heavy horse as we know it is therefore not the result of natural selection but the result of systematic human interference. The overemphasis which was laid on breeding the type with the greatest body-weight of necessity led to the exaggeration of those disadvantages which go with such a conformation. The heavy horse, kept in the stable until it had become unaccustomed to being turned out (even in the grazing season they spent far too little time at grass), did indeed attain a huge stature, but became soft and lethargic and unsuited to prolonged exertions. In the beginning of the Age of Chivalry, when this process of 'inflation' had barely begun, the 'heavy' characteristics were not nearly so conspicuous as they are in, say, the Shire or the Noriker of today, and indeed did not begin to predominate until the thirteenth century, as is apparent from the evidence of art alone.

[In the English context the Bayeux Tapestry makes this very plain. The war-horses at Hastings look like miniature Clydesdales, about the size of Welsh cobs. But they are not so hairy about the heels, and they are galloping in a way no Clydesdale could ever move. *Tr.*]

There must certainly have been intermediate types between these and the common horses, as well as crosses between light and heavy strains.

On the march the destrier was led in hand, while the knight rode a light horse specially bred for this purpose to give a comfortable ride. This was the *palafridus*—palfrey in English. The knight did not change horses until the last moment before going into action; and the only parallel to this procedure is to be found among the Arabs.

It is therefore understandable that mounting the destrier—'getting on to one's high horse'—acquired a certain symbolic significance within the Order. The Emperor Frederick I's standing orders laid down that if a strange knight approaches the camp unarmed and shieldless on a palfrey (*in palafrido*), then he is to be peaceably received, but if he rides up with slung shield on his fighting stallion (*in dextrario*), then he is to be attacked.

The Palfrey

The speciality of the palfrey was that it paced where other horses trotted. This gait is now largely obsolete in Europe, but it once lay at the foundations of a whole department of Western horsemanship.

Most quadrupeds at the walk and the trot put one fore- and one hind-foot forward simultaneously—or nearly so—but diagonally, that is, left fore and right hind or *vice-versa*. Even the erect biped human shows vestiges of this habit when he swings his arms on the march—as one leg goes forward the *opposite* arm swings forward. But in pacing the limbs on the same side of the body go forward together—left fore and left hind, then right fore and right hind.

This gait could either be induced by training, or to a certain extent by breeding, and it was prized because it was so comfortable for the rider. Mechanically, a stretcher carried by two men marching in step gives the same sort of 'ride'. So does a camel.

The heavy horse which is incapable of a sustained gallop or canter can yet cover long distances at the trot, a gait which to the heavily armoured rider on a horse with the action that the destriers had would be sheer torture—and, indeed, Field Punishment Number One in the severe disciplinary code of the Teutonic Order consisted of trotting in full armour by the hour. For this reason the moment of changing horses was postponed as late as possible, and when the chivalry attacked they did so at a gallop, or more likely a slow canter, rather than a trot.

The palfrey was also the travelling horse for civilian purposes of all who could afford it in the West. From the Latin *paraveredus*, later *parafridus* and *palafridus*, are derived the French *palefroy* and the English 'palfrey'. Strangely, in the German language the old word *ross* for horse in general was displaced by an adaptation of *paraveredus*—*Pferd*. *Palefrenier* in French means a groom. So, originally, did the English surname Palfreyman. A slower, but also easy-going, type of horse was called in Latin *gradarius*, in French *ambleur*, and in English 'ambling pad'.

The other 'easy' gait, more showy and used more often in the West for civilian than for military purposes, was the rack, now almost exclusively practised in the United States and Iceland. It is a four-beat motion, in which the feet are set down in the series left hind, left fore, right hind, right fore, not in pairs but one after the other; and it can take place at any speed from that of a walk (which it much resembles) to the equivalent in m.p.h. of a fast gallop. [The sight and particularly the sound of a good racker accelerating from 3 to 20 m.p.h. without changing step is a unique experience. *Tr.*] According to Ursula Bruns, there are natural-born rackers, among some pony breeds of Western Europe, and such are highly prized for breeding purposes in Iceland.

[The fact that usage among Latin-writing clerks was not uniform from country to country in the West does not make historical investigation easier. Throughout the period the Vulgar Latin *tolutarius* was current, and was used in Scandinavia, and probably in England, to mean 'racker'. But since the French verb *trotter* is probably derived from *tolutare* it seems probable that by this Latin word the French clerk meant a trotting light horse of the kind called in English of the period a hakenay. This latter word is itself derived from the French *haquenée*, which meant some sort of soft-paced light horse, either pacing or racking. Thus the disciplines of etymology and semantics run dead contrary to the current of hippology! *Tr.*]

The Arts of War

In the revival of armoured cavalry there was necessarily an element of deliberate imitation of antiquity, since the Roman and more especially the Byzantine Empire had adopted this mode of warfare, and there was unbroken continuity between the armoured *infantry* of Roman legions and early medieval hosts. But the fighting power of the medieval armoured lancer in comparison with that of his counterpart in antiquity was much higher because, if his discipline was inferior, his equipment was superior.

This was primarily because of the saddle. The war-saddle was brought to perfection in the West, even though its origins lie somewhere in the East, probably among horse-breeders of the settled peasant rather than the nomadic herding tradition. Most likely the Arabs brought it to Europe. Its earliest form, as a true saddle, consists of a felt pad either side of the spine and united by wooden bows, as in the Pazyryk saddles discovered by Rudenko (1951). The saddle of chivalry was a very elaborate derivative of this, consisting of two enormous rigid 'bows', the hinder one of which 'embraced' the pelvis of the rider, united by wooden bars which are more like planks. The seat was stuffed, as was the inside of the saddle next to the horse. The high, wide pommel rose sheer in front of the rider's stomach, with only just room for him between it and the cantle. [Since, presumably, saddles were made to order for individual customers, it would in practice have been impossible for a thick-set knight to use his thin colleague's saddle—he would simply

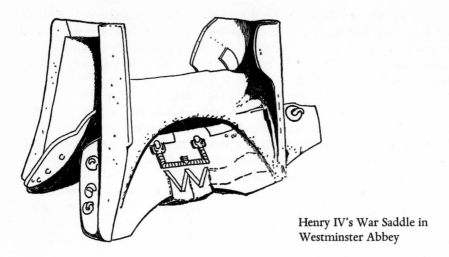

Henry IV's War Saddle in
Westminster Abbey

not have been able to get into it. And that is the point—one rode *in*, not *on*, the
medieval war-saddle. *Tr.*] Most saddles used on the march, for travelling and for
hunting, seem to have been of the same pattern. They were not really practical or
comfortable for either horse or rider, but in comparison with Roman models they
did represent a technical advance.

The rider sat with a long, straight leg—the feet sticking forward in a style that
was used for both military and civilian purposes. We think of this as the 'chivalrous'
style, but it was not in fact peculiar to the armoured horseman, and it was practised
both with and without stirrups, which had probably been introduced into Europe
by the Avars: but their use became general only very slowly, especially when one
considers their importance as an aid to riding. It was centuries before they had been
adopted by all the Germanic tribes, even the Franks, who became the great equestrian champions of Europe. They cannot be definitely shown to have been used in
the West until the defensive battles against the Magyars. Probably loathing and
contempt for the enemy led here, as long ago in the case of the Jews *vis-à-vis* the
Egyptians, to a reluctance to adopt his equipment and habits.

The tactical employment of the 'armoured wall' of knights demanded an open
ground on which to ride down the enemy. The knight fighting alone or in small
groups had so little effect that he was no match for the light cavalry, which would
quickly overcome him, as can be seen in many historical instances. He was like a
tank that has lost contact with its unit, or has blundered on to difficult going and
become immobilized and more or less defenceless. Light cavalry, on the other hand,
even when dispersed in open order, are still formidable individual opponents.

It did not take long for the vulnerable points of the 'armoured wall' to be
detected, and more or less successful means to prise it apart to be devised. Ambush
was the most common of these, in which connection the tactics of the White Huns
against the Persian armoured cavalry, anticipating European tactics by about a
thousand years, are of interest. (Note 9.)

The appearance of firearms solved at one blow the problem of how to break up
the close array of armoured horsemen. More particularly this was the tactical role
of artillery rather than hand-guns. The total collapse of heavy cavalry in the face of
cannon-fire of necessity brought an end to the art of war as practised by chivalry—

and the end of chivalry as a practical military technique. The knight now survived in an unreal world, as is very evident from the literature of the sixteenth and seventeenth centuries, where he appears either as the central figure of an artificial pastoral romance (say Spenser's *Faerie Queene*) or as the butt of some satirical mock-epic (say *Don Quixote* or *Hudibras*). From the middle of the fifteenth century onward the light horseman replaced the armoured knight, just as he had done centuries before, in the armies of Khorasan, of Rome, and of Byzantium.

The Breeding of Half-bred Horses

With the decline of chivalry horse-breeding in the West took a new turn. Interest was focused on the Andalusian horse of Spain. The breed had been widely distributed in the Mediterranean (as far east as Cyprus) during the time when the cold-blooded heavy chargers were being bred up to their maximum size, and was esteemed (but scarce and expensive) in northern countries. The first recorded in England are the two black chargers ridden by William the Conqueror at Hastings. The Andalusian was as fast as Oriental horses, as handy, as pleasant to ride, and was up to weight. It was the first representative in the Western world of what in German are called 'warm-blooded' and in English 'Half-bred' or 'half-blood' horses—that is, a mixture of cold-blooded Great Horse elements with the Oriental (Barb, Arab, or Turk). In practice the Andalusian had all the properties of the best examples of such a mixture, but probably its genetic make-up was quite different. It was almost certainly descended from a breed indigenous to the southern part of the Iberian peninsula, and described in detail by the younger Pliny. It was the normal mount of Roman generals, with a straight facial profile, or a slightly convex one like that of the Nisaean horses of Persia.

The history of Spain and of the West generally is shot through and through with this breed. It was the great weapon of the Reconquista against the Moors, and of the conquistadores against the Incas; the mount of the Cid and of Pizarro. It was also the charger of the Christian armies of the Danube region confronting the Turks.

Its dispersal in the modern era was due to the rule of the House of Aragon over Naples and Sicily, and the House of Habsburg over Spain, but it had been widely distributed throughout Europe, at the top level only (because it was always expensive) from the early Middle Ages onward. [Indeed, one may say of the eleventh and twelfth centuries that the successful Western general was typically a Norman mercenary riding an Andalusian horse. *Tr.*] It was, of course, the stallions, not the mares, that were exported, and the pure race continued to be bred principally in Spain. Maximilian II brought Andalusian sires to the foundation of his studs at Lipizza, in Istria, and Kladrub, in Bohemia, and the famous breeds which bear these names are descended from the progeny of Spanish stallions out of mares of other races. Both became uniform throughout the extensive Habsburg domains, from the Danube to the Low Countries, as carriage horses and officers' chargers.

Half-blood breeding in France was on a somewhat different basis, and associated with the earlier rulers of the Bourbon dynasty. Henry IV (1589–1610) was a true horseman, and laid the foundations of French warm-blood breeding, on the basis of the light horse native to his homeland of Navarre. This Navarrese horse, close to the Limousin in type, and indeed to the regional varieties of South-west France generally, had many Oriental attributes which were no doubt the legacy of Moslem invasions in early Carolingian times. With such horses it was possible to practise an entirely new school of horsemanship. (Note 10.)

The abundant equestrian portraits of the period prove the widespread use of half-blood horses. Whether in battle, hunting, or on the march, the person of substance is always riding a horse of the same stamp, in Britain or on the Continent, and it is a horse with all the hallmarks of Iberian origin. [And this is the great difference between medieval and early modern times. The Western aristocrat down to about 1500 rode different types of horse in battle, out hunting, and on the road between one of his estates and another. But now he was able to use one stamp of horse for all these purposes—the Andalusian was indeed 'the horse for all seasons'. Tr.] The Andalusian, and more so its derivative the Neapolitan, was unmistakable with its 'presence', the high carriage of its head, often with Roman nose but never large, on a muscular neck, rather hollow back, very broad breast, sloping croup and luxuriant tail set on rather low. It figures prominently in pictures of the battles against the Turks, in which many painters and engravers with a good eye for a horse bring out very clearly the Oriental characteristics of the Turkish horses, in contrast to the Iberian features of what we must regard as 'the Occidental hot-blood'.

The Spanish High School

It is appropriate to mention here the High School or Spanish School of Vienna (ultimately of Naples). This is a particular branch of the art of training and riding horses, the ultimate goals of which are utterly contrary to the horse's nature, and which therefore demand an extraordinary degree of strength, intelligence, and perseverance. For this discipline the Spanish horse was well suited.

This decorative, spectacular mode of riding was not at first intended as a mere display of equestrian science. The various exercises at the walk and the trot lead to complete harmony between horse and rider, and in the literally higher branches (such as the 'airs above the ground') they preserve vestiges of a manner of mounted combat in which the horse was to some extent a weapon, used to ride down the enemy. A horse that had done this course of training was worth a great deal in difficult country, among obstacles, and in close-quarter fighting. This world-famous legacy of the horsemanship of former days now survives only in two centres; the Spanish High School of Vienna, and Saumur in France. Both schools as the preservers of a living tradition are of enormous historical worth, especially in the case of Vienna, which is horsed from its own stud of Lipizzaners (now at Piber), and directly descended from Maximilian's foundation stock. These horses, which are physically exactly suited to the task, carry out with baroque formality all the evolutions of the equestrian art as it was elaborated in the seventeenth century, in the dignified setting provided by the Emperor Charles VI, who in 1735 commissioned Fischer von Erlach to design the Spanish Riding School at the Hofburg.

Open-range Breeding in America

We have seen that the primary expansion of European horsemanship and horse-mastership in the New World was Spanish, and over the American continent as a whole the Spanish influence has been the predominant one, exerted alike on the

Indians, in so far as these took up horsemanship, and on Europeans of extra-Iberian origin. It was above all Spanish horses which, escaping from settlements in Mexico, California, Texas, Florida, soon populated the central plains with their feral descendants. Here the climate, soil, and herbage closely resembled that of the Eurasian steppe which had been the home of the horse before domestication. But this relapse into the primeval freedom did not entail also a physical recession to the original steppe type; the Mustang remained merely feral, merely a domestic horse run wild.

It was primarily with the aid of the mustang that the Plains Indians of the prairie region became mounted nomads, though probably the core of their horsemanship was formed by means of horses broken to ride and stolen from the Spaniards. The Indians invented nothing new in horsemanship or horsemastership so far as we know: what they did not learn by imitation of the Paleface horseman they learned empirically all over again—but nothing in excess of what was already known and practised. What is remarkable about the equestrian revolution among the Redskins is the speed with which it happened, and the absolute transformation of their way of life which the acquisition of the horse (far more so than the introduction of guns and whisky) brought about. Whole nations abandoned the practice of settled agriculture and became totally dependent on the horse, with the aid of which alone they could effectively hunt the bison all the year round. After the adoption of hunting as a way of life, war as a pastime and a prestige-giving occupation followed. Some tribes between 1720 and 1890 (when the 'horse-fever' had run its course) became quite sophisticated practitioners of line-breeding—for instance, the Nez Percé tribe, which produced the spotted Apaloosa breed, and became so emotionally bound up with its survival that after their war-bands had surrendered (severely outnumbered, and within sight of the Canadian frontier) to the U.S. Cavalry the American commanding officer perceived that the quickest way to achieve the complete psychological collapse of the red men was the immediate slaughter of their treasured spotted horses before their eyes. The desired effect was produced—there were no more Nez Percé risings—by this refinement of brutality, which hardly has its parallel even in the bloody chronicles of Eurasian mounted warfare.

On the grassy plains of the Americas, North and South, open-range horse-breeding on a large scale found a new home in the eighteenth and nineteenth centuries, alongside the extensive breeding of cattle and sheep. Apart from navigable rivers—mostly flowing from north to south, whereas the tide of migration ran from east to west—there was no alternative in transport and communications to the ox-wagon and the ridden or driven horse. The bell-mare as leader of the half-wild herds reassumed the key position she had occupied on the Eurasian steppe, and the conditions of nomadic stockbreeding were reproduced over again.

But only in terms of numbers and form. Otherwise American open-range breeding had little in common with the Central Asian prototype. Although the rough life of the prairies threw up a special type of man, the cowboy or gaucho, the horseman of the New World, whatever his ancestry, was dominated by Spanish tradition; his manner of breeding and breaking horses, style of riding, saddlery, accoutrements, all bore traces of Spanish origin, from the crown of his sombrero to the nails in his horseshoes (if his horse was shod at all). This is still evident in the United States, and even in Canada, in so far as the prairie way of life survives at all.

The breeding of heavy horses in modern times is an essential feature of the equestrian civilization. At the moment when the armoured mounted lancer left the military scene his horse took on a different role, primarily that of a harness horse. In England this change came about (though it was not fully completed) in the seventeenth century, and its crisis may be equated with the years following the Civil War. Here as in many European countries the ex-destrier displaced the smaller native breeds in the shafts of the cart, and the draught-ox before the plough. The release of the Great Horse from military service also made possible the increase in carriage traffic characteristic of the seventeenth and eighteenth centuries in the West. But the general trend of heavy-horse breeding was to an even heavier, even slower, animal of gigantic proportions with the pulling power of two oxen.

Pride of place in Europe as a whole still went to the North French breeds, from the Pas de Calais to Brittany. The Ardennais, widely known outside its native country simply as "the Belgian Horse", has contributed genetically to the foundations of every heavy-horse breed in Europe. In England, under the name of the Flemish Horse, it is an element in the foundation stock of the Clydesdale, the Shire, and even the Suffolk, the last of which probably owes much also to the Jutland breed of Denmark. Even in the Alps the influence of this lowland breed was felt, since the Austrian Pinzgau agricultural horse derives from a cross of the Ardennais on the indigenous mountain-bred Noriker.

The Arabian Tradition

The last sortie from the heartland of mounted nomadism reached the Near East in the thirteenth century. Crossing the mountains of Iran and Afghanistan, the Mongol hordes repeatedly plundered the Islamic lands. This brought about crises in the Near East which had fundamental changes as a consequence.

Cairo, which was then the seat of the Arab Caliphate, and with it the whole Islamic empire, suffered a like change in political direction. The Caliph's praetorian guard, which consisted of slaves, instituted a palace revolution in 1250, deposing the last of the Ayyubid Caliphs, Tur-in-Shah, taking power to itself. Now, this corps of guards, known as Mamelukes, consisted originally of Kipchak Turks who had been taken prisoner by the Mongols and bought from them by the Caliph El Malik el Saleh at some slave market on the Black Sea for his Cairene household. This take-over by Turks from Central Asia of Egyptian sovereignty brought with it many changes other than political. Turkish technique in military and transport fields took firm root in Egypt, and there now began that march of events which brought to the fore the Arab horse and the Arab style of horsemanship in that part of the world where the Cyrenaican and Barka horses had once had their being.

This Turkish influence was no isolated phenomenon in the Arab world of that time. Different elements of a Turkish realm that was disintegrating over a period of some centuries found a new home in the Arab world. Most of the Turks reached the Near East as mercenaries or as slave-soldiers, but they also appeared as conquerors, as for instance in the eleventh century, when the Seljuks left Central Asia, overran Asia Minor, and entered the Holy Land. The influence of Central

43 (above) Sir Geoffrey Luttrell of Ingham, Lincolnshire, departing for the wars, *c.* 1340.
From the Luttrell Psalter. *The British Museum*

44 (below left) State Saddle in Ivory, made in 1396 and captured by the Turks from the Emperor
Sigismund at the Battle of Nicopolis. *National Museum, Budapest*

45 (below right) Western Saddle of Baroque Period

Overleaf:

46 (above) Dressage on Black Andalusian Stallion, late Eighteenth Century
Engraving by J. Froschel junior

47 (below) Dressage Work on the Pillars, with Andalusian/Neapolitan Stallion, late Eighteenth Century
Engraving by J. Froschel junior

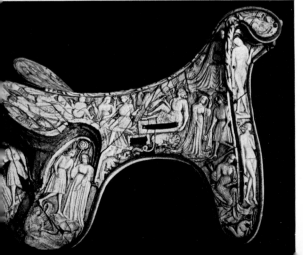

Overleaf:

48 (above)
The Spanish Riding
School, Vienna, in
1826
A. Kuntz

49 (below)
The Spanish Riding
School Today

50
French Light-horse Trooper
Early Seventeenth Century.
He is still wearing a cuirass,
the last vestige of armour.
From a lithograph by F.
Gerasch.
National Museum, Budapest

51
Austrian Dragoon of the
Early Nineteenth Century

Asia had therefore been preponderant in the Levant before the time of the Mameluke *putsch*.

This penetration over the centuries by Turks meant that from the ninth century onward a Turkish minority had been able to seize power now and again. The Ayyubid dynasty itself was of Turkish origin, and so had been that of the Tulunids (868–905). Like the Mamelukes themselves (who were to reign from 1250 to 1517), they brought many distinctively Turkish political and social influences to bear which reflected conditions of life in Central Asia, now to be imposed on the Arab society. The Fatimid Caliphs (969–1171) were supported by the Turks, and in other countries too the Turkish minorities managed to seize power. Thus in 1017 Mahmud of Ghazni, descendant of a slave bodyguard, became ruler of Afghanistan and Persia. Indeed, this syndrome of seizure of power by Turkish minorities amounts almost to a historical rule, so that historians have attributed a 'state-founding capacity' to this people. But if we take into account that the other nomadic stock-breeding peoples of Asia, such as Huns, Ephthalites, Mongols, have played a similar part in the history of India, of China, of Manchuria, etc., then this assumption can scarcely be valid for the Turks alone, but for all who practised the original Turkish way of life.

The prime reason for the important political function of the Turks lay simply in the fact that at that time the epitome of a ruling class was conceived of as a mounted warrior. We shall often have occasion to remark on the ideological side-effect of the equestrian civilization. It had occurred before and was to occur again, many times over.

These Mamelukes came from Central Asia, and their ancestors had migrated westward in successive waves until at the end of the twelfth century they were settled on the steppes east of the Carpathians. Their way of life and economic structure were no different from those of other mounted nomads; their own name for themselves was Kuman, but neighbouring peoples called them by many different names; in Greek, 'Turks', in Slavonic tongues 'Polovec', in German 'Falb', and in Hungarian 'Kun'. They made repeated attempts to cross the Carpathians and press on westward, but all were opposed by the Hungarian army, and frustrated.

The Mongols led by Batu Khan into Eastern Europe dealt a mortal blow to this steppe people in 1240. Part of the dispersed Kuman army under their prince Kuthen requested leave to pass into Hungary, and such of the remainder as had not been massacred or enslaved sought safety in alliance with the Mongols. Despite all their misfortunes, however, this nation of horsemen had preserved, together with their military virtues, a love of liberty. Just as they had been unable to reconcile this with life under the Mongols, so they found it impossible to adapt themselves either to the world of Islam, or to that of Christendom.

The admission of the Kumans to Hungary led to an internal political crisis, with tragic results, which were hastened by the battle on the Sajó mentioned above (p. 66). The reason was, once more, a dispute about grazing rights, a commonplace of nomadic history, but this time also about the slave trade and the kidnapping that went with it, combined also with religious intolerance. There were repeated armed clashes. Surprisingly, the Kumans gained a great influence in the political and social life of Hungary in a very short time; so much so that King Stephen V (1270–71) did not attempt—as the Arpad dynasty had done for so many centuries up to his time—to contract a marriage alliance with some royal house of Christendom, but married a Kuman girl and had her crowned queen. Their son Ladislas IV was called "The

Kuman", and when he succeeded to the crown of St Stephen (which he wore from 1272 to 1290), he adopted Kuman clothes, observing Turkish customs, and chose his immediate entourage from among the Kuman nobility. The Papal Legate sent urgent and repeated dispatches to Rome, reporting that the manners of the Kumans were gaining the upper hand, and that the Magyars were turning away from Christianity. But Kuman influence did not stop here; it extended, at least superficially, to the West, where the pointed Kuman cap and long cloak became fashionable.

In Egypt the Turkish conspiracy was touched off by the murder of Tur-in-Shah, heir presumptive to the Sultanate, and the last scion of the Ayyubid line. Like the Hungarian King Ladislas IV, he was the child of a Turkish mother, Chadjarat el Dur, by the Sultan Malik Shah. Events in Egypt and Hungary are paralleled also, in so far as in both cases the ruler was murdered by his Turkish subjects.

Tur-in-Shah's orphaned heir arrested Chadjarat el Dur, who had been implicated in the murder of her own son, and shared power with a Turk of noble birth as consort. But their reign was short, because the people would not tolerate a female ruler. The great period of Mameluke rule is undoubtedly represented by the reign of Sultan El Nasser (1291–1341), a son of El Mansour Kalaoun of the Bordj Ogly clan, a slave bodyguard who came to power in 1279. His nickname El Elfi ("Thousand") commemorates the price of one thousand gold pieces for which he changed hands as a slave [and reminds us that Mameluke means literally 'that which is bought and sold' Tr.]. Among the Turks this price was looked on as the measure of the wealth and noble descent of the prisoner, and this was the value all such prisoners retained so long as their identity was known, and they were not too far removed from the original scene of capture. While their status was still to some extent that of a hostage, and the possibility existed that their family would ransom them, the price paid really represented the option to obtain a much greater sum by way of ransom. [In this respect the slave-markets of the Turkish—or Turkish-dominated—world that eventually stretched as far west as Tangier, and always handled a certain proportion of West European—even British—'goods', differed radically from the slave markets of the ancient world, or even those of the Black Sea area, where in the early Middle Ages Varangian traders had brought Irish slaves for sale to the Arabs. In the old markets there had been no such 'fringe benefits', and the price of the anonymous slave was fixed solely by the potential of the man as, say, a swordsman or a wrestler, a labourer or a musician, and of the girl by her probable worth in bed. Tr.] The great sum paid for Kalaoun reflects the fortune which a feudal lord among these nomads possessed. It fell to the lot of that late scion of a highly respected Central Asian stock, El Nasser, to restore the Arab Empire, the legacy of the Prophet, to its ancient glory. But this involved also transplanting the equestrian civilization of Turkestan to an alien soil.

The best authorities for the reign of El Nasser are Ibn Batuta, Abu Bekr ibn Bedr, Makrizi, and El Damiri. The French author Perron made a special study of their contents in so far as they concern horsemanship, studying the relevant manuscripts in the library of Cairo at the beginning of the first century. His work has since been forgotten. The present writer found a digest of it in a German review of the 1850's. As such, the digest hardly fulfils the requirements of a source such as is demanded by the disciplines of modern scholarship; it nevertheless sheds much valuable light on Arab practice of the medieval period.

Horse-breeding by the Arabs, at any rate in terms of quantity, had not in El Nasser's time attained the standards of Central Asia. Even though the Bactrian horse had been acclimatized for two thousand years in the Near East and North Africa, so that the Roman Empire and later Western Europe had drawn their *materia generosa* from thence, this did not represent progress from the point of view of the Arab horseman. In general horse-breeding, riding and driving (there was very little driving) in this region, as well as fighting and games on horseback, were much the same as they had been in antiquity. One instance of this, among others, is the late adoption of the stirrup. Whereas Western horsemen had from the tenth century onward all adopted the stirrup, originally introduced by the Avars and again by the Magyars, the only people in the Arab world to use it were persons of Turkish origin, as late as the twelfth century. This may not seem so important today, but it has its significance in terms of world history, for at the time of the Arab expansion in Europe the West owed its military superiority to the more modern equipment of its cavalry, including stirrups. There can be no doubt at all that the political and cultural history of Europe would have taken quite another turn if Islam had then (say in the days of Charlemagne) got the upper hand.

The Arabs as Horse-breeders

The Arabs, like the Turks of Turkestan, were primarily nomad shepherds. The conspicuous difference is in the relatively small number of horses kept in proportion to other livestock. An Arab owning great herds of sheep and camels might have no more than four or five horses. Mahomet himself had a hundred sheep and sixty camels, but only seven horses. This is a consequence of the fact, mentioned earlier, that the Arab countries, including the Moghreb, lie outside the post-glacial boundaries of the wild-horse habitat.

For this reason even at the present day the manner of keeping horses, both in the Near East and in North Africa, is the manner characteristic of settled farmers, even though the Bedouin way of life is entirely nomadic. The Bedouin (and the Touaregs in the Sahara) keep their horses either near the tents or sometimes actually in the tents. They are hand-fed on cereals, gruel, milk, dates, even fish and meat, as well as the scraps of the master's meal. Meat as a food is considered especially important, because according to Arab ideas it induces courage.

Despite the wide difference between the Turkish and the Arab method of keeping horses—which is due primarily, of course, to the fact that the Turkish technique presupposes a supply of grass, which no pasture in the Arab world affords —signs of Central Asian influence appeared early. According to Islamic doctrine, it is an offence to sell a horse to an unbeliever, a foreigner, or any foe of Islam. This is on a par with the ban on horse exports by certain mounted nomad rulers. This dogma went so far that in Egypt down to the reign of Mehemet Ali (1805–46) no Frank and no Jew might ride a horse in public. The use of the Turkish loanword *at* in the enormous Arabic vocabulary of synonyms for 'horse' is also significant. The ordinary Arab word for horse in general, *faras*, is replaced by the Turkish term *atik* when referring to a well-bred animal, and the word has overtones suggesting purification and pure blood. A half-bred horse by a blood stallion is called *hedjin*, but if half-bred out of a blood mare, then *mukrif*. There are abundant sources to prove that these expressions were already current in Mahomet's day.

With the accession of El Nasser a new era in Arabian horse-breeding began. This far-sighted and highly gifted ruler was interested in everything that could be called progress. He was also an enthusiast in the matter of blood-stock, and open to new ideas that might be conducive to the improvement of cavalry technique, communications, and equestrian sports. The first years of his reign were devoted to warfare by way of consolidating his power. After seeing off the Mongol invaders and disposing of the Mameluke sultans, as traditional enemies, he began the re-organization of his kingdom. There is an old saying *cuius regio, huius religio* that is valid for the fifty-year reign of El Nasser. His reforms left abiding traces in many spheres of Arab life.

If his father and predecessor had preferred the Barka horse, El Nasser ibn Kalaoun promoted the use of those pure-bred Arab horses which were then bred principally by two Syrian desert tribes, the Beni Fadl and the Muhanna; both tribes came originally from Tajikistan, having migrated to Syria some three centuries earlier.

El Nasser devoted enormous energy and huge sums of money to the purchase of blood-horses. His agents were perpetually on tour, sending him regular reports of the stock available from horse-breeding tribes. He set high standards, being himself such a connoisseur of horses. If he once set his heart on an *atik*, he would stop at nothing to acquire it. Granted his enormous riches, and the extraordinary devotion of the Arabs to their horses, it is not surprising that some of the prices paid were astronomical. Kalaoun in his day had paid 5000 drachmae for an outstanding Barka horse, but El Nasser was to pay as much as seventy or eighty thousand; often, indeed, up to a hundred thousand. Mostly the money was paid in gold dirhems, and over and above this the vendor fitted out with a complete suit of clothes and his wives regaled with sweetmeats. There was hardly a tribe in all Arabia that could not boast of having sold this prince a horse.

He was especially interested in breeding problems, and made a point of visiting the leading sires at all the studs, witnessing the covering of the mares in person. If a mare were proved in foal he had to be the first to be notified, and he awaited the birth of the foal with almost childish impatience.

What is of supreme importance is that El Nasser set up a special department which maintained a register and Stud Book of pure-bred horses. So today strains of Arabian horse which are known under the collective term Kehailan, such as the O'Bayan, Seglawi, Hamdani, and Habdan, can trace their ancestry back to the days of El Nasser. Since his time it has become customary that the serving of a pure-bred mare should be witnessed by a committee, and witnesses are also summoned for the birth of a foal. Progeny of a mare which have been foaled other than before witnesses are not recognized as pure-bred, and are designated *kadisl*—that is, crossbred. It is by such means that the Arab horse has been able to preserve the eminent characteristics of its Turanian ancestors down to our own day.

Together with the expanded breeding of the pure strain of horses, there were other extraordinary developments in the field of horsemanship. Close by El Nasser's court at Cairo there was stabling on a luxurious scale for some three thousand horses. There were race-tracks with ornamental trees, fountains and grandstands, dressage arenas, and every facility for cavalry exercises and mounted sports. We may mention specifically the Maidan el Nasri for mounted spectacles and equestrian sports, the Maidan el Mahari for breaking colts, the Maidan el Kalah for horse-racing, and the Maidan el Kabak for cavalry exercises, which included archery from the saddle. Kabak is the Turkish word for a pumpkin. The target used was a gold or silver cage in the shape of a pumpkin, and containing a dove, which the competitors had to shoot at full gallop.

El Nasser took great pains to arouse interest in the Arab horse among his people. It was customary to brand yearlings in the nomad manner, and the operation took place with some solemnity, in public accompanied by the formal gift of some of the yearlings. It was a mark of especial favour to receive an Arab yearling, and most of them went to Mamelukes. Foreigners, and the less esteemed subjects of the Sultan, had to content themselves with Barka colts.

Facsimile of Arabian 'Pedigree'
This is not a pedigree in the Weatherby sense at all: more like an affidavit that the horse was bred in the stud of such and such a tribe.

Besides horse-breeding, this ruler also patronized camel-breeding, likewise favouring Turanian strains. Camel-breeding in the higher branches, as in the case of all domesticated animals, depends on the propagation of certain valued strains, and, for instance, in Central Asia down to this century a select 'Bactrian' two-humped camel has been bred for transport purposes alongside a one-humped riding camel, both by the Turkomans. Of the latter, a refined variant is dispersed through the Near East, known in Arabia as Mahran and in North Africa as Mehari. The racing camels bred by El Nasser and known as *Badjdah* could match horses for speed.

Here we may mention a curious fact in the history of warfare. The Arabs used their pure-bred horses just as the Western knights used the destrier—as a charger exclusively in battle—apart from its use as a racehorse. Generally the Arabian warrior rode a camel on the march and only mounted his horse immediately before going into action. The difference was that the Arab war horse was by custom a mare, because stallions made too much noise.

When El Nasser died there were 4800 horses and 5000 camels in his stables. Even though his immediate successors did not keep up his expensive hobby, they kept along the lines of his more important innovations.

The ascendancy of the Turkish Mamelukes did not in any case last long. In 1384 a new Turkish group, the Circassian Guard, seized power. One of them, Sultan Barkouk, known as 'El Malik el Zahar'—that is, "The Glorious King"—was the first of a dynasty of twenty-six Circassian Mamelukes to reign.

Under Barkouk's rule Central Asian traditions of horsemanship bloomed anew. His passion for stockbreeding is proved by his ownership of seven thousand horses and fifteen thousand camels. The codification of the rules of racing is also associated with his name. At that time the traditions of horsemanship had taken firm root in all ranks of Arab society, as is proved by the writings of the Arabic historian Makrizi (d. 1442) alone.

Early in the sixteenth century the Osmanli Turks put an end to the hegemony of the Circassians, and Sultan Selim I (1512–20) forced the last Mameluke prince to abdicate, so that Cairo and the whole Arab caliphate fell under the rule of Constantinople. In order to have done once and for all with the power of the Mamelukes which had endured for three centuries, their leaders were invited by the Turks to a feast and thereafter murdered—all except one who managed to mount his horse and, leaping over a high wall, made his escape. The memory of this feat lingered for many generations as a legend, and the same story was acted out again in the days of Mehemet Ali.

The Turks revoked the centuries-old Arab embargo on the export of horses, and henceforward Arabian horses were to be seen in the stables of the sultans of Constantinople, and of his pashas and beys. In the Turkish Empire Arabia figured as the reservoir of the noble *bedevi at* (Bedouin horse). With the Turkish expansion into Europe the Arab horse also won further renown in the West. Europe was then in a posture of defence *vis-à-vis* the advance of the Osmanlis, which involved changing over to light cavalry instead of chivalry, and this led to a great demand for 'Turkish' horses (by which was meant Turkish and also Arab horses).

The Arabian Horseman

In the mass of writing by Europeans who in the nineteenth century travelled in Arab lands in search of horses we find frequent mention of a peculiarity of Arab horsemanship, or rather horsemastership: to the Arab, his pure-bred horse was one of the family, and shared the tent with him. These animals are besides extraordinarily tame and intelligent, and deserve the care which is lavished on them. A high-bred horse is to the Arab a property whose worth can only be matched in refined gold, weight for weight, and on which all his pride is set. In it he sees the incarnation of all his skill in breeding. The Arab never has a rough word for his horse, and he could never bring himself to strike one.

Thus to him the horse is a domestic animal in the narrowest sense of the word; it shares his dwelling, whether this be a house or a tent, and is only to be compared, in Western terms, with the pet dog. It patiently allows the children to play between its feet, and when it lies down it allows its master to recline against it. It is also the watchdog of the black tents, and their inmates. Its acute senses apprise it at once of the approach of strangers, or of any danger, and it sounds the alarm by snorting, or by other conspicuous behaviour.

Of course, many anecdotes of miraculous performances by Arab horses are sheer fantasy, but many have been attested by reliable witnesses.

The Arab horse, with its utter emotional dependence on and loyalty to its master, is perfectly aware of what goes on when the owner is in treaty to sell it. It shows its unease by restless behaviour, threatening the buyer with teeth and hooves, so that he cannot approach it. But once the deal is clinched its behaviour alters; accepting the inevitable, it hangs its head and lets the new owner lead it away in all obedience. Cases have been known in which the rider has lain down in the shade of the horse to escape the singeing rays of the sun, while the horse stands rigid as a statue, watching over its resting master. There are horses, too, which in consideration for the squeamishness of the rider have refrained from performing their natural functions so long as he is in the saddle. But it is in perilous situations that the almost human intelligence of the Arab horse comes to the fore. Its spirit of sacrifice then becomes heroic. Whereas other horses wounded in battle run madly away in terror and pain, throwing their riders or rolling on the ground, the Arab horse endures to the last breath. According to one report, an Arab horse whose rider had fallen wounded to the ground picked him up with its teeth by his clothes and saved him out of the mêlée.

The legendary belief in the extraordinary powers of the Arab horse has also left traces in mystical belief. Thus the Arabs are convinced that no evil spirit can approach a man seated on a high-bred horse, or any house in which such a horse is stabled. Among this legendary lore coat-colour plays a large part. Greys are the mount of kings and princes, black horses are to be ridden at night, roans are the best for hunting, light bays are especially swift. Apart from colour, distinguishing marks—stars, blazes, socks, and the like—together with the partings of the hair, have a special significance. The Arab recognizes eleven such marks which have mysterious properties.

The very rare double, horn-like protuberance on the forehead is especially baneful, auguring misfortune and death to the rider. Horses born with this blemish are called *kabr maftuh* (open grave). Just as bad is the *bokh nikhan*, a horse with two hair-partings (vortices) on the cheek. White socks are thought to indicate the individual performance of the horse; three white legs are the most prized, but four mean that the horse is completely inferior.

After all that we have said above about the Arabs, their horses, and their tradition of horsemanship, it seems superfluous to adduce further proof of the enormous reserve of equestrian lore in the Near East and its ultimate origins in the traditions of Central Asia. Arab horsemanship fits in like a link in the chain of historical development whereby those long-dead nomadic herdsmen bequeathed their legacy of horsemanship to the Near East, and thence to all the world.

Horsemanship in Central Asia

After their settlement in the Carpathian region the Magyars were the most westerly of all nomadic herdsmen. The westward penetration of Oriental fashions in war and communications came primarily through Hungary. For our knowledge of the development of the equestrian civilization, therefore, Hungarian historical documents are invaluable.

The Magyars are the only pastoral people who possess written evidence of their centuries of nomadic stock-breeding. These documents have a bearing on the horseman's way of life, which was uniform throughout the vast area between the Great Wall of China and the river Leitha, and which is founded on the stock of the Sayan reindeer-culture. Hitherto historians (with some notable exceptions) have hardly taken account of the great significance for humanity of technical progress in the field of horse transport: and so it comes about that these documents have not yet been fully exploited, and the archaeological material that matches them has been somewhat neglected.

This material comes primarily from burial sites, dating from the era of settlement by the Magyar horsemen. It tells us much about their daily life, and also something of their beliefs, and hence of their intellectual life in general.

Ethnologically and linguistically, the Magyars belong to the Finno-Ugric family, and had a prehistory of hunting and fishing. Apparently their original home lay somewhere on the East European Plain, which was woodland interspersed with grassland. The horse would only be known to them as game. In the first centuries of the Christian era these people came in contact with Turkic tribes of pastoralists, the former probably becoming subject to the latter. There then began a process which has often been repeated in the history of mankind: the subject people took over the more advanced way of life from their overlords, but did not in the end adopt their language. The Hungarian tribes, having finally coalesced as one ethnic unit, became an equestrian people with a 'Turkish' pastoral culture but a Finno-Ugric language. Even today the anthropologist can trace these two threads in their make-up.

Attitude to the Horse

Traces of the fifteen-centuries-old Asiatic tradition of the Turks are hard to find today, due to the cultural attrition of the endless wars which the mounted warriors waged among themselves.

What few remain, either in the form of inscriptions or of folklore, tell us something not only of early Turkish history but of the mental attitude of the equestrian peoples. The oldest writing by Asiatic Turks, known as the Runestone of Orkon, is especially valuable (it is not, of course, a Runic inscription in the sense usually understood in a Scandinavian or West Germanic context).

In Mongolia, where nomadic pastoralism began, a prince of the Central Asian Turks, Kagan Bilge, raised a memorial to his brother Kül Tegin on the banks of the river Tola in the eighth century A.D. Inscriptions on the stone mention the Turkish campaigns and the deeds of Kül Tegin. The characteristic esteem of equestrian peoples for the horse shows clearly here. We learn the names of Kül Tegin's horses. In action against Chacha Sengün he rode his bay, Tadik Chur, and when it was killed under him he rode the grey Jamtar; after the loss of this again he fought on, in the saddle of the bright bay Kedimlig, property of Jeginsili Beg. Names are recorded of his grey horses, Basgu, Alp Salchi, Asman, and Ögsis, and his brown horse As. These 'runes' point clearly to the former connection between the Turks and the

Magyars, for such characters were still used for inscriptions by the Sekler of Transylvania in the sixteenth century.

A few lines of the ancient Turkish legend of Köroglu also deal with esteem of the horse. Oral versions of this legend were still current among all Turkish tribes from the Oxus to Syria in the second half of the nineteenth century. According to Vámbéri, it must go back to the time before the dispersal of the Turkish tribes. In it the hero laments the loss of his grey horse Kirat as follows:

> O thou whom I won in Turkestan,
> Come, Kirat, nourished with my life!
> Thou whom the hostile Tekke took from me,
> Come, Kirat, nourished with my life!
> O thou whose bit is heavy as a hundredweight,
> Who cravest no food after a three-day fast,
> Who tirest not after a forty-league march,
> Come, Kirat, nourished with my life!

The line about the bit is not meant to imply that the animal is hard or 'dead' in the mouth, but simply that it is so light-mouthed that the bit is a burden to it. This mental attitude is evident among Magyar horsemen as late as the eighteenth century; when the exiled adherents of Prince Rákóczi were passing through France on their way to Turkey, where they settled, one of them, Kelemen Mikes, kept a diary of his impressions in which he amended the seventeenth-century epigram about England and Italy to read "France is a paradise for women and a hell for horses; Turkey, a paradise for horses and a hell for women".

Of course, this is not quite accurate, since then at the French Court and among the upper classes generally horsemanship was of a high standard; the 'chivalrous' ideology of East and West has seldom been so trenchantly epitomized.

This mental attitude has survived in the East almost into our own day. Taboos of almost religious rigour surrounded it in Central Asia. Among the Siberian Yakuts it was not only forbidden to strike a horse but it was a misdemeanour to speak roughly to one. Among the Kirghiz, according to Radloff, striking another man's horse or making slighting remarks about it was as ill regarded as if the insult had been offered to the man himself. To them the horse was the pearl of creation, and the worth of a man could be expressed in terms of it alone. The dowry, or *Kalim*, was reckoned as so many head of horses, and so was the blood-price, which corresponded to the Anglo-Saxon *weregild*. Atonement for the death of a freeman cost 100 horses, what they called a whole *kun* (drove); for the death of a slave, a woman or a girl, half a kun; for that of a child under ten years, a quarter-kun; and so on. This reverential attitude extended also to mare's milk, to products derived from it, and even to horse-meat. It counted as an insult to set before a distinguished stranger anything but *kumis* (fermented mare's milk), and this had to be offered in a certain ceremonial form (as tea in China). Horse-flesh was chiefly eaten, as archaeological findings confirm, at religious ceremonies, and was part of the ritual of the funeral feast.

As among the Arabs, so among the Hungarians, belief in the supernatural powers of the horse flourished. Thus among the ruins of buildings in Hungarian villages dating to the eleventh century horse-skulls have been found fixed to the timbering of living-rooms; obviously as talismans against evil spirits. Both Hungarian and Arabian customs indicate a common origin in Central Asia.

This extraordinary esteem for the horse among the Turks and those people who took over their traditions hints at a further essential element in equestrian nomadic pastoralism; in the world of the nomad herdsman *mounted* nomadism was the 'higher' life, and for him the horse symbolized not only a superior standard of living, in war and in peace, but was an accessory of the 'superior person' in general.

Like other wandering herdsmen, the Magyars buried their dead with horse and saddlery, which is also a Central Asian custom. It was practised by the reindeer-breeders of Sayan, who used to sacrifice a white reindeer at the graveside. Ethno-graphic research has long since shown the connection between reindeer-sacrifice and horse-sacrifice. In both cases it is meant to provide the deceased with a mount for his journey in the next world.

This custom was similarly observed throughout the region traversed by the equestrian peoples, from the barrows of Pazyryk to the late medieval burials of Kuman Turks in Hungary. The grave-goods consisted above all of cavalry weapons and equipment: bow, arrows, quiver, valise, saddle, and so on. These are attested by surviving metal parts, such as sword-blades, arrowheads, snaffles, stirrups, as well as the metal ornaments that had once been fixed to saddlery, clothing, and accoutrements.

Among the Hungarians the manner of burying a horseman had its particular symbolism. The horse chosen for burial was beheaded, contrary to the custom observed by previous occupants of the country—Avars, Patzinaks, Uzes, Turks—and only the skull and cannon bones with the feet attached appear in the remains. It is probable they were left attached to the hide, which was stuffed with hay and the simulated horse disposed beside the corpse. Similar customs obtained in Central Asia, widely among breeders of reindeer and horses. Plano Carpini, who at the height of the Mongol invasions visited the Court of the Great Khan on behalf of Pope Innocent IV, described the horse-burials of the Mongols as follows.

> The dead man is laid in the earth with his tent, and provisions and mare's milk beside him. A mare with foal at foot and a saddled and bridled gelding are buried with him. Then they eat another horse, stuff the hide with straw and prop it up on two or four poles, so that in the next world the dead man shall have somewhere to live, a mare to provide milk, a foal to start another herd, and a horse to ride.

The partaking of horse-meat as part of a ritual meal has already been mentioned in connection with the Turks. It is notable that this custom was discarded by such equestrian peoples as were converted to Christianity (less consistently by those converted to Islam). Thus according to Eunodius the Bulgars in their pagan days ate horse-meat. Among the Magyars a reaction towards paganism which led to an uprising in 1063 was symbolized by ostentatious consumption of horse-flesh. [Farther north at exactly the same time the crisis of conversion to Christianity in Scandinavia often pivots on the same ritual point. In Norway an evangelizing king sitting down to feast at a harvest festival with his tenants is constrained, diplomati-cally, to inhale some of the steam from the cauldron of boiled horse-flesh which is a traditional item on the menu. Before that, missionaries in Anglo-Saxon England had classed hippophagy as equally sinful with idolatry, and 'disguising oneself as an animal'. The horse-meat taboo appears to be stronger the nearer one approaches to the north-west fringe of Europe. Among the ancient Irish and the Highlanders it was absolute in pagan days, and remains so today. Tr.]

In order to account for this phenomenon we must look back to the dietary laws embodied in the Old Testament. As codified by Moses, these forbade the eating of those beasts which had cloven hoofs but did not chew the cud; those with solid hoofs or claws; and those which walked on the soles of their feet. This excluded from their diet pigs, equines, dogs, cats, all rodents, monkeys, and bears. There were similar embargoes on the eating of certain species of fish, birds, reptiles, insects, and molluscs. And it was forbidden to drink blood of any origin.

These commandments, taken over by the Christian and Islamic world and very largely observed today, simply did not impinge on the pastoral peoples of the steppe so long as they retained their old shamanistic beliefs. Julianus, a Dominican monk, visiting those Hungarians who had not migrated from their former home in Eastern Europe, noted in 1237: "They do not plant crops, they eat horse and wolf and suchlike meats, they drink mares' milk and blood".

Over and above this there was an emotional current 'away from the horse'. When the horsemen from the East entered the stage of history they were figures of terror for the Western world, to such a degree that the folk-memory of the 'centaurs' was still alive at the time of later invasions, and simply served to reinforce the bogy-image of the Apocalyptic horsemen in the imagination of the now Christian Westerners who had to face them. [We may compare this with an English phenomenon, whereby any dreaded sea-raiders become, in folk-tradition, 'Danes', by analogy with the dreaded 'heathen men' of the ninth century. Tr.] It was this image of terror which caused Moses to forbid his people to keep, let alone eat, horses. The Christians who in part conformed to Mosaic law remained *selectively* antagonistic to the mounted archer, even though they were themselves horsemen of a different stamp. The physical image of the Devil in medieval art has certain features in common with the Avar or Magyar mounted archer of real life—aquiline nose, pointed beard and moustaches à la Mephistopheles and all—as the only begetter and model of all sins and vices. He is contrasted, in Western art, with angels symbolizing Christian piety whose physiognomy might be described, in terms of physical anthropology, as 'chocolate-box Nordic'.

Horse-breeding

As horse-breeders in the Carpathian region the Magyars had for centuries recourse to wild blood. This is almost inherent in the conditions of nomadic herd-breeding, since the life of domestic horses on open range is so little different from that of the wild herds, where these exist. As often as tame mares ran away, wild horses were caught, and, if not broken, used for breeding.

At Leka the steward of the Palatine, Thomas Nádasdy, writes to his master in 1537 that he is sending back the stallion drafted to the herd, for fear the wild mares will knock him about, and regrets it is not possible to catch the said mares as ordered. (Note 11.) Nearly forty years later, in 1576, the municipal accounts of Eperjes show payment of wages to certain men for taming and herding wild horses. (Note 12.) As late as 1647 the estate accounts of Sárvár show money paid out for snares for wild horses. (Note 13.)

Later on they are mentioned only in connection with gear made from wild-horse leather, or hair. The inventory of Count Szapáry in 1671 mentions ropes made of wild-horse hair. (Note 14.) Likewise at Lublo-Szepesvárer the effects of the deceased

Count Stephan Csáky in 1685 include a wild-horse tail, probably used as a fly-whisk.

The French knight, Bertrandon de la Broquière, has something to say of Hungarian horse-keeping methods, as he was on his way back from Constantinople in 1432. "[At Szegedin] I saw"—his diary notes—

a herd of wild horses brought in for sale, which are yet well able to be haltered and tamed, which made a remarkable sight. It was told us, that if any man had a mind to buy three or four thousand horses, in this town he might do it. Horses here are so cheap, that anyone can buy a fine stallion for ten Hungarian gulden. . . . From Szegedin I came to a town [Kecskemet?] and the way thither led all through a fair plain wherein the horses like wild game live quite free, one herd beside the other. This is the cause why so many are to be seen in the mart of Szegedin. . . . At Pest there is great plenty of horsedealers; if a man wished to buy two thousand good horses, surely he could buy them here. They are sold by the stableful—that is, ten at a time. Every stableful costs two hundred gulden. I also saw horses that would fetch this price between two or three of them. The most part of them come from the borders over against Transylvania, in the mountains. There is excellent pasture for them there. Their fault is, they are somewhat froward, and principally very awkward to shoe.

The Arab traveller Ibn Batuta describes the horse-stock of the Turks in Central Asia thus (fourteenth century): "This is a land most rich in horses . . . the kind called in Egypt *akadis* (cross-bred) is one of the sources of their husbandry. They have as many of them as we have sheep, if not more. Many a Turk has thousands."

Today it would be vain to search for traces of horse-breeding on such a vast scale in Hungary. The whole technique of stock-breeding has altered, so that there are no studs kept on open range, and there are hardly any horses left that winter out, or that could do so. We can nowadays speak only of the Asiatic influence on Hungarian horse-herding of former times.

Radloff, who in the mid-nineteenth century investigated the Kazakh and Kirghiz manner of horse-breeding, describes it thus: A herd amounts most often to fifty animals, of which nine or ten are mares, each with a foal less than a year old, the rest being their yearling and older followers. The stallion as leader keeps the herd together, and also stands sentry over it. He has no fear of wolves, and it is only rarely that they manage to snatch a foal from him. And it must be a bold wolf at that. The stallion is ready to fight not only predators, but also rivals. The arrival of a strange stallion is the signal for a fight to the death. The young colts of his own herd have to keep apart from the mares, in a group by themselves. The fillies do not stand to the stallion until their sixth year, but even so the instinctive aversion to inbreeding comes into play: when his own daughters come of age the stallion drives them out of the herd.

The composition of the herds seen by Broquière, we may assume, was similar to that observed by Radloff, because the life of wild and half-wild herds is determined inexorably by the instinct to survive and perpetuate themselves, without which these equines would not have survived for thousands of years. When he writes that in the great plains the herds on free range grazed side by side we can only assume that the majority of the stallions had been castrated, for we have no reason to doubt his credibility. Otherwise he would probably have reported that half the equine population of the *puszta* spent their time fighting each other, that he saw many sick and wounded horses driven out of the herd, and that the roadside was littered with the remains of dead colts. Not only was a surplus of stallions unwanted by the breeders, it was also, as is the case with American mustangs, a plague to the countryside. The unsuccessful ones, driven off the grazing-grounds, lured away mares from the farms, and those of travellers. For this reason they were treated as beasts of prey; hunted and shot. And so gelding became an indispensable procedure in this kind of breeding.

The earliest record of castrating colts comes likewise from the pen of a Western observer who had a good knowledge of the Hungarian horse-economy. Marx Fugger, who published a book in 1584 dealing with the reorganization of Western cavalry, did not, indeed, recommend the adoption of this custom, because he considered geldings to be lacking in courage and unsuitable as chargers; yet he finds it necessary to mention that the Scythians and Sarmatians had once gelded their horses, as did the Turks in his day, as well as the Tartars and the Muscovites, and that on their campaigns the Magyars rode geldings almost exclusively.

The Chertomlyk Vase
Frieze of Scythian herdsmen preparing to cast a colt for castration

It is fairly clear that this custom of the nomadic breeders also goes back to the reindeer-herdsmen. But among them the operation up to the most recent times was performed in the most primitive way—by severing the seminal cord with the teeth. The illustration on the famous Chertomlyk Vase from the Crimea, with its Hellenistic fringe showing Scythians preparing to cast a colt, quite in the modern manner, with ropes that are not shown in the engraving, does not show the actual orchidectomy, which was bloodless, being performed by crushing the cord with a wooden mallet. Just such tools are limned in the armorial bearings of István Várallyai in 1599: he was master colt-gelder to the Prince of Transylvania. (Note 15.)

Taxonomy of Hungarian Horses

We have hardly any usable descriptions of the Oriental rider or his horse dating from the period when the art of riding began to come into its own in the West, nor are they represented in the art of the period. Part of the reason may be that those circles, restricted in antiquity, which were masters of the arts of writing and drawing or sculpture were those furthest removed from the practice of horsemanship. Be that as it may, the representational art of the equestrian peoples—such as is evident, for instance, in the tombs of Pazyryk—was entering a declining phase, and would soon perish utterly, after going through a phase of the formally fantastic, rather than the naïve realism exemplified in Plate 5. After their adoption of Christianity, and therewith of Western cultural features, the Hungarians had to grope their way for a long time to full participation in the Occidental world of art and literature.

The written documents of the centuries after the settlement of Pannonia by the Magyars are the work of clerics with an alien point of view, and the visual art dating from this period, where it is relevant, has been painted and drawn and sculpted, engraved and beaten out in metal, by artists and craftsmen who were Westerners, from the outside. Disregard of this fact, especially as it affected and purported to depict the world of the Magyar horseman, has been the source of much error.

The Magyar horses were small, the average not exceeding 14 hands. They retained the lightly built frame characteristic of the half-bred horse, century after century, as is confirmed by archaeological evidence, as well as by medieval documents. The same tendency is indicated by the surviving bits and snaffles of medieval date, which by their dimensions were made for small horses with narrow jaws. This all points to the fact that during the Middle Ages the Magyars did not use a cross of heavy, 'cold' blood—did not ride the destrier of chivalry. Research has also established the Tarpan-type of the medieval Magyar horse, which was to be expected given the nature of the wild-horse population at that time. In the marginal area surrounding the Carpathians, especially in Carpatho-Ukraine and Eastern Transylvania, where before the Second World War the old, small stamp of 'native' horse was still being bred, horses with Tarpan characteristics often occurred, showing the skull-form, the dun colour, and dark eel-stripe of the Tarpan, as well as its general proportions.

Ebhardt considers the Tarpan a mixed form. The 'wild blood-horse' living close to the tropical zone was forced northward towards the end of the last interglacial (by drought?), at the same time as the pony types migrated southward. There thus occurred wild hybrids, leading to much wider distribution of the southern form, if diluted with northern blood. This state of affairs was obviously still in force after the domestication of the Pony, and was indeed assisted by deliberate human intervention.

Hungarian written sources establish that:

Among the gifts made by Hungarian princes and kings, mostly to foreign rulers, splendidly caparisoned horses, chiefly grey, figure. In medieval documents we often read of outstanding horses, far-famed, of great price, known by such epithets as *capitalis, electus, formosus, domino aptus*, etc. Now, what would be meant, in the context of the time, by these terms 'capital, hand-picked, handsome, fit for a lord' (*Urnok valo* in Hungarian)? A chronicle of the year 1380 describes the Magyar horses as small, strong, and swift, but those of the nobility are described as tall and handsome. (Note 16.)

These data fit in fascinatingly with facts arising from the results of recent archaeological research by the Russians. V. I. Calkin reported in 1966, in his work on the animal husbandry of Central Asia in the Scythian period, that the tall, 'quality' stamp of horse (which may be identified with the Akhal-Tekke breed of today, and occurred in the whole region between the Altai Mountains and the north littoral of the Black Sea) was the mount of the ruling class. But the great mass of horses were of another stamp, not being above 13 hands 3 in. in height, with much heavier bone.

The taxonomy of early Hungarian horses is on a par with that of the horses found

MAMALVCKE

II

Etching by Daniel Hofer (seventeenth century) in the National Museum, Budapest
Misleading illustration, common in early Western works, showing Mamelukes riding
cold-blooded horses of a type that did not exist in the Islamic world.

at Pazyryk. Here too the foundation stock was ponies, more or less graded-up by a greater or smaller dash of Turanian blood; only here the foundation of 'common' blood was Pony, not Taki. The Hungarian horse inherited overwhelmingly the conformation, the temperament, and the characteristics of both these original types in varying degrees according to the laws of heredity.

This means in practice that at the time of settlement in the Carpathian region most of the horses approached the average height of the Oriental races, and like the second and third groups found at Pazyryk had characteristics proper to both types. On the one hand there were to be found tall horses of general 'Turanian' appearance, assigned to the first group (by Vitt), and on the other, small Tarpans which correspond to Group Four.

In Hungarian horse-breeding there were—though to a lesser degree—other influences, and above all that of the Taki (the wild horse of Asia). As we have hinted earlier, this influence came into play during the Mongol invasions and those of the Kuman Turks. For a long time the documentary material cites this 'Kuman' type as the opposite of the Tarpan type. Miklós Oláh, historian of the sixteenth century, describes this horse as half-wild, with a big head, which points to a high proportion of Taki blood. But it has obviously left no trace behind it.

As the Osmanli Turks advanced westward the influence of the Arabian horse made itself felt. At the same time the Hungarian language was gaining ground, orally and in writing. The earlier Latin epithets *formosus, electus, capitalis,* and *principalis* were now replaced by the Hungarian word *föló,* which is the same as 'capital'. It implied a horse of quality, suitable for warfare, fit to carry a man-at-arms or a lord; it also meant the Turanian horse.

From the names used for horses in Hungary one can often deduce their origin or the identity of the former owner. Thus in the accounts of Ferenc Nádasdy for 1570 his horses are divided into three groups: 'Capital', 'Rackers', and 'Common'. The capital horses bear such names as Huseain and Harambasha, whereas such names are not to be found among either the rackers or the common nags. (Note 17.)

The identity of the Oriental with the capital horse is most apparent in the letters of Ferenc Bebek. In answer to the request of Thomas Nádasdy to "send him two horses picked from the Turkish booty, one good racker and one capital" he says that among the loot there is nothing of that description, but "if we have nothing of the sort in hand, we have some Turkish prisoners for whom I can demand as ransom the stamp of horse required (capital)". (Note 18.) Ransom at this period was customarily asked in terms of horses.

In documents from Hungary at this time the demand for capital horses of Turkish breeding frequently occurs. So also in Poland. When the Polish prince Sigismund visited Buda in 1506 he brought with him 'badavia'—that is, *bedevi at* or Bedouin horses—from Poland, and these are shown in his account books. No doubt the reason was the shortage of capital horses of Hungarian breeding, one result of the war between the Hungarians and the Turks which lasted uninterrupted for decades. (Note 19.)

Besides Arabs from Turkish sources, these horses also reached Eastern Europe by a shorter route north from the Caspian and Black seas. As time went on the provenance of capital horses shifted farther and farther eastward. In the days of Broquière they still came from Transylvania, a hundred years later from Moldavia, then from Bessarabia, from Podolia, from Circassia, and from Tartary. Ad-

52 (above)
North American
Cowboys driving
Hereford Cattle
Railhead

53 (below)
Breeding Herds c
Cattle and Horse
on the South
American Pampa

54 (right)
Argentine Gaucho

55 (below)
A good Western 'Cutting
Horse' at Work

56
An Arab stallion
from the Stud of
Abbas Pasha I,
Khedive of Egypt
1848–54.

57
Mameluke on Arab
stallion.
Lithograph by
Carle Vernet

carle Vernet

58 Sultan Osman II, called "Genc Osman", on a Grey Arab Miniature from the
Seraglio, Istanbul

mittedly by then this stock was not nearly so uniform in type as it had been in the days when El Nasser with his deliberate breeding policy instituted his Stud Book for Arab horses, but still the high proportion of pure blood was unmistakable.

Marx Fugger describes such a horse, brought back from Poland by Henry III of France in 1574 and offered by him to Fugger for 2000 crowns. The object of this offer, which in its time attracted the attention of all Europe, is described by eye-witnesses as follows: "Turk mare, blaze on face, black mane, three white socks, eel-stripe." [The body colour most likely to occur in conjunction with the black mane and eel-stripe (which is a Tarpan feature) is dun. The white feet are characteristic of the modern Arab, but even more so of the modern *part-bred* Arab. Tr.]

We may also mention the purchases of horses made almost annually by the Transylvanian Prince George Rákóczi in Moldavia. He himself drew up the code of procedure for his agents when buying Turkish and Moldavian horses; its eight points taken together show what was expected of a quality horse then. (Note 20.)

The preference for Oriental stock is proved also by the inventory of Count Adam Batthyányi's horses, 1642. (Note 21.) Besides Hungarian-bred horses he owned Turkish, Moldavian, Podolian, Circassian and Tartar horses, as well as one or two 'Spanish'—no doubt among the earliest Andalusians in Eastern Europe. Evidence of direct importation from Turania was still to be found in the last century in some Hungarian and Transylvanian private studs. The Czindery establishment, noted for its excellent horses, boasted of its Turanian foundation stock. (Note 22.)

Summarizing, it can be established that the refreshment of Hungarian stock in the Middle Ages, contrary to what is often supposed, was exclusively of Oriental origin. The import of Western horses, and their use in breeding, as we shall show below, did not begin until the eighteenth century. More convincing is the verdict of a contemporary on Oriental and Occidental horses. When King Ferdinand of Naples sent one of his equerries, trained in the Spanish School, to Hungary, to introduce Western dressage methods at the royal Court, King Matthias (1458–90) sent him back with this message:

> With the horses which we trained ourselves we defeated the Getae [Turks], subjected Serbia, and vanquished all before us, honorably by means of our own horses. We have no desire for horses that hop about with bent hocks in the Spanish fashion, we do not want them even as a pastime, still less for serious business. What we want are horses that stride out and stand firm when required.

This is indeed a striking instance of the antithesis between the Eastern and Western conceptions of horsemanship.

Riding and Driving

But what gave Hungarian horsemanship its specifically Central Asian character was not breeding alone. East of the frontier between the two traditions that ran north and south through Europe, there was so much that pointed to the common heritage of nomadic pastoralism. All the accoutrements of riding and driving, transport technique and the art of war, have their roots in this common way of life, traces of which were to be seen in later centuries.

In an earlier chapter (1) we mentioned the origin of the wooden saddle of the Asiatic horseman, among the reindeer-breeders of Sayan. For the typological history of the two kinds of saddle and their relationship there is an objective unequivocal proof: George Almásy shows in his journal of travel the make of saddle in use among the Kazakhs and Kirghiz, which is a faithful copy of the reindeer-saddle—the difference is only in their use. Among the Kirghiz they were for children of two to five years old. It was possible to lash two rods to the crossed saddle-forks in such a way as to afford a safe seat for children. The same pattern of saddle was in use until recent times in Hungary among the shepherds, who called it a *tergenye* and used it on their pack-horses.

The archaeologist Gyula László dealt (1943) with the technical aspects of the saddles, remains of which were found in the horse-burials of Hungary, trying to reconstruct from them Avar and Magyar saddles. His attempts were very illuminating. From them it appeared, not only that the pattern of the Avar and the Hungarian saddles was identical, but that they also coincided with the make of saddle used by peoples of Turkic and Mongolian culture at the present day. László in his essay also has some interesting ethnological observations to make. He points out that this pattern of saddle has remained unmodified in Hungary since the time of the Settlement, and was still being turned out by craftsmen members of the traditional saddlers' guilds until the outbreak of the First World War. The last of these saddles was made in 1920, and has been preserved in the museum at Tisza-füred.

The essential components of the Oriental wooden saddle are the two bars which run parallel to the sides of the horse, joined by arches front and rear. The rider sat on a leather sling stretched between these arches. His feet were in two iron stirrups, the leathers of which were attached to the bars. The manner of saddling up the horse also remained unchanged for centuries. Its back was first covered with a felt rug or with a sheepskin, fleece uppermost; the saddle was made fast over it with a girth, and held in place by a breastplate before and a breeching or crupper behind. The seat was mostly reinforced with a cushion over which a fur (bearskin among the rich) was spread which afforded considerable comfort to the rider. Certainly the modern saddle is more pleasing to the eye, and perhaps more comfortable, but we can safely say that as regards practical utility and cheapness no saddle excels the Oriental wooden pattern, particularly taking into account that it avoids pressure on the spine of the horse. Its wide distribution shows its utility as an essential item of equipment for the extraordinary feats of horsemanship that have been performed by all the riding peoples of the East.

The Eastern style of riding was also utterly different from that of the West. Whereas the Western horseman, even when using the 'knight's' saddle, simply forced his extended legs outward and downward into the stirrups—that is to say, virtually stood in them—the Oriental horseman rode with a short leather and bent knee, literally *in* the saddle. The Vienna illuminated chronicle shows the difference between the two styles very strikingly, in those miniatures where Eastern and Western horsemen figure together.

However, realistic presentation of the posture of the Hungarian man-at-arms is somewhat dubious. Even among the Hungarian armoured cavalry, the stiffly extended leg was not customary. According to Broquière, the Hungarians rode with a short stirrup 'in the Turkish manner'. The master who illuminated the Vienna chronicle was probably at pains to emphasize the Christian—hence Western—quality of the Hungarian knight, even by exaggerating details.

Horse-stock, riding equipment, and the technique of equitation naturally all had their influence on performance. The horseman of the West was not as yet nearly capable of the long marches and the hours in the saddle which were common practice in the East. When in 1301 a Hungarian embassy offered the Crown to the Bohemian King Vaclav in Prague, he rejected it on the following grounds, according to the *Rhyming Chronicle* of Ottokar von Steier:

> Then said King Wenceslas:
> "And if I were to take it
> I should be robbing the Hungarians;
> For however I hastened
> So it seems most like to me,
> I am not the sort of man
> To go armed with a bow
> After the Hungarian manner
> And ride six leagues in a day . . ."

(Six Bohemian leagues is something over 35 miles.)

Accounts in later times are all in the same key. The cavalry of the Hungarian rebel leader Thököly in 1676 travelled twice as far in a day as did the Imperial horse, according to their commander, General Strassoldo. (Note 23.)

Better performance depended in part on the travelling pace. The natural gaits of Equidae are the walk and the gallop. They trot only when passing from the one to the other, more commonly when 'changing down' from the gallop to the walk than vice versa.

The Oriental horseman rode at a walk, canter, and gallop, the Westerner either pacing (earlier) or at a walk and trot. Long periods of trotting were not customary before the relatively late spread of the habit of 'posting' (known on the Continent as 'the English trot', having been invented in that country).

From fairly recent times there is abundant evidence of Oriental as opposed to Western practice. Thus according to the travel notes of Radloff, Vámbéri, Moser, and Almásy the Kirghiz and Turkomen rode only at a walk and a gallop; never trotting for long. If their horses did happen to break into a trot for a few paces they did not rise in the stirrups but just 'sat out' this unpleasant gait by leaning forward from the waist. The Turkomen also trained their horses to a sort of triple called *trapatka* in Russian. At this gait they would cover 200 versts, or about 133 miles, on their raids. [The English writer Blundeville, some three centuries earlier, no doubt meant just this when he said that the "Turk" horse went best at "a certain easy train". *Tr.*]

Travel on wheels was also different in East and West. Although some nomads took over the wagon at an early stage, for a long time riding held its pre-eminence among them. We may assume that guiding the draught animal from the saddle derives from the practice of wandering stockmen, being a transitional stage between riding and driving. The adoption of the wagon by 'riding' peoples, like the adoption of riding by peasants who for long had driven carts, was spread over a very long period.

Herodotus says that there were nomad herdsmen who had wagons as early as the last few centuries B.C., yet there were others who had none until the late Middle Ages. The Old Prussians, for instance. These Balts were introduced to the wagon in 1390, by the Teutonic Knights during their campaign against the Poles. And

Broquière says, too, that the Osmanli Turks in his time used horses, mules, and camels exclusively to ride, and for pack traffic. On the other hand, the Huns—and so also the Hungarians, who regard themselves as their descendants—first appeared in Europe complete with wagons; witness the wagon-laager of Attila at the battle of the Catalaunian Fields, and certain events concerning the Hungarians described in the *Annals of St Gall*.

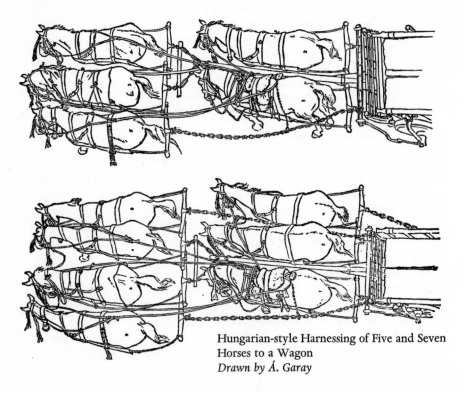

Hungarian-style Harnessing of Five and Seven Horses to a Wagon
Drawn by Á. Garay

There is much evidence of quite sophisticated wagon traffic among the Hungarians, whose wagon-train followed the armies, in rear of which it formed up when they went into action, so as to cover the rear of the host. From the twelfth century onward they had a royal corps of wagoners, and the Master of the Train (*major plaustrorum*) was an officer of the Queen's, as also of the King's, household. (Note 24.) The widespread adoption of the Hungarian pattern of wagon in the late Middle Ages bears witness to its utility, recognized by many European peoples.

The Arab traveller Ibn Battuta, visiting the Caspian region in the fourteenth century, describes the vehicles of the local inhabitants as follows:

They are called *araba* and have four wheels. According to the size of the load they are drawn by two or more horses, many being drawn by oxen and camels. One of the horses in a team is saddled, and on this the driver sits. He drives the horses on with his whip, and strikes them with a great staff if they swerve off the track.

This corresponds to the traditional method of harnessing, whereby the driver rode the wheeler. *Ductor currus* is the Latin name given to such a driver, and his special saddle is called in Hungarian *pajzán*. This rig was still common in East Hungary between the last two wars, especially in the Heiduck district.

Tibor Pettko-Szandtner, a noted whip and connoisseur of harness horses, described it in a book which Ákos Garay illustrated, and a drawing from which is reproduced here. These two rigs, rural five- and seven-in-hands, show an idea never current in the West at all. Peter Apor wrote in 1736: "At first horses were never driven from the box, but even princes' coachmen drove four-in-hand from the saddle".

Hungarian 'Peasant Coach'
Drawn by Á. Garay

Four-in-hand was the most popular rig for driving from the saddle. The driver was mounted on the near wheeler, and on the command *Tüled* ("From you") the horse on his right either drew or pushed the pole to the right, on the command *Hozzád* ("To you") he drew or pushed it to the left. The near fore-horse was called the leading trace horse because the driver, who rode behind him, had his reins in his hand. For the job a lively, active horse was preferred and his function was declared by a blanket on his back. The off trace horse had to be the steadiest, as his job was to keep the wagon rolling at the speed indicated by signals from the whip. More than four horses were harnessed together only for ceremonial purposes, especially on good roads, or when horses were being moved. The wagon with four wheels, all of equal size, was therefore what the Magyars brought with them out of the East. In the Middle Ages other types were used, the two-wheeled *kola* and *ajonca*, which on linguistic grounds may be assumed to have been taken over from the Slavs. The chroniclers tell of King Ladislas the Kuman being drawn in such a cart, whose destitute subjects pulled it for lack of draught horses themselves.

From the fifteenth century onward we hear of a new Hungarian vehicle, the *kocsi*. According to the travel journals of the Imperial ambassador Count Herberstein in 1517, it was so called after the place of its invention, the village of Kocs in Komorn county. The account by Broquière makes the difference between this and the old type of wagon clear: "They are very fair and lightly built", he says, "so that you would think one man could carry them away, wheels and body and all, on his back. The hind wheels are much higher than the fore wheels". Now the *kocsi* drivers were no longer mounted on the wheeler, but in the front of the body, if not yet on a box. Smaller fore-wheels occurred very early in the Orient. In the shaft-grave of the Sumerian king Abargi (third millennium B.C.) there was a wagon with 60 cm fore-wheels and 80 cm hind wheels.

There are many advantages to the small front pair of wheels. They make the vehicle easier to 'start', and reduce 'bucking' or pitching of the draught-pole on uneven ground or stony roads which reduced the tractive power of the horses. An even greater advantage is that it permits a fuller lock and a smaller turning-circle. It also brings the loading-surface lower, and therewith the centre of gravity, making for greater stability. It is faster and has better cross-country potential than vehicles with axles of the same height behind and before. Driving from the box is easier for the driver, and easier for the wheeler which he would otherwise ride: this is a consideration on long journeys.

A similar development is seen in the sixteenth-century Hungarian *hintó* (slung wagon), in which the body is carried on slings instead of springs. This also was four-wheeled. It was known in the West as a *calèche*. It was the combination of these two features which gave birth to the coach of Western Europe, and indeed 'coach' is only an anglicization of the old Hungarian name *kocsi*.

The coach was harnessed to the team in exactly the same way as were the country wagons of Hungary, as Broquière makes plain, however many horses were used. But in accordance with Central Asiatic practice it was still driven only at a walk or at a gallop. The Hungarian light horse, the Hungarian coach, and this manner of driving made communications inside Hungary rapid and comfortable up to the dawn of the railway era. Country wagons which are still to be seen east of the Leitha river differ little, even today, from the late medieval Hungarian *kocsi*.

The Art of War

The historical role of Central Asiatic horsemanship is most clearly evidenced in the military field. The early history of Hungarian mounted warfare is a much debated, and up to the present little clarified, problem.

However, historians are agreed on one thing: the Hungarians of the Settlement Period represented the Oriental type of 'warrior shepherd', and their fighting men were mounted archers. There is a difference of opinion as to when and to what degree the Western style of fighting was adopted. Perhaps it may be placed as far back as the eleventh century, and the decline of Oriental war-craft must be dated from then on. We incline to this view, with the reservation that armour is not a Western invention or early monopoly, but was known in antiquity and in the Middle Ages in Japan, in China, in India, and in Persia, while the Byzantine Empire employed among its manifold auxiliaries armoured Asiatic horse and foot. The fact that Germans also fought in the host of St Stephen does not by any means imply that it was from them that the Hungarians learned the use of armour; more likely the Hungarians borrowed it from either the Persians or the Byzantines, at least as the equipment of nobles and rich men and members of the princely retinue. In the period before the Mongol invasions the Hungarian man-at-arms was only distinguished from the light horseman by his wearing armour and carrying a lance. When tactically necessary, as A. Borosy emphasizes, he handled a bow also. The spread of Western armament falls chiefly in the time after the Tartar incursions, but the tactics of Hungarian heavy cavalry also had a certain Oriental character. This is shown by what Broquière says about the Hungarians: "taking part in tournaments on small horses with a saddle without high arches, dressed in fair garments according to local custom".

From contemporary accounts we get the impression of warfare waged in the style of the pastoral peoples. The first source is the Arabic historian and traveller Masudi, who described the campaign of 934 by the Magyars and Patzinaks against Byzantium.

> As day broke he [the king of the Patzinaks] formed up many bodies of horsemen on the right wing, and as many on the left. The engagement began with the horsemen of the right wing attacking the main battle of the Byzantines, showering it with arrows, and taking up a new position on the left. Then they of the left wing likewise advanced and shot against the Byzantine main battle, changing over to the right of the line. So the mounted bands kept wheeling across the Byzantine front, grinding away at it like millstones, while the Turkish main body was still not engaged. As the hail of arrows came shower after shower, the Byzantines in open order charged the Turkish main body, which till then had made no move. The horsemen did not impede them, but the Turks received them with such a shower of arrows that they recoiled. Their columns had remained drawn up in order of battle, and had not opened ranks. The mounted bands swarmed out from either flank. Now sabres were drawn. The heavens darkened and there was loud neighing of horses. . . .

The second comes after the Tartar invasion, being an abstract of Ottokar von Steier's *Rhyming Chronicle* (1312–18) concerned with the events of the defensive struggle against the Teutonic Order, who in 1286 crossed the western frontiers of Hungary. We render the somewhat pedestrian verse in prose and paraphrased:

The armoured horse of the Austrian host was some thousand strong, and composed of Austrian, Styrian, and Swabian knights. These last did not know how the Hungarians were accustomed to fight. On the news that the Hungarians were approaching, the Austrian commander wanted to sound the retreat, on the grounds that they could not be countered as one did the French (meaning that they opened fire at long range), since they would not come to close quarters. But the Swabians refused to withdraw, they formed up in close order, stirrup to stirrup, lance to lance. The Hungarians tried their usual tactics; like Turks, they rode at the enemy, yelling and shooting from the saddle, but did not close with their opponents. The battle lasted five hours, without the men-at-arms coming to grips. The Swabians took counsel what they should do. Should they disarm, to bring themselves on equal terms with the Hungarians who were fighting in their shirts? They would not take off their mail, since the Hungarians had even killed the herald who had been sent to them with an offer of peace. Men and horses were being hit by arrows, and the wounded beasts began to rage in delirium. The army, exhausted by the godless heathen, faced utter annihilation, against which it was powerless. When at last they surrendered the Hungarians approached, took away their weapons and armour, and divided the prisoners among themselves.

These two reports are by men who were not familiar with Central Asian tactics. They do not, therefore, give such insight as is afforded by the *Secret History of the*

Mongols, with Jenghis Khan's routine orders. We do not know in detail how these manœuvres were carried out, but we do know—from Villani's chronicle—that the signal to swerve aside was given by shaking a quiver, thus making a noise only audible at close quarters by the horses, when a feint was intended and the attack not to be pressed home. The horses reacted instantly, but how many men took part in each attack, and whether they discharged their arrows before or after turning away from the front, we do not know. Certain it is that this abrupt volte-face demanded a high degree of equestrian skill, for the whole squadron to turn as one man.

When we consider that the arrows were discharged at a fast gallop, throwing the reins to the horse, this is further proof of their skill in riding, their skill at arms, and not least of the state of training of their horses. There were certain risks inherent in this tactic; any confusion or hesitation among the thousands of galloping horsemen could have meant disaster in the face of an enemy who knew how to exploit it.

A hundred years later, under the Anjou dynasty, the armament of the armoured knights of the fourteenth century showed unequivocal Western influence, but the light horse still consisted of mounted archers. The Neapolitan chronicler Villani, describing the Italian campaign of Louis I (1342–82), calls the Hungarian horse lightly armed, invariably their weapons being bow, arrows, and a long sabre, their clothing being layer on layer of leather jerkins ('wambaces' in the English of the period) which acted as sort of 'poor man's armour'. Their strategic significance is stressed also in a later (1395) document of King Sigismund, in which he commanded every mounted lancer in his pay to provide also two mounted archers.

The appearance of the Osmanli Turks only increased the importance of this tried arm of the service. Rearmament against this new threat from the East became more urgent after the defeat at Nikopolis (1396). But that battle also demonstrates the difference between Eastern and Western military practice. King Sigismund of Hungary was also Holy Roman Emperor, and his campaign, which was of the nature of a belated Crusade, attracted many foreign volunteers, principally knights from France. Contemporary writers lay the blame for the defeat entirely on the French, who would let no-one deny them the honour of the first onslaught. They were the first to attack the Turks, which they did on foot, adopting what had now become the common Western practice imitated from the successful charge of the dismounted English chivalry at Crécy in 1346. In doing so they got in the way of the Hungarian light-horse skirmishers. According to the chronicle of Thuróczi, part of the Hungarian army was thrown into disarray when the horses of the dismounted French knights came into their lines and they, being unfamiliar with this procedure, thought that their riders must have been slain or unhorsed. [The question arises, what were the squires of the French knights doing? It is the duty of an esquire to take charge of the destrier at all times when the knight is not riding it. *Tr.*] It is easy to imagine what confusion would be caused by the irruption of the huge, pugnacious chargers among the ranks of Hungarian light horse, standing-to ready for action. This mishap led to a reorganization of the Hungarian army, the mounted archers being reinforced at the expense of the other arms. The Diet passed a law in 1397, whereby for the duration of hostilities against the Turks all landed gentry were to raise one mounted archer for every twenty farmsteads on their estates, and to bring him into the field. It is assumed that this was the origin of hussars. (Note 25.)

59
Hadban Enzahi, foaled in
1952, by Nazeer out of
Kamla. Standing at the
Marbach Arab stud.

60
Shari, foaled 1961, by
Hadban Enzahi out of
Hathor; Champion Arab
Female of Germany in 1968.

61
Tajar, Grey Arab Stallion,
once the Charger of a
Mameluke Officer
among those massacred by
Mehemet Ali. He was the
Foundation Sire of
Hungarian-bred Arabs

62/63 Tourney.
Illumination from the Tournament Book of Duke William IV of Bavaria, first half of 16th century.
State Library, Munich

64 Hungarian Csikos (Herdsman) with his Horse at a Cattle-trough in the the Hortogagy Puszta

65 (below) Uryanchai Girl milking Reindeer

66 (right) Mongolian Girl milking Mare

But these horse-bowmen were not conscripted serfs. The latter constituted the so-called servile militia (infantry). The archers to be raised as a part of what in England would be called 'knight service' were all freemen, experienced soldiers. Many of them were impoverished gentlemen, often refugees from Turkish-occupied territory. And so whoever was bound to find a mounted archer or hussar had not only

Hungarian Hussar with Bow and Sabre
Sixteenth-century engraving from National Museum, Budapest

to recruit him but to pay him. Such easily hired masterless men had been a feature of Hungarian life before this, especially in the cavalry of Oriental style.

The professional soldier was heir to a tradition that went back to the ancient world, for both Rome and Byzantium had filled the ranks of their cavalry with Oriental mercenaries, and still in 1259 the army of Michael Palaeologos of Constantinople contained 1500 Hungarian and Kuman Turkish horse, who by 1298 were serving the Archduke Albert of Habsburg, and in the following century were in the pay of the Pope and of many Italian city-states. Things were not much different at home. Under Andrew III of Hungary (1290–1301) and the Anjou dynasty (1307–82) Kuman archers were permanently on the establishment.

As the Turkish wars progressed their numbers grew ever greater. Refugees from the Balkans—Raizes, Croats, Slovenes, and Hungarians—all found sanctuary in Hungary, among other lands. At this time the ranks of the hussars were full of them. At the accession of Ferdinand I (1526) it was said, with reference to warfare: "It is therefore necessary to have recourse to the swiftness of doughty hussars, who can easily be had from Hungary, Slavonia, Croatia or Transylvania".

The Yugoslavs who entered the hussar bands had no influence on the development of this arm. They simply adapted themselves to the model of the Magyar hussar, riding a Hungarian light horse, in the Hungarian manner on a Hungarian saddle, equally master of the sabre, the bow, and later the hand-gun. The Hungarian army thus did not become 'Balkanized', and its tactics continued to be overwhelmingly Central Asian in style.

There is contemporary evidence in a letter of King Matthias to Gabriel of Verona in 1481, from which we deduce that the traditional procedure was still used in battle: they stationed themselves on the field in rear of the main body and sallied out at the enemy whenever opportunity offered, and when they were tired or threatened they withdrew and reformed, ready for the next assault. (Note 26.)

Increased Turkish pressure on Hungary led of necessity to further reinforcement of the light cavalry. The Diet of 1435 stepped up the furnishing of one mounted archer from every twenty farmsteads to one for every ten. King Matthias, who kept a standing army in pay, describes the hussar in the letter quoted above as the intermediate arm between the armoured cavalry and the infantry. And at this point the hussar had attained the status in Central European armies that he was to hold for the next five centuries, as the model of a light-cavalryman.

A Setback to Hungarian Horse-breeding

The life-and-death struggle against the Turks bore hard on the horse-stock of Hungary. The horses captured from the Asiatics did not go far to replace casualties. The position became worse when the centuries-old embargo on the export of horses was lifted. Under the Habsburgs the country came into the economic orbit of Austria and of the German Empire, and now nothing could stop the drain of Hungarian horses westward.

A hundred years earlier Duke Frederick of Austria was not able to find, in Wiener-Neustadt market, any Hungarian horses, their importation having been rendered impossible by the King of Hungary. But now Ferdinand I and his successor Maximilian could direct the Chamberlain of Zips to obtain horses for the Court from Upper Hungary. (Note 27.) With the lively export trade an inflation of prices went hand in hand. Whereas at the beginning of the sixteenth century eight or ten gulden was the going price for an ordinary horse, now a useful draught horse cost 150 gulden. Fugger has this to say of the prices current in the 1580's: "If it please any man to travel to the Hungarian borders, there he shall find out what horses cost; yea it is now uncommon to be able to buy a rouncy or a saddle-nag less than a hundred talers." [Even insular England did not escape this general trend of live-stock and commodity prices in the sixteenth century. It was a long-range effect of the Spanish exploitation of the Americas, resulting in a disastrous fall in the price of precious metals. Tr.]

The demand for Oriental horses was enormous. Fugger writes:

> Now latterly they bring to us many horses, much more than was formerly the case, both from Transylvania and Hungary and Poland, and also Podolian, Croatian and Czech horses . . . but those from Transylvania, Hungary and Bohemia are commonly shy and fearful, yet a good part of them are strong and bold, apt to make a warhorse . . .

The increased demand, on top of the general inflation, for light cavalry horses and fast harness horses drove the price of half-blood horses very high. The Andalusian, never a cheap horse, was simply not in this market. It was now every horseman's dream to acquire a charger that would pass muster as a 'capital' horse.

The third reason for the shrinking supply of horses in Hungary was simply the decline of breeding itself. This was chiefly the case in Transdanubia and Upper Hungary, where the grazing-grounds round the frontier fortresses had been a theatre of war for so long. Two documents of the period show this decline. A report from Zips as late as 1592 says that the serfs around Mezönánás are chiefly occupied in breeding horses, and get their living by the sale of them. (Note 28.) But on the other hand as early as 1639 the steward of the Sárospatak estate reports to Prince George Rákóczi that he is unable to procure post-horses, because the servile tenants of the Crown lands not occupied by the Turks have no horses. (Note 29.)

In Turkish-occupied territory the situation was somewhat easier. The great expanses of pasture in the depopulated lowlands became 'ranches'. Here horse-breeding flourished anew. It was easier in time of danger to bring the herds out of harm's way than in the thickly populated Crown lands across the border, where every rood of land was occupied. Droves of horses and cattle were brought to islands in the swamps, or simply driven a long way off—say sixty miles. A measure of security was to be had by a form of 'homage'; a levy paid to the Turkish overlord for immunity from sequestration of stock by the Turks. The Hungarian horse-dealer of the seventeenth century bought most of his stock from this source. Both they and private buyers favoured the southern parts of the Turkish-held territory, and sold them on from there to foreign countries. For instance, the Palatine Wesse-lényi ordered the Chamber to procure remounts for the German dragoons from Jazygia and the Kecskemét district, both under Turkish occupation in 1661. (Note 30.) Even the Hungarian magnates often kept their studs in those areas—which, however, often had undesired results, as in the case of Count Valentin Balassa, a descendant of the famous poet, who wrote to Stephan Koháry in 1677:

> although I have paid tribute for my stud, Ibrahim Bey fell in love with my mares. He sent a guard of honour of Kuruzes to conduct them via Szécsén to

Hatvan where the marriage to the Bey took place. So that is all one gets for paying tribute in respect of farm and stock. You never can trust a Turk...

(Note 31.)

Recovery in terms of numbers was not possible after the liberation from Turkish rule. Even in terms of quality, the once far-famed Hungarian horse 'fit for a lord' was gone with the wind. In its place were little thrifty, durable farm horses, quite unsuitable for upper-class use, either to ride or to drive. The landowners turned their attention to the 'Spanish' horses (which by now had become the Neapolitan-Andalusian) that now begin to appear in inventories of noble households, even in Transylvania. Even pictures of hussars show them mounted on such horses.

Finally the national interest, in both the military and the civilian transport sphere, was so jeopardized that in 1766 Maria Theresa issued a proclamation entitled *Commissio in negotio propagationis equorum* with the object of breeding stronger horses. This State intervention followed the Seven Years War, which again had played havoc with the remount services, and hence with the stock in general. The Commission laid certain restrictions on privately-owned stallions at stud. Strong stallions in State ownership were made available to cover farmers' mares. They were of Western stamp. (Notes 32, 33.)

The results appear to have been catastrophic, because no account was taken of traditional methods and conditions. Through the use of unsuitable stallions, breeding by farmers was all but ruined. Captain Josef Csekonics made a report for the Emperor Joseph II on the reform of Hungarian horse-breeding; pointing out that remount-purchasing commissions were not able to find more than two or three suitable troop horses in three whole counties.

That energetic ruler, who had ideas in advance of his age, acted in character. He introduced Government stallion depots and covering stations, founding the Mezö-hegyes stud, with Csekonics in charge to start matters on the right lines. He also founded the stud at Radauti, in Bukovina. The captain, whose services to Hungarian horse-breeding are incalculable, chose his foundation stock with great skill. In accordance with Hungarian tradition, it consisted predominantly of imported Tartar and Circassian mares, the stallions being in part Thoroughbreds from England.

Along with this reanimation of Hungarian horse-breeding there went also a reflorescence of equitation, though now vitally different from the Central Asian origins. The line dividing East from West, of which the western frontier of Hungary had so long been a sector, had been slowly fading for three centuries. And now Hungarian practice became wholly European.

A summary of the factors governing stock-breeding and transport in Central Asia among the nomad herdsmen shows the same general picture as in Hungary. After the decline of the Turkish empire in Central Asia a deliberate grading-up of steppe horses with Turanian blood can be demonstrated. Jenghis Khan's order to take all blood-horses captured back to Mongolia to be used for breeding purposes, and then the patronage of Turkoman horse-breeding by Timur-i-Leng and Nasr-ed-Din, had the same object.

The same is true of transport technique. Riding, driving, saddlery, harness, vehicles—all go back to the same source. Likewise in the military sphere. The

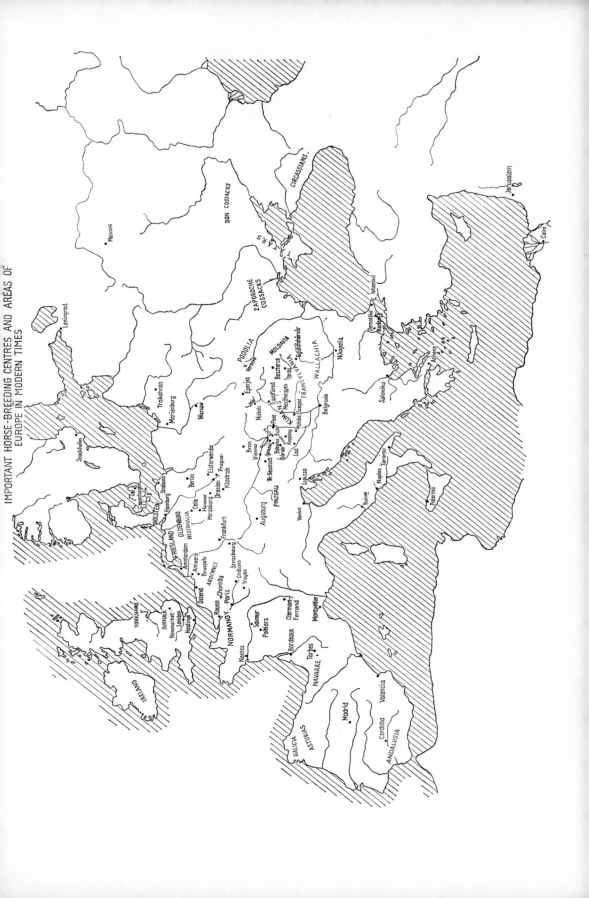

IMPORTANT HORSE-BREEDING CENTRES AND AREAS OF EUROPE IN MODERN TIMES

Cossacks in the service of the Tsar, who had originally been free-lances engaged for pay and the hope of booty, became in time troops of the line just like the hussars. Their horses, their equipment, their tactics were those of the hussars, the Cossack saddle and the hussar saddle were identical down to the last century, both being derived from the wooden saddle of the nomad herdsmen.

This equestrian culture, however, lasted longer in Central Asia than in Hungary —or the Ukraine. The last traces of it surrendered only yesterday to the overwhelming forces of the modern technical revolution.

Part IV A Uniform Europe

Contributions from East and West

Two fundamental elements of European horsemanship derive from opposite poles —East and West. There is an almost unbroken chain of development lasting from the beginning of the mounted invasions until some time in the nineteenth century, in which the Hungarians acted as the catalytic agent.

The three-hundred-year sojourn of the Avars in Europe left deep impressions behind it, more than appear to the superficial observer. It may be proved, for example, by reference to East Prussia. This was once a backwater of Europe, left almost undisturbed by the currents of the Migration Period; the civilization of the Occident reached it comparatively late, and the indigenous peoples retained their ancient customs all the longer. Our chief documentary source is the archives of the Germans—in particular of the Teutonic Order of Knights. [It is as if, in terms of English history, the last hundred years of the *Anglo-Saxon Chronicle* did not exist, and we were entirely dependent on Norman accounts of England and the English. Tr.] The specialist literature based on these archives which concerns us here is principally the study by Fritz Rünger (1925) on the breeding and origin of the war-horses used by the Order. As mentioned above, once the Order was free of its commitments in the Holy Land, it annexed East Prussia in the thirteenth century, for the furtherance of the Christian faith. In the territory between the Vistula and the Memel they came in contact with the Old Prussians, a Baltic people known as the Borussi or Pruthoni, the Central Asian origin of whose equestrian culture can be shown in incontrovertible archaeological evidence.

The Avars and the Old Prussians

The Marienburg archives of the Order point to four typically Central Asian features of the Old Prussian horse-husbandry: breeding on open range, method of castration, branding as mark of ownership (Note 34), and the milking of mares, particularly to provide kumiss, the use of which was restricted to the ruling class.

Transport and military equipment were also reminiscent of Central Asia. Their horses were small, they waged war as mounted archers, and only used pack-horses. Harness horses did not become common among them until the early fifteenth century, after the Teutonic Order's campaign of 1390, for which it did not requisition any pack-horses, as such, from its Prussian vassals, but only draught horses for the wagon-train.

So much for documentary evidence, which is substantiated by archaeological findings. First among these is the custom of equestrian burial which was customary only among the upper classes. Here Slavonic influence is perceptible; like the Slavs, they cremated their dead, burying beside the ashes both horse and horseman's gear. Gy. László points out that the Slavs of the Danube region, whose settlements alternated with those of the Avars, also followed this custom.

In the realm of ideas, too, there are certain affinities with the nomadic horse-breeders. This is evident in the hanging up of horse-skulls in Prussian stables and in Hungarian dwelling-houses, and the decoration of gable-ends with horse-heads carved in wood, in East Prussia as elsewhere in the Germanic world.

Their horse-stock, too, is what we should expect of nomadic breeders. The Ambassador, Count Herberstein, in his journal of travel through East Prussia in 1557, as well as Marx Fugger, notes that the local horses were mouse-grey or ash-grey (dun), with a dark eel-stripe. They had either domed foreheads or Roman noses, a stiff upright mane, and 'zebra' stripes on the hocks. According to Ebhardt this would indicate a mixture of Pony Type I and Horse Type III (see p. 14). In the Old Prussian language the wild horse was called *paustocaican* and the domestic horse *schweike*. But in the records of the Order the *schweike* herds were called 'wild herds'. [This apparent contradiction is explained by the widespread use of the word 'wild' among medieval and indeed later authors to indicate the technique of breeding horses and ponies on open range, and it has nothing to do with the modern biologist's definition of a 'wild' animal. It is in this sense, not in the scientific sense, that, for instance, Welsh Mountain ponies are described as 'wild'. Tr.]. We may deduce that the indigenous East Prussian horse was kept in herds on the common grazing of the wastes, and was of pony size, if not exclusively of pony type.

After the war of extermination carried on by Charlemagne in 796 we find only one further mention of the Avars: about the year 805 they sent an embassy to the Frankish Court, asking the Emperor to grant them new lands, since owing to pressure from the Slavs life was becoming intolerable for them in their old home. The Russian Chronicle of Nestor states also "When the Vlachs" [that is, the Franks] "assailed the Slavs on the Danube, subduing them by force and planting settlements among them, some of the Slavs moved out and settled on the Vistula. . . ."

Taken together, those two passages mean that Pannonia (Hungary) was the scene of repeated shifts of population in the early ninth century, and that some element of the population—either Slavs or Slavophone Avars—migrated to the Vistula basin. That there may well be some connection between the Pannonian Avars and the Prussians of the Vistula is to be assumed from the similarity of tribal names—e.g., Serb/Sorb, Abrodit/Brodnik, Prosto/Prussian.

This question can only be finally decided by a synthesis of research in the archaeological, ethnological, and linguistic fields. One thing is certain, however; that one of the routes by which the technique of Central Asiatic horsemastership reached Europe (and probably Scandinavia in particular) is through East Prussia. This made a fruitful contribution to material civilization, and probably even the practice of the Teutonic Order was influenced by its taking over, in the course of centuries of living side by side with the Old Prussians (so long as those survived at all), much of their legacy of mounted pastoralism. This may explain the community of outlook between the Hungarian landowner and his Prussian counterpart, the Junker, whose traditions seem to be derived not so much from his German forebears, whether these were Saxons or immigrants from "High Germany", as from the Old Prussian ruling class of Baltic speech and culture whom they had displaced.

The first hundred years following the advance of the Order into East Prussia were filled with continuous warfare. In the early stages the tactics of the Knights were rather primitive, and some of them still fought on foot. The Borussi, who were at the same time fighting the Poles on another front, held out heroically for a long

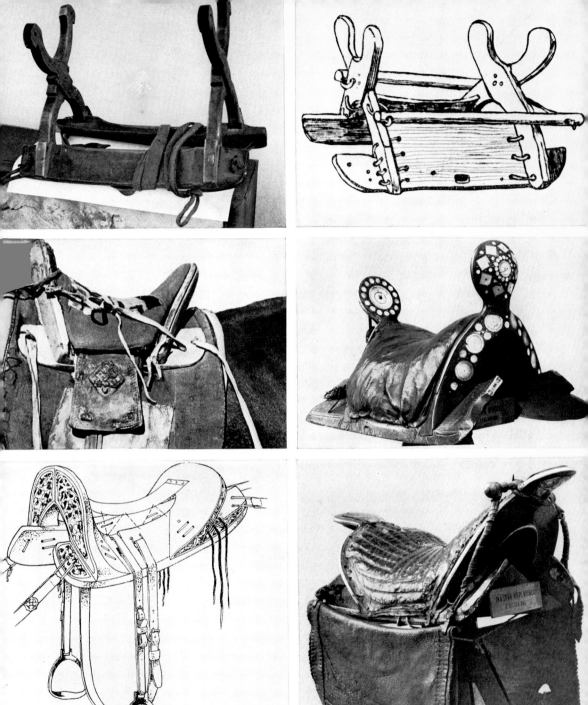

67   Evolution of the Saddle
(Top left) Reindeer saddle from Sayan Mountains. 68 (top right) Kirghiz saddle for
children. 69 (centre left) Mongol saddle. 70 (centre right) Nineteenth-century Turkish
saddle. 71 (bottom left) Reconstruction of Magyar saddle at time of settlement of
Danube plain. 72 (bottom right) Hungarian country saddle of nineteenth century.

er Anfall ist gewagt; die möchten mit angreiffen,
Es zappelt Mann und Pferd und ist schon auf dem flug,

Doch, da der fällt, hält Sie zuruk der kuglen pfeiffen,
Als die bey hiz und Muth zugleich auch schlau genug

73   Hungarian Hussars, Eighteenth Century
Engraving by G. P. Rugendas

74   Hungarian Coach, 1563. Engraving by J. Schemel.
National Museum, Budapest

75   Kuman Peasant, Early Nineteenth Century Drawing by Bikkesy.
National Museum

76   Hungarian Country-bred Horses Early Nineteenth Century.
National Museum

77　Stag Headdress from the Pazyryk
Horse-burials
Hermitage, Leningrad

time. Rising after rising ended at last with the almost total extermination of their ruling class. The last of the Old Prussian nobility perished in the rebellion of 1322, after which the Order was able for the first time to set about the building up of a systematic economy. At this period they founded the studs of heavy horses to provide chargers, a characteristic manifestation of the Occidental 'Frankish' mode of military life, existing side by side with the Oriental practices of the indigenous population. In some respects tactics and equipment of the Teutonic Order resembled that of contemporary Hungary. On the wings of the heavily armed 'main battle', mounted on destriers, there were bodies of light horse drawn from the freemen among the subject Old Prussians, the *equites pruteni*, with an important tactical role. Besides its studs of heavy horses the Order also had herds of *schweiken* running in the woods and on the heaths. As might be expected, these latter provided them with palfreys. Every Brother of the Order had to maintain one destrier and two *schweiken*; their squires were mounted on light horses of the same stamp.

The Oriental influence already evident in the fields of transport and warfare spread into the social sphere of everyday life. Out of the constant necessity to maintain everything on a war footing there arose a way of life characteristic of the army-as-State or the State-as-army which has been the baleful legacy of the Asiatic equestrian warrior-peoples to posterity. For the individual, this meant the wholesale adaptation to the 'chivalrous' way of life, at a time when—in England, for instance —the rigid bonds of feudal society based on land held by military service and the 'knight's fee' were beginning to loosen. Even the obligatory embargo on horse-exports was introduced into the Order's dominions—a little late in the day, indeed —being first mentioned in a document of 1386. At first this law discriminated solely against the Polish enemy, but by 1414 it was also directed against the West. [The Prussia of the Teutonic Knights really represents an anachronism, and as such may have been welcome to certain elements outside Germany. Thus in the *Canterbury Tales*—actually composed in the 1380's—Chaucer's Knight, who is obviously somewhat ill at ease in the increasingly un-feudal atmosphere of contemporary England, and would have been happier in the days of Edward I, had actually served as a volunteer under the banners of the Order "in Lettow and in Pruce". Tr.]

From then onward Prussian horsemanship played a significant part in the events of the West, and still today the Prussian horseman and the Prussian horse are important in the international equestrian field.

The Vikings

We mentioned above that the East Prussians and other Balts who were in contact with the horse-culture of Central Asia had passed on a certain part of this technique to Scandinavia, among other places. [Archaeology shows that Sweden and Norway, far from being the home of a North Germanic language group living in isolation after one definitive migration, had since the Bronze Age—the Age of the Charioteers —been continuously refreshed culturally by a series of immigrations from the south shore of the Baltic which sometimes had their point of departure as far west as Mecklenburg, sometimes as far east as Estonia. Even as far east as Estonia, and as late as the ninth century, we have an account of the part played by horses in the social customs of the Baltic peoples by a Scandinavian traveller who contributed this item to King Alfred's English edition (it is more than a translation) of the *History* of Orosius. (Note 34a.) *Tr.*]

If the Northmen depended for communications principally on their superbly built ships and their skilful seamanship, they were no strangers to the horse, and it is significant that the sea-going ship begins to appear in Bronze Age rock-carvings of Scandinavia at the same time and in conjunction with the pair-horse chariot. Their ships took them to every coast where they had hopes of either profitable trade or still more profitable piracy. But when they came to the head of navigable water, whether in Ireland or Apulia, then they took to horse. "This year", says the *Anglo-Saxon Chronicle* so many times, "the heathen men went up on land and stole horses". In every capacity, as merchants, as pirates, as slave-dealers, as hired swordsmen, their calling brought them into contact with the great masters of the horse, such as the Moor in Andalusia and the Khazars and Turks of the Caspian region. The eastern branch of the Scandinavian expansion, mainly of Swedish origin, is known to us as Varangians, forming among other things the guard regiment of marine infantry at Constantinople—the Polekophoroi, or wielders of the two-handed axe. In this service they learnt, as infantry, the tactical lessons of co-operation with both heavy (Fancopouloi) and light (Turcopouloi) cavalry; but the Varangian—or Variag, as the Russians called him—was also a merchant doing business along the great inland waterways of the Kievan kingdom, and, less well-known to us in the West, in Hungary, where the place-name Varong occurs frequently. Those who came home to a wealthy and honoured retirement brought with them knowledge of Eastern horse-lore, and Norway and Denmark must be regarded as the entrepôt of equestrian knowledge, which by this northern route was passed on to the West. It contributed much to the last, most momentous, and yet most indirect of the Viking expeditions. When the clan of Tancred de Hauteville took service with the Pope in Southern Italy against the Emperor of Constantinople (or occasionally vice-versa, when the latter paid better wages) they set out not from Norway but from Seine Inférieure, and no longer as their forefathers had done as marine infantry who might out of tactical necessity now and again perform a strategic march on horseback, but as knights armed and fighting in the 'Frankish' manner.

Equestrian burial with certain Asiatic elements was already an ancient institution in Scandinavia, well attested by archaeological evidence and mentioned in Northern literature as early as the days of the legendary Harald Hilditönn, slain in battle by Sigurd Ring (reputedly the father of the Viking Ragnar Hairy-Breeches who ravaged Northumbria in the first wave of westward expansion from the Fjords). Harald was an old man, who only went out to this last battle because his peasant subjects were about to offer him as a ritual sacrifice to ensure the fertility of their fields and flocks, and to take a younger and more vigorous prince as their sovereign. After the battle his enemy Sigurd Ring had him fittingly interred together with his horse, throwing his own saddle into the grave, so that his dead rival could make a fitting entry into Valhalla. [Horse-burial in the North is associated primarily with the devotees of Odin and of Freyr, and has many features in common with the funerary rites of the steppe horsemen as far east as the Altai. *Tr.*]

The Western Vikings sacked and burnt Antwerp in 836, Rouen in 841, Nantes in 843, Paris in 845, Hamburg in the same year, and Bordeaux in 847. They had in the same period destroyed the headquarters at Dorstad of their principal commercial rivals, the Frisians, who were also horse-breeders. The Duchy of Normandy, on the

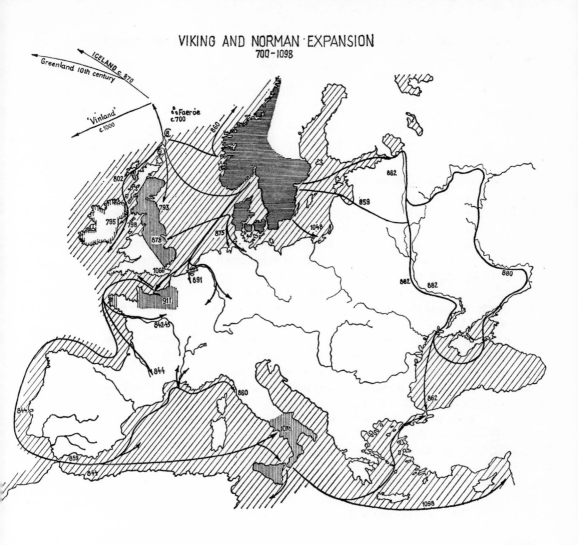

south shore of the English Channel, was founded in 911, and thence was mounted not only the Sicilian adventure mentioned above but William the Bastard's Enterprise of England.

It was the Viking incursions which caused the Frankish King Charles the Bald to summon his vassals to take the field on horseback. They were among other things the challenge, a response to which was the Frankish institution of chivalry, which they so successfully adopted themselves. The core of the Crusading armies was formed of Franco-Norman knights or knights armed and operating in this manner —the most spectacular and prolonged confrontation of East and West that the world has seen.

Thus among European equestrian peoples we may say that three above all have spread the technique and the principles of Asiatic horsemanship and horsemastership through the breadth of this continent—the Avars, the Magyars, and the Norsemen (with their half-bred descendants the Normans). To this was added—principally in the Modern period—the Near Eastern or specifically the Arab element. Traces of all these legacies are still perceptible in the world of the Western horseman today.

Eastern Customs

Burial with Horses

The earliest indication of the spread of Oriental customs is in the religious sphere. It is typified in the survival of the Oriental custom of horse-burial in symbolic form. At the time of the Scyth invasions carts, wagons, and chariots were being buried along with the dead, at least as far west as Burgundy. The mode of entombment differed somewhat from the practice of the steppes, since though the corpse was often placed in a vehicle as in a bier, the wheels being detached and placed at the side of the burial pit, the horse or horses were usually interred outside the actual tomb-chamber, and the entire carcass was not invariably present. However, the intention is obviously the same—to provide the dead with the means of travel to the next world.

Vestiges of this custom were present in the funeral pomp of the Romans, in which the dead man's horse was led, though no longer to be sacrificed at the graveside. Signs of a more recently imported Oriental custom are to be seen in the mortuary dedication of a horse, customary in the West from Germany to England inclusive in the late Middle Ages. One German example will suffice:

The German anti-King, Johann Latomus Günther von Schwarzburg, was buried in 1349; records state that two torch bearers led five horses to the altar, where they were symbolically offered, and then bought back by the next-of-kin for four hundred gold pieces, which was paid to the Church. [English wills down to the Reformation often contain similar bequests. Tr.] Plainly the symbolic offering of the horses goes back to some kind of funerary sacrifice as at Pazyryk, while the burning torches may either be a reminder of cremation as practised by the pagan Prussians or an echo of classical mythology; Artemis, who was among other things the Queen of Night and of Death, is often represented as driving in a wagon with torch-bearers attendant. And she was also the patron goddess of horse and hound.

In the West this custom remained a privilege of the landowning class which the burghers were reluctant to recognize—perhaps a prolongation of the antithesis between nomadic pastoralists and settled husbandmen. Thus in 1356 the city of Frankfurt passed a by-law specifically forbidding its citizens to claim this privilege. "Nyman vor keiner lych keyn roz adir pherd lazsen fueren mit eyme gewapetin mane"—No man is to have led before the corpse a destrier (roz) or palfrey (pherd) by an armed man. [The charger was led, at English funerals, by a man in full armour as late as the seventeenth century, as notably in the cortège of Sir Philip Sydney, of which contemporary pictures exist. The continued use so late as this, in Germany, of the word Pherd (parafridus) in its restricted sense of ambling palfrey, and not in the more general sense of horse, is interesting. Tr.]

If a Frankfurter wished to bequeath a horse to the Church he might do so, but it was to remain in ecclesiastical hands, and the family were forbidden to buy it back on pain of a fine equal to the price of the horse.

It is not yet clear by what means this Asiatic custom became diffused through the West, but it may well be the combined effect of Avar, Magyar, and Viking influence.

It may be helpful to refer to Hungarian practice. We may begin from the horse-burial as found in Hungary. The Hungarians themselves had this custom until the days of St Ladislas (1065–95), but later waves of invaders from the East—notably Patzinaks and Kumans—kept it up until the fourteenth century. Joinville, in his life of St Louis, says of the Kumans who were settled in Egypt that they were wont to bury their chief men together with their horses, but with this cruel variation, that the living horse and a groom, also living, were buried or walled up along with the dead. These Turks were nominally Muslims, and such elaborate practices are diametrically opposed to the bare simplicity of orthodox Mahomedan burial.

Both history and archaeology confirm that among the Kumans of Hungary this procedure did not apply, yet some elements of it persisted into the mid-fourteenth century. Another French source quotes a letter from the Abbot of St Geneviève at Paris to the parents of a Hungarian youth by the name of Bethlehem (Bethlen?) who died there in 1180; among the list of presents sent by the bereaved to the church where their son was buried he mentions a white horse and a lance.

A Hungarian will of about 1270 by Bezter, son of Demetrius, commands his body to be buried in the chapel of the Franciscan abbey at Ofen; he left his best horse, with saddle, accoutrements, and arms, to the Church. At the funeral of King Charles I of Hungary in 1342 three horses trapped in black were led in the cortège, carrying his arms and armour. The will of his widow Elizabeth, proved in 1380, desired that six of her twelve carriage horses should be led in the funeral procession. [This is also significant in another context. The earliest mention of carriages *at all* in English documents is in 1381! *Tr.*] (Note 35.)

Symbolic horse-offerings occur regularly in Hungarian wills of the fifteenth century. As in Germany, the importance of the offertory is emphasized by the quality of the horses and arms concerned. Not only are the horses made over to the Church, but the amount for which they are to be redeemed is specified. Johan Ernuszt, who rose from obscure circumstances to become a high dignitary (he was, incidentally, of Jewish origin), points out in his will that the offering of a horse is obligatory on persons of baronial rank.

A German ballad on the funeral of King Albert, who died in 1439, shows how important this horse-offering was in royal obsequies. It blames the Hungarians for the King's early death, and reproaches them for showing their spite by not bringing out either chargers or armour in his funeral cortège.

Pomp of all kinds, including the funeral, reached its height in the Age of Baroque and the funerals of Hungarian landowners of this period were no exception. See p. 118 for a panoramic view of the cortège of four sons of the house of Esterházy killed at the battle of Vezekény against the Turks in 1652—a veritable equestrian spectacle. Even now, three centuries later, many people find it goes against the grain to accept the motorized hearse.

Still very occasionally a horse is led in some funeral procession (usually a State funeral) with the boots fixed in the stirrups, the toes pointing backward. The reason for this lies far back in the past, among the beliefs of the steppe herdsmen, who thought of life in the next world as the reverse of this one, and used to put the saddle on the funeral horse back to front with this significance.

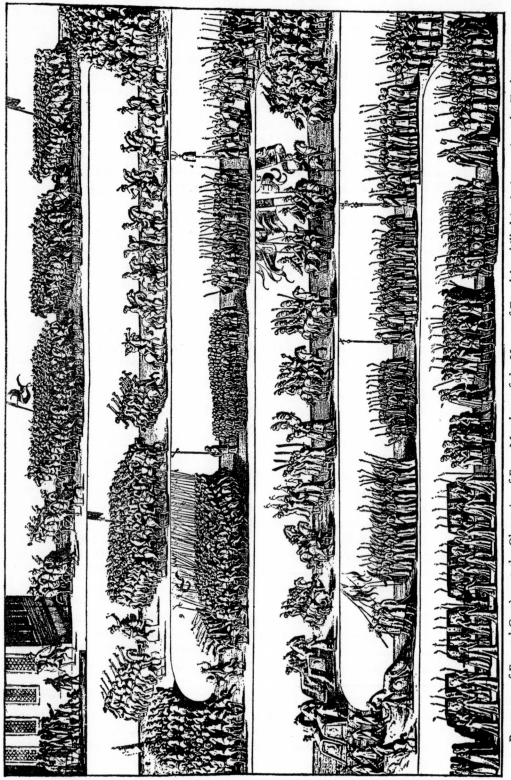

Panorama of Funeral Cortège at the Obsequies of Four Members of the House of Esterházy, killed in Action against the Turks, 1652

Copper engraving in Library of Academy of Sciences, Budapest

Oriental influence was not confined to the mental attitude of the horseman, but also to the technique of driving. The adoption of the Hungarian style of harness represents a diffusion of Eastern technique.

West European harness in the early Middle Ages differed little from that of the Romans. Vehicles were the single-axle cart and the four-wheeled wagon having fore- and hind-wheels of the same size. When driven from the vehicle itself, these equipages were clumsy, and only suitable for good roads. There were few good roads, and fast wheeled traffic did not exist.

The earliest indication of adoption by the West of driving from the saddle is our Plate 81, the journey of St Elizabeth. This Hungarian princess, a daughter of King Andreas II of the House of Arpad, went to visit her father, accompanied by her husband, the Margrave of Thuringia, in 1225. The picture dates from the early fourteenth century, and though it still shows fore- and hind-wheels of the same size, the driver is mounted on one of the wheelers, in Danubian fashion. The tubular tilted wagon-cover is of a type still used in Hungary until recently, and is mentioned both by Ibn Batuta and by Broquière as typically Hungarian. During the next century driving from the saddle became much more widely diffused.

According to the historian Domanovszky (1917), distribution of the sprung carriage also began from Hungary, and followed the same route. The first such vehicle in France is mentioned in the *Grande Encyclopédie* as having been brought by Isabella of Bavaria on her way to her wedding with King Charles VI. The second to be seen was in 1457, sent by King Ladislaus V of Hungary to the Queen of France, when sueing for the hand of her daughter, the Princess Madeleine, in marriage.

There is much evidence of the capabilities of Hungarian wainwrights during the next century. A letter from Count Ferenc Batthyány of 1559 mentions one who would deliver an iron-tyred sprung wagon to Count Arco for 25 gulden. (Note 36.) At that time the sprung wagon was used only by royalty and nobility. It was usually driven six-in-hand. (Note 37.)

The next development was the diffusion of the Hungarian *kocsi* throughout Europe. In a previous chapter we traced its origin to Oriental prototypes, and drew attention to the peculiarity of this Hungarian speciality in having smaller fore-wheels. Furthermore, it was no longer driven from the saddle but from the box, which may be regarded as a concession to Western custom.

While in Hungary the great advantage of this novel vehicle lay chiefly in the fact that the wheeler no longer had to carry a rider, it led in the West to a complete revolution in transport. Feats unimaginable by means of the clumsy Western wagons became possible at one blow by means of the coach. Fast and comfortable (by their standards) travel became a commonplace. This new mode of travel made new demands on the Western horse-stock. A demand soon arose for horses that could gallop or trot for long stages, in harness.

The *kocsi*, under various names closely resembling the original Hungarian, was distributed throughout Europe in the space of a few decades in the sixteenth century. But while it facilitated travel it also brought problems in its train, especially on the military side. So long as everyone had been accustomed to travel on horseback, there was no lack of horses "apt for service in the wars", or of horsemen to ride them in battle. But as soon as men took to travelling by coach, both sources began to dry up. Many European Governments intervened directly, among them German principalities, Italian cities, England; all passed laws restricting coach traffic, and inveighing against this new fashion which tended to make men effeminate, and was the cause of senseless luxury. In 1588 the Duke of Brunswick directly reproached his subjects: "young and old, they are turning into idlers and coachgoers". A remount crisis and a dearth of horsemen for military service arose during the reign of Queen Elizabeth of England [at least, this was the official view, though it is doubtful whether her parsimonious regime would possibly have produced the money to pay the number of horsemen who were actually available for service, if all assessable persons had made a true return of horses in their possession and men in their households able to ride. In fact, out of the whole kingdom only 3000 horsemen and suitable horses for them existed *on paper*; this was the ostensible cause for the moving in the House of Lords of a Bill to restrict the use of coaches. Another consideration was the traffic jams which coaches caused in towns still built on the medieval plan (or no plan) with very narrow streets. In fact a true return would probably have shown more than 3000 horses and riders 'apt for service in the wars' north of the Trent alone. *Tr.*] But there were many published works making the same point, such as the oft-cited book by Marx Fugger. He too sees in the rise of coaching the reason for the recession in Western horsemanship: "Yea, these Gotzis serve so much towards idleness, that a man will lead his whole household, even to the cook and the cellar therein." He proposes that in order to preserve the art of horsemanship and maintain military virtues "we should do as in Spain, and forbid the riding of asses under the saddle, or else allow it only under license at a heavy fee"—but the fee is to be for coaches, and in fact many countries now began to introduce the coach licence. He thought that the principle being that those who could afford a saddle could also afford something better than a donkey to put it on, this principle could well be applied to coach-owners, and pointed out that those who formerly bred horses were now giving it up, and "they yearn so for a Gotzi, either to sit in by themselves or with three companions and so journey through a whole province!"

The basis of his argument in favour of half-blood horses is especially interesting; at that time a hundred thalers was being asked and given for Hungarian, Spanish, and Italian horses, though not every horse was suitable for the campaigns against the Turks. "What chance would I have of riding down a Turk on the Hungarian plains, were I mounted on a Frisian or a Dutch stallion, or even on one of our German rouncies, much less if I were loaded on a coach? None, you may be sure."

Marx Fugger was not alone in his strictures. There was a flood of pamphlets and proclamations against the fashion for coaching; many mounted with such fervour that they landed on the far side of the horse. In 1673 an Englishman even went so far as to say that coach-driving was a menace to English trades and harmful to the health.

Incomprehensible as all this is today, it is a significant stage in the evolution. Though more than five centuries had passed since the days of Charles Martel and the Magyar raids, the way of life which they had introduced had not permeated all classes of society. With few exceptions, in the West equitation and the lore of the horse remained the privilege of the knightly class, of the nobility and certain of their specialized servants, and it was among this section of the population that the

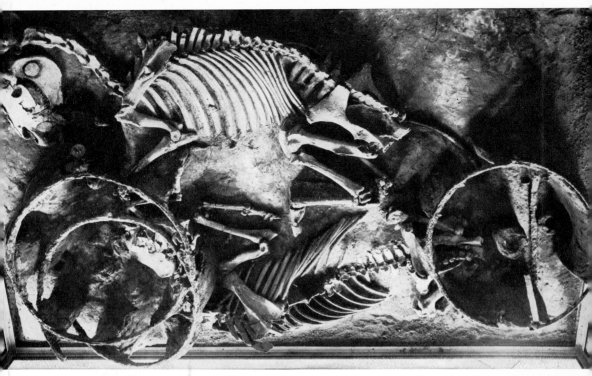

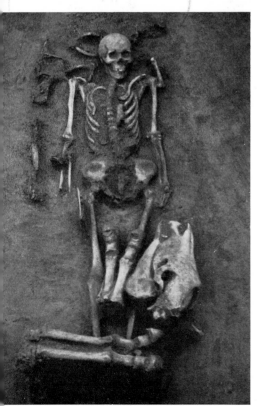

78 (above)   Scythian Grave from Szentes-Vekerzug,
     Typical Wagon-burial with Horses

79 (left)   Magyar Horseman's Grave from the
     Settlement Period
     Excavated at Oroshàza, 1961

80 (below) Ceremonial Wagon from the Ship-grave
     of Oseberg, Norway

81 *St Elizabeth's Journey to Hungary*, 1225
Painted panel in choir of Holy Ghost Hospital, Lübeck

82 Ferdinand of Tyrol dressed as an Eastern Horseman, in the Style adopted by Light
Cavalry in the Sixteenth Century.
National Museum, Budapest

83 Friedrich von Rittlitz in Eastern Horseman's Costume
Sixteenth-century drawing from National Museum, Budapest.

84 Hungarian Hussar
Engraving by Engelbrecht

85 Prussian Brown Hussar

86 English Officer of XIth Hussars

87 Count Valentine Esterházy, Proprietor of the
Esterházy Regiment of Hussars in France, 1784

Ein Husar von des Herrn von Geschrey Freÿ Compagnie
Wann der Husar vom Gschrey auf seine Feinde jagt
Und eins noch gegen Sie mit der Pistohle wagt,
So faßt er den Palasch so eifrig als vermeßen,
Zum Schröcken in das Maul, als wolt er solchen freßen.

88   Hussar of the Geschrey Free Company in Bavarian Employ.
Engraving by Engelbrecht

89 (left)   Polish Lancer of the 3rd Regiment, 1816–31   90 (right)   Polish Lancer in the Prussian Royal
Service, 1742
National Museum Budapest

91   The Turkoman Stallion Turkmain Atty, 1791–1806

92 Early-seventeenth-century
Travelling Carriage
*Cabinet of Engravings,
Berlin*

93 The Queen of Spain's
Berline, with Special
Suspension for Long
Journeys
Mid-eighteenth century.
*Musée de Tourisme et des
Voitures, Compiègne*

94 Swiss Alpine Post-wagon
for five-in-hand, 1830–40
Deutsches Museum, Munich

95　Express Mail-coach from Hungary. Lithography by J. Backer. *National Museum, Budapest*

96　The Emperor Franz Josef travelling in Hungary, 1852. *National Museum, Budapest*

new fashion of coaching had made the greatest impact and led to a numerical decline of men accustomed to the saddle.

In Hungary travel on horseback was part of the daily background of rich and poor alike. It is true that a law was passed in 1523 obliging the gentry to take the field either on foot or on horseback, and not in a coach, as many were already doing. But this was only a war emergency measure, and was not intended to maintain the permanent supply of men who could ride. At the time of the Diet of Rakes (1525) there were assembled, according to the Nuncio Burgio, ten thousand horsemen "all equipped as light horse after the Hungarian manner", quite in the tradition of Magyar and Hunnish antiquity.

Horse-breeding

The demand for fast light horses—not so much, as we have shown, for harness work as for light cavalry—led throughout Europe to the inflation of breeding Andalusian and Oriental horses. Chief among the Oriental hot-blooded sires used was the Arab.

To those two chief sources of hot-blood—the Arab and the Andalusian—a third was soon added. During the first half of the eighteenth century, Prussia, once the home of the Borussi, with their Central Asian traditions, saw the beginnings of a breed of light horses of such quality as to afford a landmark in the history of horse-breeding. Not only was it built up on a basis of Oriental horses with *some* Turanian blood, but it used sires which actually came from Turania. In 1732 King Frederick William I founded his famous Trakehnen stud with stock mostly imported from the East. The Turanian line was represented by Persian and Turkoman stallions which reached Prussia by the most varied and devious routes. One of them was the stallion Turkmain Atty who came long after the days of Frederick William I, having been foaled in 1791; a sire of such prepotency that he stamped his quality on the whole breed. He was a present from the Tsarina Catherine II to the Chancellor, Prince Kaunitz. His name is Turkish, and means simply Turkoman Horse, from which we may conclude that he belonged to the Akhal-Tekke breed.

The Trakehnen foundation stock had never before moved outside the confines of the original habitat of the wild horses—the same is also true of all the Hungarian breeds—and hence had not been subjected to the influence of an alien environment, as happened in the case of the Arab and the Barb, and has had an influence on their evolution.

Not only hot-blooded horses but also Oriental breeding techniques were borrowed, as is evident in the method of selecting breeding pairs, so also was castration, the product of which in Continental (but not Scandinavian) languages betrays its Oriental origin. Thus in French there is a verb *hongrer*, to castrate, and two nouns *hongre*, gelding, and *hongreur*, colt-gelder, both derived from *Hongrie*, Hungary. In German the gelding is called *Wallach*, showing that the custom must have been borrowed from the Wallachians (Vlachs) and Transylvanians, no earlier than in the days of the Teutonic Order. But in the extreme west of Europe—the Iberian peninsula—castration is reported by Fugger as being performed in the same manner as Hungary, with a wooden mallet, though not in the intervening countries. The explanation must lie in Arab intermediaries by way of North Africa.

Eighteenth-century tactics necessitated the employment of light cavalry after the Oriental pattern, of which the prime exemplar was the Hungarian hussar; but an equally important one was the Polish lancer. Significantly, the word *Ulan* means 'lancer' in Polish, and *Ölan* means 'nobleman' in the language of the Tartars.

A retrospective view of the development of cavalry warfare over several thousand years enables us to determine a certain continuity; as the people whose livestock husbandry was of the settled-farmstead type, both in prehistoric times and in antiquity, adopted the fighting technique of the mounted pastoralists, the mounted soldier of Oriental type remained a factor in Western armies down to modern times, and long after the bow had yielded to various types of firearm. During the century and a half of conflict with the Turks on Hungarian soil, this 'light-cavalry spirit' was not merely kept alive, it was intensified. In the Middle Ages the commitment of the light horse was initially in skirmishing—but it was more than skirmishing, it was a form of attrition which in later periods could only be achieved by harassing fire or the more intense bombardment of artillery. The light horseman 'ground away'—the very words of an Arab historian quoted above—the resistance of the enemy line-of-battle by long-range arrow-fire, and did not close with him until his stock of arrows was exhausted and the enemy physically weakened and morally shaken. The hussar's forte was a new element—a lightning attack not preceded by any such preliminary 'softening-up'. This became known throughout Europe as the *coup d'hussard*.

Two examples of this gambit may be cited. In the War of the Austrian Succession in 1743, Count Ferenc Nádasdy swam his regiment of hussars across the Rhine without losing a man or a horse, overran a line of field-works regarded by the French as impregnable, and compelled the fortress of Lauterburg to capitulate. (Note 38.) So much for the military axiom that it is useless to employ cavalry against fortifications! Again in 1757, in the Seven Years War, Count Andreas Hadik appeared with 3400 men before Berlin, suddenly, from Elsterwerda in Saxony, overpowering the garrison of the Silesian Gate with his Croatian infantry and Hungarian hussars, and swept away a counter-attack at the Kottbus Gate by a mounted attack ("I ordered the hussars and cavalry to attack with the sabre at a gallop"). With that, the garrison's resistance was broken. He levied a contribution of 700,000 gulden and set off on another forced march in order to escape encirclement by two converging Prussian armies, reaching his original base in three days. (Note 39.)

What opinion was held of hussars in the West we learn from a report by Marshal Villars:

> I feel obliged to state, that there are no troops who will serve with greater courage in the face of greater danger or will stand heavier fire or more severe losses in men and horses. There never were soldiers that fought better than these. I would to God our own cavalry had such spirit.

The pioneers of hussar expansion in the West were the small units which served as mercenaries in various European armies for regular pay in peace-time supplemented by loot on active service. (Note 40.) As every employing state was anxious to keep its hired sabres happy, so their established customs were respected. War as a regular profession was characteristic of, if not peculiar to, the Eastern horseman's way of life. [The obvious parallel in British terms is the companies of Irish and Highland swordsmen in English, French, and other foreign employ, who gained their living in this way without necessarily being political exiles like the famed Wild Geese brigades. Tr.] Both their scale of pay and the manner in which they drew it differed from that of the regular troops of the employing Power.

For instance, in France they were compensated for the customary perquisite of ransom for captured enemies by a bounty for every severed enemy head they could produce. [It is said, with or without foundation, that Senegalese troops of the French army were also remunerated for such trophies in this century. Tr.] (Note 41.) In the Prussian Army standing regulations laid down: "What the hussar can get by his sword from the enemy he is to keep for himself, without anything being withheld, and no difficulties are to be made." This order forbids, in the case of hussars, the forming of a common pool of loot, as was customary in other units. In 1759 Frederick the Great reactivated an old standing order which brings out the special status of the hussar. "Officers, NCOS and War Office officials are not to wound the pride of the Hungarian hussar; they are to be strict in their behaviour towards him, but must avoid humiliating reprimands and they are never to thrash such a man."

The first Hungarian officer to be seconded together with his troops to a Western service was Colonel George Ráttky, who entered the French service in 1692, and who after the battle of Höchstädt took command of a unit of 300 hussars formerly in the service of the Elector of Bavaria. From 1704 to 1710 Baron Gabriel Bellay-Bellawitz was in Dutch service with 150 hussars, but then went into Danish employ, and after many years returned home by way of Poland. (Note 42.)

After the Peace of Szatmár which brought the rising of Ferenc Rákóczi II to an end in 1711, officers and other ranks of his disbanded force took service with foreign Powers by troops. Thus Ladislaus Bercsényi, son of the Kurutz general Nikolaus of that name, joined Ráttky's regiment in 1713, followed by the two Valentine Esterházys, a son and a grandson of the rebel Anton Esterházy, then living in exile at Rodosto. With their collaboration the first three hussar regiments in the French service, which bore their name, were formed on the Hungarian model. It is significant that the oath of allegiance on attestment was taken in Hungarian down to the French Revolution. But these three regiments survived the Revolution, as the Swiss Guard did not, and still existed down to the end of the First World War.

The first regularly paid hussar unit in Prussia was raised in 1721 by refugee Hungarian officers, and it served the celebrated military maniac, King Frederick William I of Prussia, as a model for his "Black", "Brown", and "Death's Head" hussar regiments among others. In the roll of their commanding officers we find such names as Sigismund Halász of Dabas, Paul Werner of Györ, Michael Székely, Ferenc Carol Köszhegy, and Michael Kovács, the last-named being killed in the American War of Independence. Until 1743 there was a recruiting office in Vienna where officers and men signed on, but in that year it was abolished. No wonder that in 1757 the hussar regiment "Yazyg and Kuman" in the Austrian service called the Prussian hussars opposing them "Black Kuruzes", referring to Rákóczi's rebels. (Note 43.)

The third outlet for East European light horse was in Holland, where in 1743 Count George Frangepani took over the legacy of Colonel Bellay; like Ráttky, he had been in Bavarian service. In the roll of Hungarian officers serving in the Dutch army we find between 1745 and 1752 such names as Michael Zsigray, Gregor Sándor, Michael Ersey, Johann Szakáy, Alexander Jármay, Baron Josef Waha, Samuel Patonay, Ferenc Asztalos, Johann Sándor, and many others. By their aid regular hussar regiments were raised, the new arm being introduced partly by Hungarians, partly by French, Prussian, and Dutch intermediaries, into the establishment of the Russian, Polish, Swedish, Danish, Bavarian, Wuerttemberg, Baden, Saxon, Hanoverian, and British armies, as well as those of minor German states such as Weimar, Kassel, and Hesse-Darmstadt, the episcopal principalities, and Nassau; also Portugal, Spain, Modena, Piedmont, Naples, the Papal territories, Sardinia, some Balkan kingdoms, and—Japan. Besides the uniform, which imposed itself with greater or less completeness on various units, even to the Horse Artillery of the British Army, and (in some respects less suitably) the full-dress uniform of the Royal Air Force, the tactics and sundry customs of the East European light horseman penetrated in the wake of the hussars. In the eighteenth and early nineteenth century the hussar was regarded as the embodiment of the 'modern, progressive' soldier, which of course he was, by contrast with the traditional musketeer fighting in close order and firing by volleys, supported by slow-moving dragoons who were not really cavalry at all. (Note 44.)

Saddlery, Accoutrements, and Riding-Style

Along with the spread of light cavalry the use of the gelding for military purposes went hand in hand, but much more so there grew the use of the Hungarian saddle. The heavy demand for wooden saddles brought an unprecedented revival—indeed, boom—to the Hungarian saddlery industry, and the products of the workshops of Tiszafüred and Igmánd become known throughout Europe, and sought after. J. N. Máttyus, a lieutenant of hussars, wrote in 1828 a cavalry manual dealing comprehensively with this saddle. He wrote in his preface:

> Because of its practical design the Hungarian saddle is the best to fight in, it is the cheapest and the most durable . . . but since, abroad, it has become fashionable to modify and adapt it to locally current fashion, I think it relevant to set forth the essential features of its design, which were probably first introduced into our country by Asiatic peoples, and by us to foreign nations. . . .

By modification, by mass production, by the exaggeration of certain peculiarities which originally had been merely decorative, the foreign-made 'Hungarian' saddle lost much. Count Joseph Gvadányi wrote in 1788 in *Journey of a Village Lawyer to Buda*—a rhyming narrative—

> I think that when they are mounted on their horses, the saddles on their backs will be of Igmánd or Füred make, the bridles hung with fringes in the shape of swallow-tails, the cheek-pieces ornamented with thongs or gold thread with gold or silver agrafes, or decorated with sea-shells—the whole inlaid with coloured strips of leather. This was once the custom of our famous ancestors . . .

The best Western versions of the wooden saddle retained only those features which were of practical use.

Just as the hussar brought new tactics to cavalry warfare, so the Hungarian saddle had its influence on Western riding. We saw above how the Western rider sat with his legs stretched out, and this seat—which now seems so alien to us—was only displaced by the Hungarian style. Now henceforth the European rider began to draw up his knees after the Hungarian manner. Significantly, when Robert Shaw was visiting Yarkand and Kashgar in 1868, having ridden all the way from India, the Turkomans asked how it came about that he rode like a Turk, but his Indian escort in another manner.

When in 1809 the Hungarian pattern of saddle was taken into service by the Austrian army the dragoon saddle was described as: "Hungarian, wooden, the fore-arch (pommel) cut quite short. The stirrup leathers are hung further forward on the bars, and slantwise, so as not to make the man ride too far forward in the saddle." In the second half of the nineteenth century the Hungarian saddle was widely replaced by a modified version of the English saddle, while in Hungary itself the traditional design was still in military use during the Second World War, but by this time some of its originally wooden components were made of steel.

Western Influences and their Historical Effect

Hitherto we have only treated of the Eastern element which went to make up the final European synthesis of horsemanship, but now we will trace the development of some Western traditions which made their way eastward.

The Spread of the Pacing Horse

Armoured cavalry, its characteristic skills at arms, and its tactics, had been gaining ground in Eastern Europe since the thirteenth century, while the Western custom of jousting became the amusement of Eastern courts. The Hungarian Order of the Dragon, founded in 1404, was one result of this; and thereby the principles and customs of chivalry gained a firm footing in what had been hitherto the European stronghold of Eastern practice, in equestrian matters. This relatively late cultural influence had as its corollary the expansion of the palfrey into Hungary.

The pacing gait, as unnatural as riding itself, was still quite unknown to the peoples of Central Asia and those who rode like them in the Middle Ages, and no mention of such a fashion there is to be found either in Oriental or in Western documentary sources. Nevertheless, it is probable that it originated in Western Asia, possibly in imitation of the gait of the riding-camel.

The Romans knew it, and apparently all Mediterranean peoples whose pre-equestrian past included chariot-driving. According to Pliny, it was a speciality of the Celtiberians whose pacing ponies (known in their own language as *thieldones*, and called by the Romans *asturcones* after the province of Asturias) were presumably bred to pace. But they can also be trained to do so, and this was done in Hungary, where the strain of horse genetically *inclined* to pace was less common than in the Celtic west. Training was done before the foal was a year old, by joining fore- to hind-leg on each side with an inflexible link. But since not every horse will perform equally well at this gait, even if successfully trained, efforts were made to breed the right sort, one of the specifications for which was a short body. In Hungary the counties of Doboka and Beszterce Nazód were noted for their pacers. Breeders and trainers bought foundation stock from there. In 1499 King Wladislaw II forbad any more to be sent out of the counties, lest the reservoir of breeding stock should fall below the danger-mark; or else possibly because he did not wish this foreign custom to gain a hold on his country at large. (Note 45.)

The first illustration of an ambling palfrey in Hungary is an illumination in the *Vienna Illustrated Chronicle,* showing the train of the Bohemian King Wenceslaus to Hungary in 1301. The first documentary evidence comes in 1335, in which the pacing palfrey is called "parefridus" and the ambler "dalm"—a word of totally unknown etymology. (Note 46.) It does not seem that the gait became much more widespread until the second half of the fifteenth century. (Note 47.)

Some estimate of the palfrey's popularity is afforded by the price of 100 gulden, asked at a time when other sorts of horse—good ones—were fetching 20 gulden. By the sixteenth century almost all the better-off gentry possessed a palfrey. In 1537 Ferenc Batthyány wrote to his young brother: "When I was your age I would never get on a palfrey, I wanted horses that stepped out more. And such I prefer now. You will be wanting a ride in the Queen's Cage next." By the "Queen's Cage" he meant a litter, borne by two horses, in general use in the West, but especially in mountainous countries such as Spain and Wales, where it survived longest.

It is probable that the pacing/ambling/racking tradition of riding came to Hungary from the south, brought by Yugoslavs displaced by the Turks. Philological evidence, often inconclusive, points if anything to a Slavonic origin for the Hungarian word *poroszka*—palfrey, in the South Slav *pruszati, prusszka,* even though these have been glossed as 'trot' and 'trotter'. The same inference may be drawn from the Hungarian word *paripa* for an ambling horse (*gradarius vulgo parypa* in 1579), derived from the Greek word *parippi* (Note 48), which seems to be a contraction of the Graeco-Latin *paraveredus.* But by contrast with the West the palfrey enjoyed only a short spell of fashion in Hungary. Many deemed it unmanly to ride so, and it is little mentioned towards the end of the sixteenth century, and not at all by 1700. Indeed, the times of the Turkish wars were not at all propitious for the keeping of horses that could not be turned over to military use, and were only suitable for peaceful journeys or for hacking about at home. [The same concentration on *trotting* horses adaptable for light-cavalry use is observable up to about 1600 in Britain, on the marches of Wales and of Scotland, with their endemic state of minor frontier warfare. *Tr.*]

The combination in the West of travel on wheels and the adoption of the 'hussar' style of riding with shorter stirrups also tipped the scale in favour of the trotting horse, though somewhat later. The palfrey decline was steep throughout the eighteenth century, absolute by the nineteenth, by which time it had been stigmatized as 'ugly', and unsuitable for a cavalryman.

The 'five-gaited horse', to use an all-embracing American term, held its own almost everywhere where carriage travel remained difficult. Nineteenth-century travellers describe it as current in the Balkans, the Near East, and in the Far East (pacing was inbred in the now extinct Indian Kathiawari strain), and it may be connected with Arab expansion. From Spain and from Britain it spread to the Americas; in Latin America the *Caballo de paso* and its counterpart the pacing mule still flourish; while the Anglo-Saxon tradition of the palfrey is nowadays confined to such territories as Tennessee and the Carolinas. (Note 49.)

The Spanish School

The other variant of Western horsemanship, the Spanish School, had even less success in Eastern Europe. King Matthias of Hungary (1458–90) not only rejected its method, but refused to accept any Spanish horses "hopping around with their bent hocks". On the other hand, a bare fifty years later most of the higher nobility had Spanish horses in their stables. (Note 50.) Yet the Spanish High School never really caught on east of the Austrian border. The primary reason was that the training method was regarded as a 'purgatory for horses'. Young Ferenc Nádasdy, studying at the University of Vienna, wrote to his mother in 1669, more or less laying this bogy: "I saw how they were trained, and Your Grace may believe me when I say that the Spanish and Italian trainers do not use the horses brutally" and he asks her to engage such a trainer. (Note 51.) We do not know whether the lady did comply with his suggestion; be that as it may, throughout the rule over Hungary of the Habsburgs who were its greatest patrons, the Spanish or Neapolitan High School never took firm root in Hungarian soil.

Driving

What the Hungarians and their neighbours in Eastern Europe thought worth adopting were Western innovations in the harness field. Many technical details were adopted, such as the solid-bar driving bits which automatically "gave the horse a good head-carriage" (Note 52), Western types of hame collar (which are nevertheless ultimately of Turkish origin), French traces and draft-chains—not least horseshoes of modern type which cover, not the whole sole as formerly, but only the rim of the hoof.

Of the Occidental innovations the new-style carriage was unquestionably the most important as a means of locomotion.

While the wagon and the coach, once the most advanced in Europe, had undergone no modification in Hungary since we last noted their appearance—inventories enumerate exactly the same parts under the same names all through the sixteenth and seventeenth centuries (Note 53)—coaches and carriages in the West had developed greatly, if not in the direction of travelling efficiency, at least as far as the comfort of the passengers was concerned. Hungarian light coaches and travelling wagons, the same in 1500 as in 1900, developed in the West into the very heavy caross which had great capacity, and ultimately into such variants as the Victoria, the Berline and Coupé, the Calèche, and the Mail-coach. These and many others have as almost their sole common factor the smaller fore-wheels.

Vehicles designed for comfortable travelling, such as the post-chaise and the 'glass coach' of the nobility, appeared in due course in Hungary, and with them came the more powerful type of carriage horse, often with Andalusian or Neapolitan blood. Whereas the mail-coaches were still harnessed four-in-hand and driven from the saddle by postilions according to old Hungarian usage, the greater landlords drove six horses in three pairs in Western style. Only the leading pair were driven by an outrider on the near horse, the other four being driven by the coachman on the box. This way of driving is not demonstrable in Hungary before the middle of the seventeenth century, but some form of six-in-hand, the exact nature of which is not known at the present day, existed there before that.

The steppe fashion of driving was still evident in the harnessing, of country carts only, in the nineteenth century, using vehicles whose design and the nomenclature of whose parts has remained unchanged from the seventeenth century to the present day. The carrier, driving three horses at the gallop, provided a means of rapid public transport down to the beginnings of the Hungarian railway system. Count Dénes Széchenyi, in his day a great expert on horse transport, mentions in his book (1892) the old Hungarian style of driving, or what was called 'mixed driving', as already outmoded: it consisted of alternate spells of walk, trot, and gallop.

The Battle of Mohács and its Consequences

This chapter, which deals with the expansion of Western practices, would not be complete if it did not point to the historical consequences of such influences. An example, drawn from the Hungarian past, is the calamitous death of King Louis II during a mounted action. We may consider what caused the death of this king on the field of battle, and why he did not succeed in escaping from Mohács in the same way as three hundred years earlier his predecessor King Béla IV had done, under much more adverse circumstances, in getting clear away after a defeat at the hands of the Mongols. Louis II of Hungary (1516–26) was the son of Vladislav II of the Jagellonian dynasty and the French princess Anne de Foix. He was married to Maria of Habsburg, sister of the Emperor Ferdinand I. With this overwhelmingly Western background, appropriate influences prevailed at the Hungarian Court, and the King's death on the field of Mohács can be attributed in some degree to the consequences of adopting Western customs.

This is the sequence of events: on the news that the Turkish host was approaching, the King took the field himself on June 15th, 1526, in order to hasten the concentration of troops from all parts of the kingdom. On his departure from Buda he was riding, according to the Chronicle of Dubravius, a black Frisian horse. The King at the head of his army did not get far on this horse, which according to Istvánffy died under him a mile out of Buda, at the village of Érd. This was regarded by many as an ill omen, nor was the King himself unmoved by it.

On August 29th the two armies were facing each other at Mohács. The battle did not start until three in the afternoon, neither side being fully prepared before then. On the Hungarian side a guard had been detailed for the King, all mounted on fast horses so that if need be the King could escape on one of them, and they had been given the mission, in certain circumstances, of rescuing him from the mêlée and escorting him to a place of safety.

At three o'clock, then, the glitter of lances was observed opposite the Hungarian right wing. The Turkish cavalry was advancing. The Hungarian commander, Archbishop Tomori, at once sent a cavalry unit to oppose them, but this, to the general consternation, was none other than the royal guard. Since at this critical moment no-one wished to commit an apparent infraction of discipline, nobody disputed this ill-considered order; and consequently from the outset of the battle the King was deprived of his escort. At almost the same time the Hungarian vanguard attacked frontally, and with such fury that they almost reached the pavilion of the Sultan. On the heels of this success the King led the main battle to the attack.

A Turkish source continues, with Oriental floweriness: "Recking naught of arrows or bullets, the king put his piebald to a gallop and like a raging evil spirit rushed on to the post of glory." On this attack followed the decisive turn of the battle: the cleverly masked Turkish batteries came into play, opening flanking fire on the attackers, the Hungarian right wing recoiled, bringing the Hungarian centre into

97 Racing at Datchet, near Windsor, 1684

98 Painting by Rosa Bonheur of Stallions fighting, reputed to represent the Duel
between Hobgoblin and the Godolphin Arabian

99 The Thoroughbred Stallion Eclipse, 1764–89   100 The Thoroughbred Mare Kincsem, 1874–87

101 Racing at Epsom

102 Fox-hunting in England.
The Kill, by Byron Webb, 1851

103　*The Carriage Drive in the Prater*, Vienna, 1885.
Watercolour by G. A. Wilda

104　The Same

disarray, so that though some smaller units fought on, panic engendered by the unexpected Turkish artillery fire decided the issue of the battle.

Subsequent events are recorded in the dispatch by the Papal Nuncio, Burgio, dated from Bratislava and forwarded to the Holy See. He reported that Ulrich Czettricz, Chamberlain and confidant of the King, had told him on his arrival at Bratislava how he, the King, and Stephan Aczél had got free of the mêlée and were getting clear away when they came to the Csele brook, a tributary of the Danube that was normally quite small, but was then swollen by a recent cloudburst. As they were about to cross, the King's horse became refractory and reared up in the water, so that his rider (who was already exhausted) slipped from the saddle and was drowned by the weight of his armour. When Aczél saw the plight of his master he jumped in after him, and was also drowned. (Note 54.)

Czettricz set out at the Queen's behest some two months later, to search for the body. Arrived at the scene of the disaster, he found the dead horse stuck in the bog, and he and his following thought at first that the King's body must be underneath it. But all they found was the weapons. Finally they came on a newly dug grave, and the King's body in it.

Although all the available evidence is that of eye-witnesses, or at least as first-hand as that of Burgie, speculation was rife for centuries because the testimony was so conflicting. The common people simply did not believe that the King could have come by his death through the obstinacy of his horse. The Treasurer Thurzo in a letter to the King of Poland ascribed the accident to the wounding of the King's horse, while Turkish accounts say the King himself was wounded. Istvánffy the historian maintained that the horse came over backward in trying to climb the steep bank. The picture becomes clearer if one takes into account how people rode in those days, especially at the Court of Louis II.

The account books for 1526 show purchases of horses for royal use from Moravia. They are described as "equi armigeri", and, more significantly, they were attended by German grooms (Note 55), thus leaving no room for doubt that they were heavy horses trained in the German manner—in short, destriers intended to carry a man in full armour. But since it is well known that Louis' predecessors Vladislav and Matthias had ridden nothing but Hungarian, Transylvanian, or Turkish horses (Note 56), it therefore follows that these were the first heavy horses to have formed part of the royal establishment.

We noted above that Louis II had set out from Buda, contrary to Hungarian custom, on a Frisian horse, the collapse of which at Érd was probably due to haemo-globinaemia to which heavy horses are subject. It is especially prevalent among highly fed horses that are kept up in stables all the time, and the symptoms appear consequent upon sudden exertion; in acute cases death occurs very quickly.

Plainly, the King took no warning when this first horse collapsed on being galloped straight out of the yard, but once on the battlefield he mounted a fresh heavy horse—a piebald destrier—while at the same time fast light horses were being kept in readiness for him. He was simply following established custom; the Western convention was to ride the destrier only in, or in immediate anticipation of, action, and the other horses afterwards.

This had been the case with the Emperor Otto II, as with all Western knights. And in a like situation Otto had survived. It is always possible that in the confusion Louis was not able to get near the fast reserve horses in order to change on to one of them, so turned to flight on his heavy charger. This is the more likely since his guard had been prematurely committed to action, and since the horse he rode seems to have been wounded. (Note 57.)

The immediate cause, therefore, of the disaster at Mohács, which had portentous consequences both for Hungary and for Europe, may be the death of the King's horse under him, which by its breeding and type was not equal to the task, and probably succumbed to a heart-attack. But the underlying cause was the 'Westernization' of the Court, with its French Queen-Mother and German Queen, both in civil and in military matters. Louis had not the sharp, objective eye of Matthias fifty years earlier, enabling him to see the unsuitability of Western techniques for his purpose. If it were then true that the welfare of the State depended on a horse's back, as the proverb ran, this was a classic example. By the death of the King a successful counter-attack became out of the question and the balance of power in Eastern Europe was permanently upset. The old Magyar dominion was now to be shared by the Turks on the one hand and the Habsburgs on the other, until the defeat of the former a hundred and fifty years later, which would lead inevitably to the formation of a new Great Power, Austria-Hungary. [All through the choice of the wrong stamp of horse. One is reminded, in some respects of the old English proverbial jingle:

> For want of a nail the shoe was lost;
> For want of a shoe the horse was lost;
> For want of a horse the rider was lost;
> For want of a rider the battle was lost;
> And all for the want of a horseshoe-nail. *Tr.*]

The Thoroughbred

Towards the end of the seventeenth century there began, with the introduction of Arabian and Barb horses into England, a unique stimulus to horsemanship in that country, which also added a new branch to the family tree of the Turanian Horse: this branch is called in most countries—but not in England—the English Thoroughbred (*il Purosangue inglese*, etc.), and its half-bred derivatives are known as 'Anglo-' whatever—*e.g.*, Anglo-Norman, Anglo-Khabardin, etc., etc. This new kind of hot-blooded horse was a milestone in the history of European horsemanship.

The history of riding in England, as in Western Europe generally, goes back to the days of the Roman occupation and beyond. Riding had become more and more common since the end of the Bronze Age, but for military purposes it only became practicable to the extent that larger horses became available, a process probably accelerated during the Belgic invasions of south-eastern Britain in the last two centuries B.C., and culminating in the introduction of full-scale riding-horses by the Romans, mostly from Iberia.

The medieval or feudal phenomenon of chivalry—that is, a social order which hinges, in military as in civil life, on the armoured mounted lancer with his Great Horse—was only fully developed in England under the Normans, though it had been foreshadowed during the reign of Edward the Confessor (1042–66). There is documentary evidence for the importation of Andalusian stallions in the reign of William the Conqueror, though the most successful use of these as sires was due to the Earl of Shrewsbury, Robert de Belesme, who flourished in the reign of Henry I (1100–35), breeding 'steeds' for knights and 'rouncies' for squires.

King John in the early thirteenth century spent a great deal of money on horses for hunting, and Richard II on 'coursers'—which among other things were race-horses, though we really know nothing about racing as it was in his day (1377–99). The King of Navarre gave him two such horses described as 'Spanish' but more likely belonging to one of the light-horse breeds of South-Western France. The statute books of the Tudors from the reign of Henry VIII to Elizabeth abound in ordinances laying down the minimum height for stallions depastured on common grazings, the object the production of horses "apt for service in the wars"—i.e., capable of carrying a man in half-armour—and the repetition of these enactments over and over again for more than three-quarters of a century shows how ineffective they were. It was in fact impossible to breed potential war-horses except in the traditional manner—in a park, usually attached to a royal castle, kept up in winter and fed with a quantity of protein and an allowance of hay which was quite beyond the resources of ordinary freeholders to provide. More significant, as a foreshadow-ing of the Thoroughbred, are the efforts which Henry VIII made to import horses of Oriental stamp from North Italian sources such as Padua. Royal patronage of racing began seriously with the accession of the first Stuart king, James I, formerly James VI of Scotland, and it may be significant that at the end of the sixteenth century fast horses of native breed were commoner in Southern Scotland than in any part of England. Under James I, importation of Oriental horses from the classical source—Aleppo market—began; declined during the reign of Charles I, who had a penchant for Andalusians; came almost to a standstill during the Civil War of the 1640's; and was resumed on a greater scale under the Commonwealth.

The Ancestors of the Thoroughbred

Oliver Cromwell, Lord Protector, was fond of hunting and racing, although for political reasons he forbade the latter sport during a great part of his years of office, because race-meetings offered too great an opportunity for 'disaffected persons' or 'malignants' to meet together. Place, his Master of the Horse, bought him an Arab known as the White Turk, but unfortunately we do not know by what route it reached England. Its success on the Turf, however, was undoubted. Imports con-tinued on a mounting scale throughout the reign of Charles II.

The first Arabs mentioned in the Stud Book came to England by way of Turkish and Hungarian intermediaries. Thus the Lister Turk was part of the booty taken at the fall of Buda in 1686, and likewise the mare Belgrade Turk at the recapture of Belgrade (1707), presented by General Mercy to the English owner. Of the three stallions who are the corner-stone of the General Stud Book, two came from Turkey; the Byerly Turk imported about 1680, and the Darley Arabian in 1705.

The third was the celebrated Godolphin Arabian (or Barb) who was discovered by a Mr. Coke drawing a water-cart in the streets of Paris. Coke was sorry for the bay stallion, bought him for 75 francs, and brought him to London. As later ap-peared, either the Bey of Tunis or the Sultan of Morocco had sent this stallion to King Louis XV as a present. He gave him to his cook, who sold him to the carter. In England he came into the possession of Lord Godolphin, who used him as a teaser for his stallion Hobgoblin. This was in 1730. In the next year, the mare Roxana was to be served by Hobgoblin, and was first tried by El Sham (the Godolphin Arabian's real name), who tore loose from the stud-groom and attacked Hobgoblin, killing him. He then covered Roxana. The result of this union was a colt named Lath. Among his grandsons was the famous Matchem, from whom many Throughbreds today are descended.

[A certain confusion arises from the fact that in Restoration England the words Turk and Turkey were very loosely used. Thus the Darley Arabian was bought at Aleppo, which was in Turkish territory. But he was actually foaled, in 1700, in the Syrian desert among the Fedan Bedouin. *Tr.*]

The system on which Thoroughbred breeding in England was organized might accurately be called Egyptian. Records in the private stud books of the eighteenth century, and of the General Stud Book in due course, were made on the principles laid down by El Nasser some centuries earlier, to which we have referred. The only animals admitted to the General Stud Book, from the beginning until today, are those all of whose ancestors are entered in that Book, which records all the Thoroughbreds all over the world. Any horse, one of whose ancestors is of unknown origin, is regarded as half-bred, and so are all its descendants, no matter how brilliantly they may perform.

Although the Arab was a formative factor in the creation of the Thoroughbred, it was only *one* factor. The mares put to the three foundation sires were mostly of unknown origin; primarily the 'Royal Mares' about whose breeding there has been much dispute. Probably they represented the cream of all those horses which had been presented to the Royal Family over many generations, or their descendants, including also those purchased by Henry VIII from the Gonzaga family of Padua. The stud was in fact dispersed by public auction after the execution of Charles I, and it was not possible, after the Restoration, to reassemble more than a certain proportion of these mares and their progeny. But considering the nature of royal gifts and purchases over the preceding hundred years, it is likely that the great majority of these animals were of Oriental origin. Count G. Wrangel, writing in 1888, said: "Charles II, who re-activated the Newmarket races instituted by Charles I, was the first to import [Oriental] mares". This may be true so far as deliberate purchase is concerned, but it takes no account of mares coming into the possession of previous monarchs by way of gift.

He continues:

> Unfortunately we lack detailed information about the number and breeding of these Royal Mares. It has however been asserted on the strength of oral tradition, that they came from the Orient, yet there are other circumstances which make it appear more probable that they came from Hungary. What is certain is that the Royal Mares cannot all have come from one source.

Wrangel's assumption is credible in the light of the general picture of European racehorse breeding at that time. If it were justified, then the 'unknown Oriental factor' in the Thoroughbred would be identical with that in such European 'warmblood' studs as Trakehnen and Czindery; that is to say, descendants of the Bactrian horse which had arrived, not by way of Arabia or even North Africa but by a more northerly route via the Caspian and the Black Sea. That there must be some other factor (and this is most unlikely to be a 'native' element) is proved by the fact that it has not been possible to breed up an animal of Thoroughbred type on a basis of pure Arab foundation stock, either in England or elsewhere.

Erika Schiele, in her book *The Arab Horse in Europe* (London edition, 1970), represents the view (put forward by Carl Raswan, among others) that the genesis of the Thoroughbred was due to the influence of the Muniqi stock of Arabs. The Muniqi, as opposed to the Seglawi and Kehailan types, reached its present form only in the seventeenth century, when the tribes who bred the original Muniqi and Jilfan types migrated to Northern Mesopotamia, where they came in contact with Turkoman nomads, and put some of their mares to the Turkoman stallions. The cross of Muniqi on the other two 'classic' Arabian types is said to produce foals that look more like Thoroughbreds. This theory rests on the same basis as Wrangel's quoted above, pointing to an out-cross of Turanian blood, without which the descendants of the Darley Arabian, Byerly Turk, etc., would without exception have looked like pure-bred Arabians or pure-bred Barbs.

The capabilities of the Thoroughbred on the Turf, in the hunting-field, and in harness are common knowledge nowadays. Nevertheless another proof of their capacity to do everything that a horse can do was given by an experiment which Sir Charles Bunbury made in the last century. He made a bet that his TB mare Eleanor—one of the few females that have won both the Oaks and the Derby—could carry a greater weight than a working horse. Now, this was still in the era when the 'professional' weight-carrying packhorse was an everyday sight in England. A miller's horse, accustomed to carrying great loads of corn and meal, was put up against Eleanor, who walked away quietly under an enormous load, under which the pack-horse could scarcely stand upright, let alone step forward.

The Arab horse which had been pure-bred since the time of El Nasser underwent in England a modification quite apart from the effects of cross-breeding. The biological effect of the changed environment, even taken by itself, would have been very powerful. In terms of climate, of vegetation, of ecology, the English countryside resembled the original habitat of the wild horse much more than the Arabian desert, and those characteristics which the Arab horse had acquired in response to the arid climate of Arabia, with its sparse vegetation and lack of shade, and the very different chemical content of the soil, it would in any case have shed after some generations of life in a more humid climate, with abundant grazing, a different kind of protein (oats instead of barley), more drinking-water with a different mineral content, and a soil containing entirely different trace elements. The only common factor that remained between Arabia and Britain was the close proximity to the human race, the frequent handling from birth, and the amount of time spent 'indoors'—whether in the black tents or in loose-boxes. The average height of the Thoroughbred increased by eight inches in two hundred years; its performance, especially over short distances, improved; and its conformation altered so as to approach nearer to that of Central Asiatic breeds such as the Akhal-Tekke. This combined influence of climate and soil is observable to a greater or less extent in horses of partly Arab descent throughout Europe, as for instance at the Bábolna stud, which has had very frequent refreshments of Arab blood, so that its characteristic Shagya breed is in effect an Arab in all but name. We may well ask ourselves what would happen if a herd of registered Thoroughbred horses were kept in an extensive park without hand-feeding, in a temperate climate, mating being determined by the preference of the mares and the fighting ability or 'pecking-order' of the stallions. Obviously there would be a reversion to the wild type—but what would this wild type be like, if the original components consisted exclusively of

Thoroughbreds? Would it in fact become identical with the 'wild blood-horse' whose existence in the remote past is believed in by some? This would indeed be a costly experiment, but probably not much more costly than those which have gone to the 'breeding-back' of such lost races as the Tarpan and the aurochs. In this age of scientific research it seems that such an investigation might be as rewarding as the two mentioned above, which apart from their objective (pre) historical interest have provided information which is of direct utility in the field of genetics and stock-breeding.

Distribution of the Thoroughbred

The unique English successes soon had their effect on Continental horse-breeding, and a massive importation of Thoroughbreds began in the second half of the eighteenth century. Despite its favourable effect on the balance of trade, British Governments did not welcome this traffic, and a new embargo was imposed. It was so strictly enforced that a ship in which Count Ferdinand Kinsky was personally escorting a stallion and four mares across the Channel was fired on by coastal batteries, in 1760. Restrictions were so far loosened as to permit the export of blood-stock in particular cases, except for certain lines which were deemed too valuable to allow out of the country. With this reservation, it was now possible for blood-stock to reach any country in Europe and any British colony without let or hin-drance. Its rapid spread was due to the popularity which horse-racing—English style—soon attained abroad. Another cause was the demand for blood-horses for crossing which arose in many countries, but especially Central Europe, from the remount crises brought about by repeated wars.

But the production of half-blood horses made great strides in Britain and Ireland also. Crossing with the larger 'indigenous' breeds produced the Hunter, the Hackney, and the Coach-horse, especially the Yorkshire Coach-horse which was a cross of the Thoroughbred on the Cleveland Bay, itself a fixed type of uniform colour that was the result of a cross of Barb and (probably) Andalusian horses on the pack-horse mares of North-eastern England, taking shape about 1670.

On the Continent the Electorate of Hanover and Duchy of Brunswick were pioneers in bloodstock breeding. The proximate cause was, as so often, a political event. By the accession of George, Elector of Hanover, to the British throne on the death of Queen Anne in 1714, the thrones of Britain and Hanover were united until 1837. In 1735 the Hanoverian stud of Celle was founded, drawing some foundation sires from England. The Hanoverian half-blood owes its existence to King George II and his son the Duke of Cumberland. It has since become world-famous [and the wheel has come full circle. During the 1960's Hanoverian stallions were standing at stud in England, primarily with the object of getting heavyweight hunters and event horses. *Tr.*] The story was repeated in East Friesland, once the home of heavy destriers, whose descendants were crossed with Hanoverians to produce a heavy-duty coach-horse. In other North German principalities such as Mecklenburg, Holstein, and Oldenburg, where since the decline of chivalry the emphasis had been on the breeding of Andalusian or Neapolitan chargers, Thoroughbreds were now imported to impart quality to the local stock. From the beginning of the nineteenth century onward German horse-breeders with half-bred stock on either a Thoroughbred or Trakehner basis attained a standard that was not only valuable from a military and transport point of view at home, but became of international importance.

What Prussia was for Germany, what Yorkshire was for England, Hungary for the Habsburg monarchy, Normandy was for France. From the days of the half-Norse Norman Duchy onward, chivalry and horsemanship had been engrained in the Norman people. In the departments of Orne and Manche a heavy horse had been bred time out of mind, and side by side with it a lighter riding type, especially in Merlerault and the Cotentin. A dash of the Thoroughbred here gave rise to the Anglo-Norman, valuable alike as a coach-horse, a hunter, and nowadays as an event horse or show-jumper. Nonius was an Anglo-Norman entire. During the Napoleonic Wars he fell into Austrian hands and gave his name to a whole breed which had its origin in the Imperial stud at Mezöhegyes, where he was sent to stand, so impressed were the authorities by his performance and conformation. This Nonius strain is today a working horse of great substance, which has long proved itself to be of equal merit with the North Star and Furioso strains, likewise bred in Hungary and partly of Thoroughbred ancestry. [North Star was a trotting 'roadster' bred in East Yorkshire. Tr.]

The Thoroughbred appeared in every corner of the world where the military and commercial interests of the British Empire required its presence. The combination of sea-power and horse-power was an essential prerequisite of colonial expansion, just as it had been in the days of the Normans.

When the American colonies united and became independent they soon worked out their own varieties of half-bred horses, a combination of the Thoroughbred with stock mainly of Spanish origin. Here we need mention only the Quarter-Horse, the Morgan, and the American Saddle horse, ridden mostly for pleasure, and the Standard-bred, used for trotting-races. The Standard-bred in its turn has spread to all countries of the world where sulky-racing is carried on. All Standard-breds are descended from the Thoroughbred Messenger, who came to the United States in 1788; his sire, the grey Mambrino, is well known to all admirers of equestrian art through the splendid portrait by Stubbs, which shows him to have been one of the most Arabian-looking racehorses that ever were foaled.

The picture of Thoroughbred breeding would not be complete without some account of the two individuals which are reputed the best horses the world has yet seen. One was bred in England, a great-grandson of the Darley Arabian named Eclipse, foaled at the Duke of Cumberland's stud, in 1764; he lived to the age of twenty-five. The other was the mare Kincsem (1874–87) bred in Hungary by Ernst von Blaskovich. Both were chestnut, both were unbeaten on the Turf throughout a long career. The career of Kincsem in particular is unique. With her 54 wins, some on Hungarian courses but also in Austrian, German, French, and English races, she proved her invincibility against the best horses in the world.

European travel by road, in the saddle or on the box, was pretty much the same in every country, at the time when the Thoroughbred was spreading across the Continent, due to the widespread imitation of English habits which now set in. The admired pattern of a 'horsy' individual, whether riding or driving, was the English Meltonian or Corinthian with his characteristic clothes, mannerisms, saddlery, harness, method of putting the team to, type of carriage driven, rules of sport, and even the custom of rising to the trot which now for the first time became common in Europe. [Both in civil life and in the Army, even though English cavalry, to the present day, differ from civilians in *not* rising to the trot. *Tr.*]

Road traffic made new demands on the horse-breeder throughout Europe as the nineteenth century opened, since the new network of completely metalled roads called for a different pace. The Continental *pavé* was not suitable for galloping stages, either for riders or for drivers, so that the traveller had to trot his horses for long distances. [To what extent the Scottish invention of the Macadam road surface, which was more like the original rammed-gravel surface of Roman roads, made the British Isles an exception to the general rule, is debatable. *Tr.*] Since the once almost universal travelling pace, the 'easy-gaited' lateral amble, had vanished from memory, the 'English trot' called in England 'posting' (because it was originally the habit of postilions) was the only tolerable means of progress. But it presupposes a slightly bent knee and a certain amount of weight placed in the stirrup, so that the rider can clear the saddle at every second pace of the horse; and this particular seat points backward again to the east, and the characteristic seat of the Asiatic mounted archer. Besides racing in harness, the only trotting breeds for travelling in light vehicles which challenged the English Hackney (which was essentially a cross of Arab blood on 'native' Welsh and Norfolk roadsters) were the Russian Orloff and the American Standard-bred mentioned above.

Reaction in the East

Let us now turn back and look eastward across the Leitha River, over those plains which are a continuation into the heart of Europe of the Eurasian steppe.

Count Stephan Széchenyi was, if not the first, the most successful sponsor and patron of imported English Thoroughbreds. By word and deed, and by the organization of various associations, he brought himself to the leading position among Hungarian breeders. Not only did he import bloodstock, he brought over from England hunt servants, gamekeepers, stud grooms, trainers and jockeys and nagsmen, and did all he could to further the spread of English sporting customs.

Outside the closed circle of racing and hunting, the importance of the Thoroughbred in Hungary was most apparent in the production of half-blood horses. What henceforward was to be known throughout Europe as the "Hungarian Horse" was essentially a half-bred horse of outstanding quality, and mostly bred in State studs [which have never existed in England; neither the royal establishments nor the National Stud of today are State Studs in the Continental sense. *Tr.*]

But this did not come to pass without strenuous opposition in Hungarian equestrian circles, which remained faithful to the traditions of Central Asia, and were especially hostile to this manifestation of Anglomania. Extracts from two publications of the nineteenth century will serve by their original phrasing to demonstrate what we mean, quoted verbatim:

An anonymous writer under the pen-name of "Tisza-side Hungarian" issued a broadsheet in 1846, fulminating against the English style of horsemanship as follows: "The English are obsessed by gambling. They put up men to beat each other to death with their fists, just so as to be able to bet on the issue. They train cocks to fight, just in order to bet". [Cockfighting was an Oriental, perhaps originally Indian, custom, introduced into Britain by the Roman army. *Tr.*] "They organize horse-races in order to bet. Therefore why should we Hungarians, who do not like betting,

105 Finish of a Flat Race

106
Trotting Race

107 'The Art of Falconry'
Wood engraving from Weisskunig

108 Lion-hunt, on Sassanid silver plate.
Hermitage, Leningrad

109   Assyrian Wild-horse hunt. Relief from Assurbanipal's palace. Nineveh. 639 B.C.

110   Mounted Archer shooting Hares
      Bronze strap-end from Avar grave at Klarafalva.
      Szeged Museum, Hungary

111   Deer-hunting, from Roman Tombstone in Pannonia
      National Museum, Budapest

race horses? We do it in imitation of the Germans, who thereby copy the French, who copy the English. If anyone thinks these races do the horses any good, he is mightily in error. . . ."

Speaking of the high cost of imported racehorses and the prize money at races, he says:

> Truly we pay a high price for the pleasure of seeing simian-like creatures ride horses that look more like greyhounds. There is no uglier sight in all the world than a jockey sitting in his gaudy colours on a horse fit and ready to run a race. It has come to my ears that owners sometimes ride races themselves. A worthy occupation for a Hungarian gentleman, indeed! But I also hear that they wear jockey's clothes in such cases. The dress of an English groom is a noble costume, most fitting as the apparel of a Magyar landowner. But such noble lords should have a care, lest they inadvertently attend a session of parliament thus arrayed.

Among the papers of John Pálffy, a protagonist of the national rising of 1848, there is much evidence of the distaste of his peers for this aping of English customs. The Transylvanian landowner Josef Daczó was a sworn foe of all foreign customs, but his son Ferenc welcomed them. Pálffy wrote:

> Young Ferenc is a great Anglomaniac, and so he only wanted to ride English-fashion, which consisted, on his part, of tucking his knees under his armpits and whenever the horse trotted beating time on the saddle with a certain portion of his anatomy. This made his father very angry, and he told him repeatedly to learn to ride Hungarian-fashion, as he ought to be able to do by now. But all to no avail. One day when Ferenc went for a ride, the old man lay in wait for him behind the gate. When his son trotted past him, he swung his crutch at him (he was slightly lame) and hit him on the backside just as he was rising to the trot, giving him such a fright that he lost his stirrups and came off. The old gentleman laughed and said "There's English riding for you."

Nevertheless, despite all opposition rising to the trot became universal in quite a short time. In the late 1850s it was introduced into the hussars, first of all by Colonel Baron Edelsheim. The Austro-Hungarian cavalry before that had been accustomed to march at a foot-pace, and preferably by night.

In the nineteenth century two sources of energy were discovered and exploited: steam and oil. This led to a fundamental revolution in travelling. And as once before, in the early days of the exploitation of animal power, these new resources were adapted to military use, so that they ultimately displaced the horse. The epoch that had begun with the domestication of the horse on the plains of Asia, and led to a uniform European horse-borne culture, was now brought irrevocably to an end. The Thoroughbred horse henceforward was to justify its existence only in the field of sport.

Part V Sport and Performance, Past and Present

Equestrian Sports

These have existed in every society in which riding has been part of workaday life, and in which the art has become a passion transcending its utilitarian importance. Its earliest variant was in the furthering of a widespread propensity to hunting (which in itself was originally a means of subsistence), and in the course of time not so much the hunting as the horseman-like skill displayed therein became of greater significance. [This 'hunting to ride' is still, in England, opposed to the creed of devotees of the older craft of venery, who 'ride in order to hunt'. *Tr.*]

An anonymous chronicler of Hungarian affairs in the twelfth century makes a statement that would surprise the present-day reader of any nationality when he says that the Hungarians are the best hunting-men of all, because before they migrated to their Pannonian home they went hunting every day, and so had more practice.

A Hun hunting, second century B.C.
From Chinese brush drawing

We cannot, however, measure this assertion by the standards of today. Taking hunting in the wider meaning it bears in most European languages, as *la chasse*—that is, the pursuit of game by any and every means, each of which has accumulated over the centuries a mass of custom and ritual and expert lore—the modern hunting-man or shooting-man is not a figure comparable with the onetime hunter of the steppes.

In *his* eyes, quite apart from his role as the provider of an alternative meat diet and the controller of predators, as well as of wild herbivores who competed with the domestic herds for grazing, the hunter underwent a daily trial of strength and a warlike exercise, exacting for man and horse alike. The element of danger was not absent, and the chances of the hunter and the quarry were more even than they are now. Dexterity and courage alone availed the hunter, only in a slightly less degree than they did in mounted warfare.

The skilled hunter of the Eastern peoples was therefore also a skilled warrior, who did not shrink from breakneck feats and was in thrall to the oldest of human passions, which became the most aristocratic form of sport. Mounted hunting itself arose in that 'navel of the world' above-mentioned, the Sayan Mountains, where the Uryanchai to this day approach the game on reindeer-back. In all probability it was from this ultimate source also that the Hungarian hunters mentioned by the anonymous chronicler drew their traditional skill, in far-away Hungary. Though the Uryanchai have no dogs, in the course of westward migration the use of hounds to hunt by scent or sight, cheetahs, and various rapacious birds, from the eagle to the kestrel, grew up. No longer was use made of the Stone Age devices of pitfalls, nets, or of archery from ambush; it was now exclusively a matter of hunting *par force*—the pursuit of game on horseback with (occasionally even without) hounds.

This manner of hunting justified, at princely Courts, an establishment of venery that was like an army. Marco Polo says that when the Great Khan went hunting there were several thousand riders in the field, besides the huntsmen and falconers of the royal household. The Khan maintained two Masters of Game, who had under them twenty thousand greyhound leaders alone. Even making allowance for this author, whose well-earned nickname was "Marco Millions", this is still a formidable figure, whose like is only found in medieval Europe in Hungary. The huntsmen, kennelmen, whippers-in, falconers, austringers, and keepers preserving bison, deer, beaver, and hares, maintained by the Hungarian Crown in many counties, were equal to the population of several villages, and remind one of the Oriental establishments. The King himself, devoted to venery by heredity, was the centre of this vast establishment. (Note 58.)

This hunting *en masse* persists today in Mongolia, where every man who can ride, from Cabinet minister to shepherd, takes part in the hunt, which is only now beginning to lose its traditional meaning. Thousands of horsemen surround the game, among the most prized of which is the inedible wolf.

To General Csekonics we owe a detailed description of hunting *par force* in Hungary on the grand scale. The meet was at Mezöhegyes, with a field of six hundred horsemen, and the quarry were wolves, foxes, and hares. No hounds were taken out, and the order of the day was that the game was only to be ridden down or taken with whips.

The hunt lasted two whole days and ended with an extraordinary occurrence. As the last covert of tall thick grass was being surrounded a wolf broke out and through the ring of horsemen. He had already got off to a good start when a man riding a little grey mare set off after him. The grey mare vanished over the horizon, and after five hours came in sight again, the dead wolf hanging over the saddle-bow. This achievement was crowned in the horse-race which followed the hunt, which the little grey mare won. (Note 59.)

In descriptions of these mounted hunts many extraordinary feats are enumerated. Of these it will suffice to mention only one, the most stupendous. In 1613 Bethlen Gábor, Prince of Transylvania, went with his retinue to Torda, to receive the homage of his Turkish and Tartar allies. During the formalities a single hare ran diagonally across the field which was taken as an ill omen. A contemporary witness states: "One of the Tartars, a tall fellow on a white horse, galloped uphill after the hare, caught up with it, leaned down from the saddle and picked it up running in his hand, bringing it to Bethlen Gábor and placing it, still alive, on his saddle-bow." All present were greatly relieved that the ill omen had thus been averted. Anyone who has seen a hunted hare jinking and swerving at high speed will appreciate the standard of horsemanship required. (*Materials for History of Transylvania*.)

Another Eastern technique was falconry. The first written evidence for its practice outside Mongolia is Chinese. A document of the Hsia dynasty, probably of the second millennium B.C., mentions, among gifts distributed by the ruler, trained hunting falcons. Thereafter data is scanty. Ktesias, the Greek physician at the Court of the Persian king in the fourth century B.C., calls falconry a new Indian custom, in his time still little known in Persia. Most histories of the sport say it was brought into Europe by the Huns; the evidence is not very reliable—the falcon standard of Attila is adduced as proof. Charlemagne is said to have been the first Western monarch to keep falcons.

The Hohenstaufen Emperor Frederick II did much to spread knowledge of the art in European Courts with his book *De Arte Venandi Cum Avibus*. This monarch (1212–50), who was himself of Norman descent, being on his mother's side a grandson of the Norman King Roger II of Sicily, wrote the book at Palermo, his capital. He employed Arabian falconers; he had Hungarian connections by marriage (Note 60), and so a threefold influence is perceptible here also—Norman, Arabian, and Hungarian. [If we remember that the Sicilo-Norman house of Tancred de Hauteville was of Scandinavian origin, this takes us even further back into the history of falconry. There is evidence for the domestication of falcons in the Wendel period in Sweden (seventh century), and the sport will have been brought to England and Normandy, among other places, during the Viking invasions. The fact that the falcon is mentioned in *Beowulf* may be due to this late influence, since the poem was first written down after the invasions. On the other hand, it does contain references to Anglo-Saxon customs of an earlier date, such as mound-burial. If falconry existed in pre-Viking England it will have been in East Anglia, a province which then and now abounds in the large aquatic birds that are the falconer's favourite quarry, because the royal house of East Anglia was unique among Anglo-Saxon dynasties in being of Swedish origin, and the royal cenotaph of the Wuffingas at Sutton Hoo contains many heirlooms of Swedish manufacture. It is quite possible that at the time of the last of these burials, in the mid-seventh century, contact still existed between the Swedish and the Suffolk branches of the family. But whether in the ninth or in an earlier century, the falcon, like the stirrup, must have reached England from the steppes by this northern route. Hawking was certainly unknown to the Celts of Britain, and to the Romans also. The Roman *auceps* seems to have been either a fowler with nets or a sharpshooter with bow or sling, and it is significant that the very word for falconer was absent from the Latin vocabulary, so that the Emperor Frederick had to use as the title of his Latin work the clumsy paraphrase "The Art of Hunting with Birds." Tr.] (Note 60.)

But Frederick II was not only King of Sicily, he was also German Emperor, and his household in Sicily was often the object of disapproval in Germany. There especial scorn and indignation met the wholesale adoption of foreign customs, and the Emperor was blamed for turning his palace at Palermo into a hunting-lodge, where he was surrounded by baying hounds and screeching hawks.

The Hungarian influence tending to the dissemination of Central Asian hunting techniques in the West was a phenomenon which, as Gy. Laszlo has shown, was repeated in later centuries.

The invention of firearms accurate enough to shoot flying birds dealt a mortal blow to falconry, as in all forms of hunting a principal object was still the provision of a change of diet. The pursuit of deer with hounds also declined, until it became a 'pure' sport, with little thought of the larder in mind. The English, in particular, turned to the pursuit of the inedible fox, and the English foxhunt set the tone for sporting Europe, with its scarlet-coated sportsmen mounted on horses of partly Thoroughbred blood, behind English foxhounds. Nowhere did this fashion meet greater opposition than in Hungary. The 'Tisza-side Hungarian' quoted above in his diatribe against the 'copy-cats' turned his attention from racing to fox-hunting:

> Our copy-cats will not let the matter rest there. They must needs hunt after the English fashion. Great Britain is over-populated and game is scarce there. Therefore they have developed the curious habit of pursuing the fox on horse-back, only to catch it and put it in a bag, so as to have something to hunt next time out. This all very well for a rather flat country which abounds in stretches of turf, and roads. But is it not ridiculous to imitate this caricature of hunting in our Carpathian hills, where boar, wolf and bear are to be found in plenty? Our fathers loved hunting as the image of war, making men bold and skilful. They slew the beasts of the forest hand to hand. That made sense, and he must indeed suffer from imitation-mania who would follow the example of the English who themselves would be only too glad if they had our wealth of game to hunt ...

[This Hungarian from Tisza-side is an easily recognizable type, corresponding exactly, in English terms, to the nineteenth-century encrusted Tory squire, nourished on beefsteak and port, nowadays a stock figure of heavy comedy, with his contempt for Frenchmen (and by extension for all foreigners) as "Frog-eatin' mounseers," and quite incapable of imagining that any other country can afford, or its inhabitants practise, any form of sport equal to, let alone superior to, his own. The kind of officer who 'won' the Crimean War. *Tr.*] What would he have said if he had witnessed the logical development of the synthetic foxhunt *à l'anglaise*, the drag which became fashionable throughout Europe, with its line over a prepared course of artificial obstacles following a pack in pursuit of oil of aniseed? For all that, even the drag-hunt had its uses. Like racing, it was a means of selection by performance, and thus a useful ancillary to horse-breeding, as long as horse-breeding itself had a practical aim in view.

Coursing with greyhounds, likewise of Oriental origin, survived the mounted hunt *en masse* by about a century. It was still practised in Hungary after the Second World War, but when it vanished the Hungarian breed of greyhound went with it. The greyhound is of Oriental origin, and now survives only in the West because it is easier to organize greyhound racing, and the betting that goes with it, than horse-racing. Pig-sticking, introduced in imitation of Anglo-Indian sportsmen who in turn were imitating the aristocracy of the Moghul Empire, also took root briefly in Hungary, where the pig-stickers used a special spear, weighted with a metal knob just above the point, to lend impetus to a downward blow.

Turkoman Gazelle-hunt with Falcon and Salukis
Drawing by Evert van Muyden. After Moser, 1886

There is nothing new under the sun. A relief from Roman Pannonia shows a Roman horseman hunting deer with just such a spear.

The Hungarian horse-herds (Csikós) have a mounted sport peculiar to themselves. It has become well-known through the description of the American sculptor Alexander Finta, who once lived the life of these herdsmen on the *puszta*. Under certain conditions of freezing rain the Great Bustard becomes unable to fly. Flocks of them with their congelated feathers, still able to run very fast, were herded together into circles some fifty yards in diameter, hemmed in by cracking horse-whips. As they ran round in circles, the game was to see which herdsman could pluck the most plumes from the living bird. They entered the circle by turns, each being given five minutes to pluck plumes from the tails of the bustards. The forfeit for dropping hat, whip, etc. was to miss three turns. Success depended on the ability to follow every twist and turn of the fleeing bird while bending down low out of the saddle.

Another kind of simulated hunt is that in which one rider takes over the role of the quarry, as in a paper-chase. Its earliest variety is evidently that practised by the Kirghiz nomads to this day. One of their girls will cry out to a boy "Who can catch the wolf-maiden?" and gallop off on her horse. This is the signal for a mad pursuit uphill and down dale, the boys riding hard after the girl and trying to catch her round the waist, or at least to touch her breast, while she stands them off with blows of her whip. Carl Diem, who recorded many Oriental customs and equestrian sports, thinks this a vestige of marriage by capture. For instance, the bridegroom rides a race with the bride and tries to snatch her veil. This custom persisted in Hungary down to the seventeenth century. [In England, specifically in Cleveland, a similar bridal custom derived from marriage by capture survived into the nineteenth century and involved a horse-race home from church for which the prize was the bride's garter. *Tr.*]

Eye-witness accounts of the wedding of Ferenc Rákóczi to Ilona Zringy outside the fortress of Sboró mention 'the hunting of the basket'. But this game was not played by the high-born couple themselves or their relatives but by some horsemen from their retinue. (Note 61.)

Another of these mounted capture-games is known among the Turks as *baj-rakonju*. In it a horseman holds a pennant in his hand, while two others try to wrest it from him. As soon as one of them succeeds, roles are exchanged, and he becomes 'it', and is pursued in turn. There is a European variety of this game, called in French *jeu de barre*, and played with a ribbon on the shoulder.

But all these entertainments, which might be known collectively in English as gymkhana events, pale beside the great Asiatic mounted sport called by various nomad peoples *baiga* or *kok-buri* in regard to the demands they make on riding skill. It is or was widespread in Central Asia: this is how Franz von Schwarz described the version he saw played among the Turkomans in 1900:

> The patron of the game throws a dead sheep or goat among the players, who are all mounted and armed with the inevitable whip. The object is to pick the carcass up from the ground and give it back to the patron of the game. But this is much harder to do than it sounds, for hardly has the first horseman picked it up at full gallop and laid it across his saddle-bow, than he is surrounded on all sides, by those seeking to snatch his prize from him. Often two men will gallop away side by side, both holding the carcass, tugging and heaving at either end

of it, till they pull it apart and both fall off their horses each holding a part. Every moment in the fearful press and tumult a horse and its rider comes down, and the whole troop ride over them. But I have never seen a serious accident so caused, though I must have watched hundreds of *baigas*; so great is the dexterity of horse and rider. There are no obstacles in this game: if after a long hard struggle one of the players has managed to get hold of the sheep and get clear of the others, then they all set off after him, in full career up hill and down dale, through bush and over briar, over garden walls, ditches, through deep and rapid rivers and down the steepest slopes. Mostly a game lasts several hours, until the most skillful and tireless rider manages to shake off all his opponents and throw the sheep at the feet of his host . . . As in Europe, this game was played on such occasions as weddings or to celebrate the birth of an heir. [See p. 146.]

There were various mounted ball games current in Asia, and polo is a development of one of these. It is first mentioned in an epic poem by the Persian Firdausi, celebrating the heroic deeds of the Iranian prince Sijavus (seventh century B.C.), and gives an account of a polo match between Persian and Turanian princes. In the early centuries of our era the game was known from the Pacific to the Bosporus. It has been played in Japan, China, Tibet, Turania, Iran, Asia Minor, India, and the Arab countries. In many of them it is still being played. In the 1870s it was brought to England by the 10th Hussars on their return from India, and this version of the game was reintroduced to Hungary in 1969.

If we follow the development of this game, we see that not only did its progress run parallel with the dissemination of the Turanian horse, but that the rules of the game were modified to conform with the quality of horses in various countries. For instance, in medieval Arabia polo was played in a quite different way from what it was in Persia. The ball was thrown in between the two teams, who started at an equal distance from the half-way line: it was apple-sized and of leather. The object was to drive the ball over the opponents' back-line, instead of aiming at a goal, as today. The stick used was so short that the player had to bend right down out of the saddle to hit the ball. The whole game proceeded at a sharp gallop, with many twists and turns and the constant risk of collision with an opponent, and being trampled underfoot.

The practical importance of mounted games is well expressed in a remark of Nur-ed-Din, the implacable opponent of the Crusaders. He said, when questioned about his passion for the game, which he even played at night by artificial light: "God is my witness, I do this not for pastime only; we have no time to spare. We are waiting, but we are in the presence of the enemy, and we must be ready at any time to take arms and to horse. If we kept our horses hobbled in the lines, they would get fat and soft, unfit to undergo long marches, and they would not be nimble enough for close combat. This game of ball is the best practice for our horses, hardening them and making them not only fit but handy and obedient to the rider."

Not only must the horse be trained and fit; the rider's skill at arms must be improved constantly. In the Orient the racecourses, or maidans, in the environs of every princely palace were used as ranges for the characteristic Asiatic ballistic exercise—archery from the saddle. Such maidans are found from Japan to Turkey. The Turks also used them to practise javelin-throwing from the saddle. Their popular game of 'Atli-Jerid' was played on the At-maidan of Constantinople, which

112
The Legend of
St Eustace; the
Stag Hunt Capital
of Column in
Abbey Church,
Vézelay

113 Indians and White Men hunting Bison
Indian Painting on Moose-hide
Museum of the American Indian. Heye Foundation, New York

114
Thirteen-year-old Mongol Girl,
Winner in 1962 of the Annual
Race at Archosta in Mongolia

115
Fantasia by Libyan Bedouin

116 The Rittal Ten-in-hand Coach-team, a *Tour de Force* of Driving

117 Dressage: J. Neckermann with Antoinette

was none other than the Hippodrome of ancient Byzantium. This was a contest between two teams of horsemen armed with wooden unpointed javelins. The individual victor was the one who scored most direct hits. They took turns to ride out between the opposing ranks and throw spears, to which the 'enemy' replied with a volley, and points were counted to each horsemen in turn for the number of 'enemy' spears he caught in the air or parried.

At a time when such games in the Orient could look back on a history of several centuries they began to be diffused through Europe with the Norman expansion. During the Middle Ages there spread from Normandy such sports as riding at the ring or the quintain, wrestling on horseback, and tourneys. Geoffroi, Seigneur de Preully, had codified the laws of the tourney by the end of the eleventh century, and they soon became standard throughout Christendom.

In the beginning there were mass engagements with sword and mace, but not with lances, and the duels with the lance, originally called *jeux de table-ronde* or 'jousts', were a later development. As early as 1252 French chivalry decided that the tourney should take place with the lance only, either with the blunt weapon (*arme courtoise* or *gracieuse*) or *à outrance* with a lance-head consisting of a 'crown' of small diverging points.

The tourney began in England under William I, in Germany under Conrad II (1024–39), but was specially favoured by the Emperor Henry VI (1190–97). In his reign the German knights were organized into four great jousting associations; Rhenish, Bavarian, Swabian, and Franconian, each presided over by a marshal. The rules of combat were very precise, by contrast with the practice obtaining farther east, and the institution of the tourney was supposed to embody the highest ideals of Christian chivalry.

Only those knights might compete in the lists who could show at least four ancestors of equestrian rank, but the sovereign might confer eligibility on others. They were all entered in an index of those entitled to joust. Tournament courts, consisting of marshals, heralds, and arbitrators, were responsible for law and order, the proper conduct of jousts, and the announcement of contests in advance. It was all very German and well organized, with plenty of paper-work and officials with polysyllabic titles. The lists were commonly oval, with raised seats for spectators; with a flourish of trumpets the knights in full armour entered the lists escorted by their squires, where their names were checked against the index, before the tilting began.

The object was to unhorse the opponent, by the weight and impetus of the mighty destrier. The faster the course down the lists, the harder was the impact, aided by the weight of the horse; sometimes both horse and rider were knocked over, sometimes the rider was swept backward out of the saddle, and lances shivered to splinters. In order to avoid outright collision, a barrier was erected all the way down the lists, and in the course of time tilting over this barrier became universal. The jouster took up his station on the left side of it, and kept his horse well in towards this 'pale'.

The object of the tourney was merely display, entertainment, and (decreasingly as time went on) a form of practice for real combat, but before the introduction of the 'pale' many contestants either lost their tempers or found themselves matched by private enemies, so that there were many fatalities to man and horse. Two princes of the House of Babenberg, Leopold I and Leopold the Virtuous, came by

The Game of Baiga
Drawing by Evert van Muyden. After Moser, 1886

their death in the lists. A notorious combat in 1273, known as "The Little War of Châlons", at which Edward I of England and the Count of Châlons met hand to hand, ended in blood and tears, for their retinues became so embroiled that many of them were killed. In a tournament of Darmstadt in 1408 seventeen Franconian and nine Hessian knights were left dead in the lists, and King Henry II of France was killed by Count Montgomery, jousting, in 1559.

At the time of this fatality jousting was still occasionally happening in England, at the very end of an unbroken tradition, but the occasional contests under the Stuarts were a conscious antiquarian revival, just as much so as was the Eglinton Tournament under Queen Victoria (1839). Whereas in the West mounted sports persisted and flourished as much as formerly after the decline of chivalry, in all forms ranging from the staghunt to the gymkhana, decadence in the East set in long before the advent of the machine age. The relics of Asiatic equestrian sport are nowadays more common in the museum than outside it.

The mounted sports of today differ so radically from those of the older tradition that valid comparisons of performance, past and present, can be drawn almost solely in the fields of flat-racing, hurdling, and steeple-chasing.

Carl Diem, looking back in 1960 over the development of equestrian sports, said: "The flowering of Asiatic physical culture came to pass much earlier than that of Europe, and even if it has lost much in the course of time, its seminal ideas in this field have been preserved to the present day".

How much does competitive sport, so universal and so uniform in our day, owe to this tradition of the equestrian peoples? It is not so much a question of the physical similarity between the equestrian exercises of the past and modern sports such as racing, ball games, tests of skill and dexterity, as of the fact that the internationally recognized concept expressed in the English term 'fair play' and embodying the moral essence of chivalry, the sporting ethic as such, together with the very idea of 'rules of the game', were primarily of Oriental origin. We inherit this through the channel of Greek athletics, of which the modern Olympic code is a conscious imitation.

Feats on Horseback

A comparison of equestrian performances, past and present, is not an absolutely feasible task, for it could only be valid on the basis of identical conditions and chances. If it is nevertheless to be attempted, then this is for two reasons: first, to offer an approximate picture of evolution; second, to attempt some sort of comparative scale.

Oriental practice takes into account a factor that is absent from the modern world of sport. It is important, for it serves to divide equestrian performance into two categories which are not fairly comparable, involving a concept embodied in the Hungarian word *lóhalál*, used to translate various Oriental expressions, all of which imply quite simply that the horse is regarded as expendable. This ultimate ruthlessness was implicit in the speech of English coachmen of the 'great' period when they spoke quite objectively of 'driving to death', and has no exact equivalent in Western tongue, unless it be the Spanish word *matacaballos*.

This tempo of travel, practised by the peoples of the steppe, was dictated by the degree of urgency which the Palatine Nádasdy had in mind, for example, in his direction to a courier dated 1556 (the equivalent of the vaguer English "Haste, post Haste") "Carry this letter day and night to Kapuvár, though it kills the horse." (Note 62.) The same idea is embodied in the rules of the Turkish game of Jerid, which enjoined the victor to reach the nearest city at top speed, if necessary at the cost of the horse's life, which according to Carl Diem was often the case.

Of course, this does not mean that the horse so ridden or driven must of necessity perish or founder, it simply implies limitless effort, and the condition in which the horse arrived at its destination was a function of its capabilities, its condition at the start, its constitution and state of fitness. A horse could fall dead of effort at the trot, theoretically even at the walk, if more was asked of it than its ultimate capability.

The table contains, even though the available details do not allow an exact match, four sections, each relevant to the Oriental standard of travel, each being a performance at the customary travelling pace, also examples where the horse was ridden to death, and within these examples where there was, and was not, a change of horse.

The first two parts of the table concerned with the speed of travel tell us nothing new. Hourly averages of 7 to 12 km without change of horses and 12 to 15 km with, and a daily journey between 6 and 12 hours are quite customary performances. Rides involving the death of horses, on the other hand, provide results which are worth more detailed consideration. Officers of the German and Austro-Hungarian armies took part in the long-distance rides Berlin–Vienna and Vienna–Berlin over the same route. Sixty-nine out of 97 Austro-Hungarians completed the course, and 76 Germans out of 120. Count Starhemberg, then a lieutenant of hussars, riding a Hungarian half-bred mare, was 1 hour and 40 minutes better than the first rider of the German team, Freiherr von Reizenstein, 73 hours 7 minutes. The winner's horse was one of twenty-five which did not survive the ride.

A ride from Budapest to Vienna organized by the Austro-Hungarian army had 79 entries, of whom 51 completed the course. Of these, seventeen did it in less than twenty hours. The fact that only three horses succumbed points to a fairly moderate speed in relation to the distance, always excepting the remarkably brilliant performance of the winner, a lieutenant of hussars called Bela von Wodianer, riding a Thoroughbred mare.

The long-distance ride from Brussels to Ostend showed results of a quite different order. Hardly half the sixty-one contestants completed the course, though it was comparatively short, with the loss of one-third of the horses. The Dresden–Leipzig ride with 22 entries, six of whom did not finish, and in which seven horses died, showed similar results. But here the performance of the hussar, Lieutenant Zuern of the Royal Saxon Army, on a half-bred mare from Beberbeck is well-nigh incredible.

The similarity of the results leads to the conclusion that results depended in the first instance on the overall length. This is understandable, and most obvious in the case of short journeys. Lieutenant-Colonel Count Otto Hermann Styrum made a bet in 1678 to ride from Vienna to Wiener-Neustadt, and did it in one and three-quarter hours, at an average speed of 28·5 km per hour. Classic races over shorter distances show even better averages: courses of 20 km even show averages like 40 km per hour, and better. Sprints by racehorses often work out at 16–18 metres per second, which is more than 60 km per hour.

Urgency	Performer	Route	Days	km	Riding Hr.	Riding Min.	Rest Hr.	Rest Min.	Total Hr.	Total Min.	km per day	km per hour	Source
"Normal travel" — using one horse	1244 William of Holland	Venice–Brno	16 days	736							46	not counting rest 7–12 km	RÜNGER 1925
	1301 Hungarians according to King Wenceslas	6 rasta	1 day	56.4									Austrian *Rhyming Chronicle*
	9th c. Emperor Constantine	Salonica–Belgrade	8 days	550							56.4		Emperor Constantine *De Administrando Imperio*
	1603 Sir R. Carey	Windsor–Edinburgh	66 hr.	650							65.6		Dent and Goodall 1962
	1629 Transylvanian Embassy	Constantinople–Gyulafehérvár	8 days	620							77.5		Rákóczi, B. 1577
"Normal travel" — with relays	1714 Charles XIII of Sweden	Demotika–Stralsund (driving)	16 days	2400							150	not counting rest 12–15 km	Századok 1869
	1841 Mail Coach	Budapest–Miskolc	1 day	183							183		Timetable 1841
	13th c. Mongol Post	30–40 parasangs	1 day	200							200		Spuler, *Mongols in Iran*
	1241 Subotai's Scouts	Verecke–Pest	3 days	480							160		Diem 1941
	1861 W. Russell	Smith's Creek–Fort Churchill	192		8	10	—	—	8	10	—	23.7	Pony Express Record
"Riding to Death" — using one horse	1892 Count Starhemberg	Vienna–Berlin		580	60	27	11	—	71	27		9.6	WALDBAUER 1909
	1908 Von Wodianer	Budapest–Vienna		230	14	48	1	50	16	38		15.5	WALDBAUER 1909
	1903 Long-distance ride	Brussels–Ostend		132	6	54	—	—	6	54		18.8	WALDBAUER 1909
	1895 Lt. Zuern	Dresden–Leipzig		135	5	57	—	—	5	57		22.5	WALDBAUER 1909
"Riding to Death" — with relays	1920 Tzeren, Mongol Courier	Ulias-Sutai–Peking	9 days	2800	158	—	58	—	216	—	311	17.7	DIEM 1941
	13th c. Mongol Post	60 Parasangs	1 day	341	18	6	1	—			341	18.5	SPULER 1937
	19th c. Count Sándor	Buda–Vienna		230	8	10	—	—	9	10	—	26.5	ANDRÁSSY 1857
	1830 Osbaldeston	Track		320	8	40	—	—	8	40	—	34	ANDRÁSSY 1857

In the next section, showing relays of horses ridden to death, we must remark the performances of Tzeren, Count Sándor, and Osbaldeston, if only because doubt has often been cast on the figures for Sándor. Tzeren, who was a courier in the Mongolian post service, did his ride on post-horses, having the privilege of choosing the best horse at every stage. He was also assisted by people sent in advance, who rode the relay horse alongside him so that he leapt from saddle to saddle at full gallop. In order to stand up to the exertion he was bandaged all over with woollen cloth. He galloped full out for distances of twenty-five or twenty kilometres, and took six or seven hours rest every one of the nine days. This throws some light on the organization of Jenghis Khan's post express service, with its daily stage of 340 km. (Note 63.)

The first to cast doubt on the performance of Count Sándor, "the Devil's Horseman", was Loeffler, and Diem came to share his doubts, because Sándor did the journey from Vienna to Budapest in half Wodianer's time. Their error can be ascribed to the fact that they left out of account Wodianer's single horse, whereas Sándor had many changes of mount.

According to Sándor's diary, an hourly average of 26 km was an exacting test of the rider's powers, although he did do one lap in a carriage. (Note 64.) His achievement is real enough, as is that of Styrum, and not to be reckoned among the fabulous. That Sándor very often rode horses to death is evident from the remark of a contemporary that "he alone used up as many riding-horses as would suffice to mount five regiments of cavalry".

Osbaldeston's ride in England came about owing to a bet that he would ride two hundred miles on a circular track without fences in nine hours. He changed horses every ten furlongs—that is, about 160 times. His friends provided him with the necessary changes of horse. To this, Sándor remarked that on the basis of his own time between Bratislava and Vienna—60 km in 94 minutes with an average of 40 km an hour—he could have ridden Osbaldeston's course in 4 hours 52 minutes. Although results on the racetrack and across country are not to be judged in the same class, nor yet changes of horse every twenty and every two kilometres, we can only accept this remark with reservations, since the average speed kept up by Sándor between Budapest and Vienna is much below that attained by Osbaldeston. (Note 65.)

It further appears from the table that European capabilities in long-distance riding improved in the same measure as Oriental techniques were diffused. Progress is most evident as between the first and third sections. When in Hungary the post organized on the Eastern pattern with relays of horses was introduced in the eleventh century, and by royal decree its horses were classified as able to undertake a stage of one league or only half, even forced marches in the West were scarcely achieving the average speed of the Hungarian post. In 1236 the Emperor Frederick II covered 120 km, on a journey in Italy, in two days and a night, riding say 36 hours; even with 18 hours travelling and 18 hours resting this is still only six or seven kilometres per hour. Even more significant is the race between King Charles VI of France and his son-in-law, the Duke of Touraine, in 1381. (This is the same King Charles VI mentioned in connection with the introduction of the Hungarian slung-wagon.) The chronicler Froissart says:

> The King and the Duke were travelling in the South of France. At Montpellier they made a bet, which of them should get back to Paris first. The two young men, fired by the glances of the fair ladies of Montpellier, were first impelled by

the desire to see their wives again, although the amount of the wager, five thousand francs, did not count for nothing. They each started escorted by a single knight and travelling day and night they repeatedly changed horses. The Duke won the race by taking a boat down the Seine to Melun while the King was having eight hours' sleep at Troyes; the Duke then taking again to horse did the whole journey in 4¼ days, to the King's 4½, taking driving and riding together, over the whole stretch of 150 leagues [about 469 miles]. (Note 66.)

Even if the King's time was no mean achievement, it cannot compare with the 340 km a day that were commonly being ridden at that time in Asia. The difference lay not so much in the riders as in the horses. The royal horses were undoubtedly all stall-fed palfreys and the like, unaccustomed to prolonged galloping, and the harness horses probably even slower; neither could hold a candle to the ordinary run of Mongol or Turk horses. Another disadvantage was that no-one in the West had any conception of how to organize a training programme, with which the Orientals were already familiar. (Note 67.)

A notable feat was performed in France in the eighteenth century, when a certain Count Saillant bet that he would ride from the Porte Saint-Denis at Paris to Chantilly and back (80 km) in 6 hours, changing horses. He did it with 18 minutes to spare, so that his average speed was 27.7 km.p.h., which is by and large the same speed as that of Sándor and Styrum, taking into account the disparity in length of course. Similar speeds and times during that century can be shown among other Western nations.

With the establishment of common standards of horsemanship throughout Europe the test of horse and rider could be measured in terms not only of distance run and time taken but also of obstacles cleared. This is primarily a Western phenomenon, because in the hillier and closer country of the West, often divided by hedges between arable and pasture fields, ability to jump high early became of practicable importance. Such obstacles by and large did not exist either in Western or in Central Asia; it was more important for the horse to be a strong swimmer, and the rider to know how to swim a horse, in order to cross larger rivers without a boat, and the long jump performed by the King of Urartu's horse would have come in useful in crossing a stream without wading. (Note 68.)

It is therefore not possible to cite comparisons in the past for steeple-chasing, for hurdling, or for show-jumping measured against present-day records. (The world record by Captain Alberto Larraguibel Morales of Chile in 1949 on the 16-year-old T. B. Hause—a high jump of 2.47 metres—is still unbroken.) These records were achieved by two factors: systematic training and the use of the Thoroughbred or the half-bred horse of hunter type. The art of riding perfected by hours of practice and training is no longer a monopoly of the East. The spirit in which horsemen of international calibre approach their task with a peculiar devotion is truly international, varying little within Europe, and has its exact counterpart in the American and Australasian continents, of identical historical origin.

In our day the supreme test of horsemanship forms part of the Olympic Games. The Olympic Event, called by the English word Military in most languages but not so called in English, consists of dressage, cross-country, and show-jumping phases, the last over a course comprising fourteen obstacles up to 1.50 metres high. The following table shows the first ten nations with their score in team and individual marks, in which a gold medal counts seven points, a silver five, and a bronze four.

TABLE OF TOTAL POINTS IN OLYMPIC GAMES 1912–68:
TOP TEN NATIONS

Nation	Gold	Silver	Bronze	Points
Germany	8	7	8	123
Sweden	10	2	5	100
Italy	4	7	6	87
France	6	5	3	76
U.S.A.	7	7	5	76
Great Britain	3	2	7	59
Holland	5	3	—	50
Mexico	2	1	1	23
Australia	2	1	1	23
Switzerland	1	2	1	21

The performance put up by representatives of various nations is not only a proof of their skill and determination, it is a living testimony to the survival of the spirit of chivalry in our world, in one of the few fields where a limit has been set to the possible technological advance. The breeding and the riding of horses being more of an art than a science, we may regard the combination of man and horse at international level as near the summit of what human and equine endeavour can achieve for all time.

118
Miniature from the
Duc de Berry's Très
Riches Heures,
illustrated by the
Limburg brothers
about 1415. The
month of August,
showing a party of
falconers.
Musée Condé,
Chantilly

119-120   Tut-Ank-Ahmen hunting Lions, 1358–1349 B.C. From the grave of the king.

121   Persian Miniature showing Game of Polo, Sixteenth Century
Ethnological Museum, Munich.

Epilogue

When we look back over the Equestrian Age we gain a new perspective of the march of historical events. We gain understanding of the rise of humanity from knowledge of prehistoric man's mastering of the problems of transport and communications, and of the historic role of the horse.

Where and when did man find the natural conditions that enabled him to make progress towards civilization? Why did this happen only after the end of the Ice Age, a hundred or a hundred and fifty centuries ago, whereas the remains of recognizably human beings go back hundreds of thousands of years?

These conditions were to be found only in 'the navel of the world'—the Sayan Mountains (52°–55° North and 90°–100° East), the cradle of the pastoral way of life. Only there in the post-glacial world could the flora and fauna of the Ice Age continue to exist south of 60° latitude. At the same time it was the one region that offered mankind optimum climatic conditions for the life of the wandering stock-breeder, and permitted the herding of stock on open range, the riding of reindeer, and subsequently the riding of the horse, which led in the end to the Great Migration of Peoples.

Without this development there would have been no contact within Eurasia between centres of civilization, no exchange of cultural properties, and none of the most fundamental requirements of human progress. The horse ridden by Oriental man must remain the symbol of prehistoric events, contributing decisively to the progress of humanity, east and west.

What of the future? At the end of the Equestrian Age the horse lost all practical significance, and yet its cultural status remained undiminished. It holds its own in the fields of art and literature. A civilization which is founded on millennia of equestrian endeavour still retains its equestrian habits of mind. The popularity of the horse in sport remains undiminished in the Old as in the New World. Thousands of riding clubs and horse shows, equestrian spectacles of all kinds, bear testimony to this.

The breeding of horses of quality is inseparable from the idea of an equestrian civilization. If horse-breeding at the present day has declined and must decline in quantity, it has unquestionably gained in quality, as compared with the past, even the recent past. Still as in the past those countries excel in the production of fine horses which have contributed most to the new unified horsemanship of Europe, and which over the centuries have imposed an indelible national stamp on their light-horse breeding: England, France, Germany, Poland, Hungary. I might mention here also Arabia and Spain, both of which have been the centre of an important national tradition in horsemanship and horse-breeding.

One last thing; now that the Age of the Horse has vanished we see less and less often what we too commonly saw in the past—horses going to rack and ruin through human greed, ignorance, and brutality. It is just and fair that the burden should have been lifted off the horse on to the machine. If the civilization which depended on the horse is gone for ever, it is being replaced now by a civilization which is still enriched by the horse !

A work dealing with such wide aspects of the history of civilization could never have been provided with such abundant historical data unless the author were amply supported on all sides with information and references, whether solicited or not. I wish therefore heartily to thank all those who have so kindly contributed facts and ideas that have gone to the making of this book.

Notes

1 (*page* 18)   My childhood was spent in the Hungarian countryside and my fantasy-world was innocent of the internal combustion engine. My dreams were filled with colourful visions of horses and horsemen. As to my real boyhood, I cannot remember when I first rode a donkey or a horse. I imperceptibly acquired the daily skills of horsemanship; saddling up, driving, feeding, grooming, and the rest, until at last I was fit to be entrusted with the care of fifteen half-grown colts at pasture. My terms of reference were precise: I was to keep them out of the sown and standing corn. Since grassland was not extensive with us, and surrounded by arable land, this was no easy task, and it was made more difficult by a penchant which the colts had to panic at the slightest sound, and, unaccustomed as they were to grazing in the open, to make off over hill and dale. Nevertheless, I managed to hold down the job of colt-herd for a long time, solely due to the fact that the leader of the herd was a three-year-old. It was simply a question of time before I managed to halter him and break him to ride. Once on his back I could easily lead the herd wherever I wanted it. On our migrations I always rode him in front, and my younger brother on a donkey whipped-in the stragglers. Later, when I became a breeder myself, I kept an old mare among the youngsters. With her help there was never any trouble, even on unfenced pastures.

2 (*page* 18)   Janós Kemény, later Prince of Transylvania, points in his autobiography to this equine instinct by an incident on his journey to Constantinople in 1628. Unknown to him, his horses and those of his suite ran away by night, all but one which was tied up. Awakened by its neighing, the riders set out to look for them in pitch-darkness, and on Kemény's orders tied a long rope to the halter of the one remaining horse, the end of which one of them held in his hand. The horse followed the tracks of the runaways to the place where the previous evening they had been watered by a stream outside the village. And so despite the darkness of the night and the unknown country they soon managed to recover the runaways. (J. Kemény, Autobiography—in Hungarian—Századok 1959.)

3 (*page* 24)   There was migration northward in very early times. The peoples of the late Palaeolithic, who were hunters, followed the reindeer as it migrated from its southern habitat, and according to the 'reindeer-shadowing' theory this led to the development of the Mesolithic and Kunda cultures. Therefore northward migration meant for reindeer-breeders no more the opening up of unexplored regions than did westward migration to the first horse-breeders.

Part II

4 (*page* 52)   Delbrück describes the Germans as an equestrian people and therefore discounts the evidence of Procopius and Agathius on the points mentioned. In support of his thesis he cites Aurelius (Chapter 21), who described the Alamani as excellent horsemen. Therefore he ascribes to them the victory at the battle of Strasbourg, and in his view the success at the battle of Adrianople was due to Germanic cavalry skill, and not to any failure of generalship on the part of the Romans. In the preceding chapter I have shown the origin of Germanic mounted tactics among those tribes only who were in contact with the Huns, which is in direct opposition to the view put forward by Delbrück in *Geschichte der Kriegskunst im Rahmen der Politischen Geschichte* (II Berlin 3rd ed. 1921, p. 433).

5 (*page 61*) A writ by Béla IV, King of Hungary, in 1265 shows the mutual esteem in which Hungarian and Polish horsemanship was held. It allows the population of Lipto county, on the Polish border, to trade freely in horses with the Poles. The export embargo was valid only for Bohemia and Germany, not for Poland. (Századok 1908, p. 878.)

6 (*page 62*) Again and again in medieval documents we find riding described as an upper-class custom. J. Rothe in Luciliburg's *Chronicle* (1434) says of St Elizabeth's journey to Hungary that she travelled in a wagon, but her husband, Margrave Louis of Thuringia, and his suite "came riding after the manner of gentlefolk". (Gombos I. p. 333.)

Part III

7 (*page 72*) L. S. Ruhl, Curator of the Museum of Electoral Hesse, weighed a complete set of armour, saddlery and accoutrements, with personal weapons of the same period, with the following result:

Steel chamfron for horse	5 lb.	
Bridle, bit and headstall	8 lb.	
Remainder of horse-armour, steel plate and leather	78 lb.	
Saddle, girth and stirrups	24 lb.	
Man's complete plate armour	80 lb.	
Pair spurs	3 lb.	12 oz.
Sword, mounted pattern	7 lb.	
Shield	5 lb.	8 oz.
Lance	10 lb.	
Dagger	4 lb.	5 oz.
Man's clothing	10 lb.	
Man's surcoat	5 lb.	
Housing over horse-armour	10 lb.	
Helmet crest and pennant	5 lb.	
Total	255 lb.	9 oz.
Rider, say	175 lb.	
All-up weight	436 lb.	9 oz.

These weights are in the old Brandenburg (Berlin) pound, which equalled 0·514 kg, and was practically the same as the English pound. The total weight in metric units is therefore 224 kg. It may be compared with the Austro-Hungarian cavalry manual, which gives the average weight of a trooper as 70 kg and the all-up weight to be carried by the troop-horse as 121 to 128 kg; a horse racing under Jockey Club rules was carrying about 8 st. 10 lb. (55·33 kg); or the standard English packhorse load of 2 cwt., which is about half of 224 kg.

8 (*page 73*) Mention of pugnacious horses employed in battle is rare, but it does occur after the Age of Chivalry. During a lull in the Turkish wars in Hungary Aga Ibrahim of Koppány in 1589 challenged the Constable of Tihany, István Pisky, to a duel, the provocation being a correspondence in which each had abused the other and offered severe insults. (Pisky enclosed with one of his letters a pig's tail, whereupon the Muslim retorted that he must have cut it off his own rump.) The Turkish challenge read "Fight à outrance, either with weapons or with teeth".

We do not know whether this combat actually came off, but in that same year another Constable, Mihály Bory, was at odds with the same Turk. Only this time it was agreed to settle the issue in the presence of an equal retinue from both sides. Not until the fight began did it become clear that it was not the principals who were to fight 'tooth and nail', but their horses. The Hungarian was hard pressed, since the Turkish stallion was more vicious than his. The Hungarian retainers were outraged at what they took for a trick, and attacked the Turks.

A massacre ensued from which few of the Turks escaped. The incident was construed both at Vienna and at Constantinople as a breach of the truce, and led to a diplomatic incident. (Széchenyi Provincial Library, MS letter of Aga Ibrahim 16/61. Description of fight in Istvánffy, 1724.)

9 (*page 76*)   The White Huns showed their aptitude for strategic ruses in their campaign against the Persians of A.D. 459 with the following novelty. They set up snares such as hunters use, digging pits on the battlefield, carefully camouflaged. This line could only be crossed in the middle by a passage as wide as six horses abreast. They drew up their array behind the pits, and one of their squadrons made a feint attack. When this body pretended to flee the pursuing armoured Persians were drawn into the pits.

10 (*page 78*)   The Duke of Newcastle in his *Nouvelle Méthode et Invention* described this breed, principally hailing from the Tarbes plain, as follows:

> The best of these are the finest horses in the world, for everything from the tips of their ears to their hind hoofs is fair about them. Neither so light as the Barb nor so heavy as the Andalusian (Neapolitan), for endurance, courage and docility, they excel besides by their action. At a walk, trot or gallop they leave nothing to be desired. I may say there is no horse more worthy to carry a monarch whether on the field of battle or in a triumphal progress.

11 (*page 91*)   The uncommonly high esteem attaching to the wild horses is apparent from the fact that they were bred in game preserves. Thus Tomas Móró writes to the Palatine Nádasdy in 1556: "Your Grace commanded me to release the filly in the game park that is reserved for Your Grace." This was at Sarvar, where bison, elk, red, roe, and fallow deer were also preserved. (Budapest Archives, Hungarian Chamber 185, Nádasdy Family, B 1521, misc. Hirnyk.)

12 (*page 91*)   Ditto Dl. (Eperjes municipal accounts, fol. 363.)

13 (*page 91*)   Ditto Hungarian Chamber. (185, Nádasdy family, B. 1564, fol. 471.)

14 (*page 91*)   Ditto Motesiczky. (fasc. 10, fol. 37.)

15 (*page 93*)   Ditto Lad. Col. 111. This document describes the bearings as follows (in Latin): "in the field, proper, the right hand and forearm of a man, holding a mallet upraised as if to strike the member of a horse. . . ."

16 (*page 94*)   From the mass of documents bearing on this the following examples may be cited. In 1280 four horses which were well known throughout the country were priced at 40 marks each. (Budapest Archives, Dl. 38667.) In 1317 a horse lost in battle is described as 'famous'. (Budapest Archives, Dl. 100,0041.) Again in 1557, *equus principalis . . . dignitati conveniens* (Budapest Archives, 185 Nádasdy family, B. 1526, misc. Mágocsi) and in 1579 "a horse fit for any lord." (Budapest Archives, P. 707, Zichy Family, fasc. 10, 186.) Finally, *equus capitalis*, (Ditto. E 185, Nádasdy Family, misc. Rum VI).

17 (*page 96*) The clerk Adam reported to his employer, the wife of Palatine Nádasdy, on the provenance of the horse known as Harambasha:

> There is an order that the captured captains and their horses are to be sent to the King and his son. As we have to do with the Germans (Habsburgs) things are not easy. Of good horses suitable for a lord (*urnak valo*) there are only two: one of them is with Andras Pethö; we have sent secretly to Kapuvár with orders to tell no-one that it belonged to Harem Pasha, and let no one see it . . . (Budapest Archives E. 185 Nádasdy B1534), td. misc. Adám deak.

18 (*page 96*) Budapest Archives E 185 Nádasdy Family B 1515 misc. Bebek.

19 (*page 96*) Traces of direct importation of Arabian horses are to be found even in Hungary. In 1548 the Lady Majláth wrote to her son: "Your beloved father sends you— since you have been so diligent in learning—a Saracen horse from Bethlehem, the City of David, where our Lord was born . . ." (Budapest Archives, 185, Nádasdy Family, B 1528, misc. Majláth.)

20 (*page 97*) (1) He is to buy me a quiet horse, yet fit for riding: by quiet I mean that it will stand to be mounted. Yet I wish it be a proper riding-horse, swift, with a good gallop and sound legs.
(2) The horse is not to have a hard mouth, for a hard-mouthed horse is a very foe, and if it were the best in the world, what shall that profit, if it have a hard mouth?
(3) It must be sound and not subject to lameness.
(4) It must not be too wide.
(5) It must not be an aged nag, but if possible still young, say between two and seven winters.
(6) . . . not to buy me a weak horse, but as I am a right heavy lad, it must be strong and muscular, fit to carry me.
(7) Let him not take into his head to buy me a horse with devilish tricks, that lashes out or is nappy, nor yet such a one as twirls its tail round, for that kind of horse is not suitable for a gentleman and shameful to ride.
(8) It must be fair and stately, of what colour I care not.
   (Budapest Archives 190, Rákóczi Family, B 1585, fol. 46.)

21 (*page 97*) Correspondence of the Palatine Tomas Nádasdy shows the wide range of horse exports from Moldavia and Wallachia in the sixteenth century. Writing during 1556 about the repeated purchases made by him on behalf of Archduke Maximilian, he says of one consignment "Three are Walking Horses, three pacers, the former being all Wallachian, one of the pacers is a Turk, grey with some spots; the second is a Szegh (Shagya?) from Moldavia of a striking grey colour, the third a chesnut from beyond the Alps". (Budapest Archives P 1322, Batthyány Family fasc. 112, 123.)
   On receipt by the Archduke in Vienna, he "chose three of them, two pacers including the Moldavian Szegh with a white blaze, the chesnut Transalpine horse, and the third the Walking Horse with the hogged mane". (Budapest Archives 185 Nádasdy Family, B 1524, misc. Köver.)
   The price of Moldavian horses at that time was equal to that of the Arabs. Adám Perényi paid 120 Talers to Gábor Kende for a Moldavian chestnut broken to ride in a curb in 1669. (Budapest Archives 423 Kende Family, fasc. 7/1669.)

22 (page 97) There is a hint as to the breeding of the "Ertzel" horses bred in Lad parish, county Somogy, in a Hungarian sporting periodical of 1857. The stud-owner added the following to a description of the horses advertised for sale:

> This stud traces to the stallion and twelve mares which Ignatius von Czindery brought back from Greater Tartary in 1736, and which have been kept pure since then without admission of other blood. The result of this inbreeding is a uniform strain, conformation and performance do not vary as between individuals. The half-bred progeny out of farmer's mares show the prepotency of the Ertzel stallion, as he can get foals of passable quality even out of the commonest mares. (*Lapok a Lovástat es vadaszat köreböl*, 1857.)

The Czindery stock was still important among private studs during the nineteenth century, or at any rate among some of them. It is incomprehensible why the authorities of that day did not further the propagation (together with that of the TB and the purebred Arab) of this strain which had been bred on Hungarian soil for more than a century. This principle of Hungarian horse-breeding was still well understood about 1800. Baron Josef Wenkheim, a generally acknowledged specialist in this field, deplores, in the book which he published at Pest in 1815, that the once free trade from Tartary, Caucasia, Bessarabia, Poland, and Moldavia is now blocked and impeded to the detriment of Hungarian horse-breeding. He says:

> The history of our indigenous horse shows . . . that the Hungarian horse is closely allied to the Arab, it comes from the same stock of a warm climate. We must therefore only use as foundation stock horses from such a climate or one similar to our own. But hold aloof from all other strains and try to eliminate them, for they bring us nothing but trouble; they may have a showy exterior, but they beget nothing but bastards. Little by little they will be the ruin of our stock.
>
> Therefore for our purpose the most commendable are the Turk, the Barb, the Persian, Circassian, Caucasian, Turcoman—all the Russian breeds of the South like the purebred Donskoy, specially the Zaporozhie—also the Andalusian and the Neapolitan. . . . But all Northern breeds we should eschew, they have no common ancestry with ours and they degenerate in our climate. . . .

General Csekonics was of the same opinion, saying (Pest 1817) that the Transylvanian horse was "of authentic ancient pure lineage, able to contest the palm in light-horse breeding throughout Europe against all comers, including the English Thoroughbred". This high esteem for the Transylvanian horse runs like a bright thread through the whole tradition of breeding in Hungary. As we have seen, it is evident in the fifteenth-century French traveller Broquière's notes, and occurs again in the histories of Miklós Oláh, who esteemed it even above the Turkish horse. So long as the homeland of the Turanian horse had not been engulfed by Tsarist expansion, even the Russians drew their best horses from Hungary in great measure. This esteem was confirmed by the Russian General Piscsevics, when in 1758 he was ordered by the Tsarina Elisabeth Petrovna to acquire horses from the Transylvanian stud of Count Mikes for the Court of St Petersburg. He was of Yugoslav origin, and had once been in the Austrian service; he noted in his memoirs that they were without fault, and of such quality that he had never in all his life seen better or finer horses. (*Memoirs*, Hungarian trans., Budapest 1904.) His purchase aroused great admiration at St Petersburg.

In the second part of the nineteenth century the same revolution took place in Transylvanian horse-breeding as had happened in Hungary fifty years earlier, but in this case the damage could not be remedied after the extinction of this valuable strain of horses.

23 (*page 99*) "The aforesaid enemy . . . who can cover in one day a distance that we could hardly perform within two days, because they are equipped as light horsemen. . . ." (Budapest Archives, E 245, Rep 3242, fol. 203.)

24 (*page* 100)   Budapest Archives, Dl. 1154 and 2135.

25 (*page* 104)   The proverb "No prophet hath honour in his own country" is also true of the Hussars in Hungary. For decades a lively controversy raged as to whether the hussars were of Hungarian or external origin, and only came to an end—alleviated by the reduced strategic value of cavalry but aggravated by the jealousy of other arms—with the denial of their traditions rooted in the soil of Central Asiatic horsemanship. It is significant that between the World Wars the term Hussar was not used to describe the Hungarian Army (Honved) cavalry. The horse soldiers who in the history of European warfare had won such renown were strangely repudiated in their own country.

There is no hint in contemporary documents, or even a shadow of circumstantial evidence, that the hussar as such was of Balkan origin.

Bonfini, in his account of King Matthias' mercenary troops, mentions three nationalities—Bohemians, Hungarians, and 'Raizes' (Yugoslavs). The King's letter to Gabriel of Verona sets out his order of battle as consisting of heavy cavalry, light hussars, and infantry.

26 (*page* 106)   "Our armoured cavalry are accustomed to stand their ground, though they be all cut down where they stand. But the light troops attack whenever opportunity occurs, and when they are exhausted or menaced by some grave danger they withdraw behind the main body and there re-form, and when their morale and physique is restored they pass again to the offensive."

27 (*page* 106)   Budapest Archives E 254. fasc. 2956. 1574. nov. 8.

28 (*page* 107)   Ditto E 254. fasc. 3188. fol. 582.

29 (*page* 107)   Ditto E 190. Rákóczi Family, B 1584 fol. 146.

30 (*page* 107)   Ditto R 224, 1661, pall. 97.

31 (*page* 108)   Ditto R. 224, 1667, pal. 97.

32 (*page* 108)   Ditto, C 35, Lad. D. no. 18.

33 (*page* 108)   At this time Western stud methods were gaining ground in Hungary. In 1715 the steward of the Zichy estate of Zsámbék wrote to his employer: "The mares will not stay in the herd, but scatter all over the place", and asked him to send them a stallion without delay. (Budapest Archives P 707. Zichy Family, fasc. 126, nb, 17626.) In 1777 the Master of the Horse to the Károlyis was sent round the neighbourhood "to find out how people manage mares and stallions when covering in hand or running free." (Budapest Archives, 398. Kárólyi Family, misc. Mlinaricz.)

Baron Wenkheim (1815) and General Csekonics (1817) both lay the blame for the decline of quality in breeding which went hand in hand with the cessation of horse-keeping on open range on the fact that mares were no longer covered at their own will. Both stress the importance of mares being served in accordance with their own inclination, that of the stallion, and natural selection. Wenkheim recommends for this purpose four stallions to a herd—Csekonics even more—on the ground that, in any herd, sub-herds tend to form round each stallion, whereby there is more opportunity for insemination according to natural impulse.

Csekonics continues:

As horses have a natural instinct whereby each sire attracts or wins by fighting a given number of mares, according as he feels he is able to serve so many, and thus assert his rights... Therefore I make so bold as to say, that all breeders should—nay I beseech them, rather—to give up the half-wild husbandry and revert wholly to the totally wild . . .

Now consider all the light cavalry of Europe. Nearly all their remounts are the progeny of wild herds . . . and all civilian horses such as cobs and the like in commercial use, down to cab-horses—you will find that most of them are of wild origin.

Nowadays not only in Hungary, but wherever horses are bred, all is changed. Present experiments, and the practice of artificial insemination, are in complete opposition to all that were once considered fundamental principles. The horses are deprived of their last opportunity to refuse a coupling repugnant to Nature, or to avoid it. I call this a senseless affront offered to Nature, the consequences of which will probably not be realized until the resultant damage is not to be repaired.

34 (*page 111*) There is medieval evidence for branding of horses in Hungary. In 1270 horses from the village of Barcza were marked with *signum in scapula in parte sinistra per modum furce* (fork on near shoulder) and then with *signum in sinistra parte in latere admodum virgule* (twig on near flank), and lastly with *signum in dextro femore 2 ferramenta equorum* (off thigh, 2 horseshoes). (Budapest Archives Dl. 84214 and 84198.)

In 1336 Peter Nagysemjén recognized a horse in the royal camp near Kreisbach which bore the well-known Kállay brand *signum falcastrum luporum* on the near side (a wolf's paw). (Kállay Family archives, 497.) The branding of horses in the Trakehnen and other German studs is a relic of the time when herds were kept on open range, and the practice is still common in the British Isles (*e.g.*, Wales, Exmoor, New Forest) where herds run on common grazing.

34a (*page 114*) "Estland is swythe micel" says the West Saxon king, reporting his informant, the Norwegian merchant skipper Wulfstan (Ulfsteinn):

Estonia is a big country, full of towns, and to every town a king. There is much honey there, and good fishing. The kings and the rich men drink mares' milk, and poor men and serfs drink mead. There is much fighting among them. The Estonians brew no ale, for they have mead enough instead. It is the custom among them, that when a man of any consequence dies he lies in state uncremated in the house of his friends and kinsmen a month and sometimes two, and in the case of kings and nobles as much as half a year. And all the time the body lies in state there are drinking bouts and sports and gambling, till the day of the cremation. And the day they intend to carry him to the pyre, they take all such of his property as is left after the drinking and the gambling, and part it out into five or six lots, or sometimes more, according to how much of it is left. And they put the largest share a mile from the town where the corpse lies, and the other shares in diminishing order between that and the town, so that the smallest lot is nearest the town. There then assemble all those men that have the fastest horses, some five or six miles outside the town. And they all ride at full speed towards the property; and he that has the fastest horse comes first to the outermost share which is also the greatest, and so one after another until it is all taken up. And he that comes fifth or sixth, as it may be, takes the smallest share nearest to the town. Then they all ride on their way with their winnings, for nothing is held back. This is the reason why fast horses are uncommonly dear among them. When all this treasure is dissipated they carry out the corpse and burn it, together with weapons and clothing. [Preface to Orosius' *History.* Tr.]

Part IV

35 (*page 117*) Budapest Archives Dl. 6692/1.

36 (*page 119*) Budapest Archives E 185. Nádasdy Family., B 1514, misc. Arco.

37 *(page 119)* Budapest Archives, Dl. 26171. The six-in-hand slung wagon was in daily use among the more considerable Hungarian landowners in the fifteenth and sixteenth centuries, for travelling. According to a fifteenth-century account book, the Imperial Palatine once progressed through Upper Hungary with five such wagons.

38 *(page 122)* From a deed of grant by Maria Theresa to the Counts Ferenc and Josef Nádasdy of 1744. (Budapest Archives P 507, Nádasdy Family, series 2. no. 46.)

39 *(page 122)* *Leith von Hadik to His Royal Highness concerning the Expedition into the Mark of Brandenburg and the Storming of the Royal Capital and Residence of Berlin.* (Copy of commander's report, made contemporaneously, and in possession of the author.)

40 *(page 122)* The Tschunkenberg case will serve among many examples to demonstrate that the demand for Hussars was not directed exclusively to Hungary, but to Oriental horsemen in general. He was a Turk, his real name Mehmet, and was present at the battles of Kassa, Buda, and Vác; in 1685 he was the last Turkish defender of the fortress of Nógrád. He was very popular among the Hungarians. Fighting bravely, he lost his right arm in battle, and was consequently known as 'Csonkabég'—that is, "the One-Armed Bey". At the storming of Nógrád by the Christians he, his wife, and his son were taken prisoner, and he was brought to interrogation at Wienerneustadt on November 14th, 1686. Ten years later he and his family embraced the Catholic faith. The Emperor himself stood godfather to him, and he was christened Leopold Josef Balthasar Tschunkenberg. An Archduchess stood godmother to his wife.

In the War of the Spanish Succession there were four regiments of hussars, as early as 1702: the Ninth (Czobor), the Eighth (Pál Deák), and the Kollonits and Ebergényi Regiments. In the same year four more regiments were raised; by Simon Forgách, Imre Gombos, Péter János Loósy and Gábor Esterházy, son of the Palatine, the last being commanded by Colonel Tschunkenberg. His new name is of course a Germanization of the old nickname Csonkabég. He became a favourite of Prince Eugène of Savoy, who once freed him after he had been taken prisoner. In December 1704 a second regiment (Lehoczky's) was placed under his command, and this brigade was then attached to the English force fighting on the Moselle. On 16 Feb. 1705 Field-Marshal Groensfeld wrote to Prince Eugène; ". . . poor old Csunkabeck who was commanding the light horse on the Moselle front, was murdered by franc-tireurs, together with Lt. Col. Rudnai of Esterházy's whose son in retaliation burnt six villages to the ground. . . ." to which the Prince replied on Feb 25th: "It is not certain . . .". (Vienna, War Dispatches, 1705.)

Old Csonkabég's son, Ferenc Leopold Tschunkenberg, was made an Austrian baron. No doubt he grew up in Hungary, for like his father he wore Hungarian costume, wrote letters in Magyar, and felt himself a complete Hungarian. He served in Sicily, and in Upper Italy. He died in 1735 at Klausen, in South Tyrol, without male heir extant, and was thus the last of his line. He bequeathed his estate to the founding and endowment of a church at Wienerneustadt. Takáts the historian says that portraits of the Tschunkenbergs, father and son, were to be seen in the Town Hall there.

41 *(page 123)* Moreri: *Dictionnaire*, 1732. When they return from the war the general gives them as many gold pieces as they bring back heads.

42 *(page 123)* Budapest Archives E 169 Bellavitz Family B 1532.

43 *(page 123)* From a contemporary letter in possession of the author. At the time of the Napoleonic Wars we also find hussars serving abroad called 'Kuruzes'. A letter of 1800 mentions the 'Red Kuruzes' in French pay. (Budapest Archives, Jeszenák Family, P 1398, cs. 10. fasc. 12, 1062.)

44 (*page* 124)   The popularity of the Hungarian hussar at that day is expressed in a Rhineland folksong of the eighteenth century:

> Now the Hungarian hussars ride
> From Hungary to the Rhine
> All in red breeches
> And a grass-green cloak about them.
> If a hussar falls, then he rides to Heaven,
> And another loses an arm or a leg;
> What else are chaplains and surgeons for?
> They are well served, body and soul.
> Many a heart these hussars have broken
> Between Hungary and the Rhine
> And many a nut-brown maid asks,
> "Where will my hussar be now?"

From the locally collected and published *Zupfgeigenhansl*.

45 (*page* 125)   Károlyi Family Archives, vol. 3, p. 40.

46 (*page* 126)   Budapest Archives, Dl. 14545.

47 (*page* 126)   The late spread of the pacer to Hungary is evident from the lack of skill in training it, which lasted for a long time. The Master of the Horse at Sárvár, the Nádasdy estate, wrote to his employer in 1557 that he had harnessed three carriage horses in a team with the pacers, and hobbled them near fore to near hind, etc., but had no success, as the mares never did learn to pace, but broke the hobbles. (Budapest Archives, Nádasdy Family. misc. Pálffy János.) The Hungarian proverb "It is hard to make an old horse pace" echoes the English fifteenth-century saying:

> As hors that ever trotted, trewely ich yow telle
> Ful hard were it to teche hym, after, to amble well.

or more succinctly, in the sixteenth century

> Trot sire, trot dam, how shall the foal amble?

and shows the belief then prevalent, that horses could only be bred, not trained, to pace or amble.

48 (*page* 126)   Budapest Archives P 707, Zichy Family, fasc. 10, 186.

49 (*page* 126)   The use of horses of different gaits, in the manner customary in the Age of Chivalry, is now only found, apart from examples in the southern U.S.A. and South Africa, in Iceland, which was settled a thousand years ago by Scandinavian, British, and Irish colonists, with horse-stock drawn from the entire north-west coastal region of Europe. In Iceland, pacing and racking are inbred in some strains of pony.

50 (*page* 127)   It was said of Palatine Nádasdy's horses kept at Sarvar in 1561: "The brown mare has foaled to the King's horse. It is a good colt, like the sire. I have foreborne so far to show him to anyone, for fear of the evil eye" (Budapest Archives E 185, Nádasdy Family, 8, misc. Pálffy János.)

51 (*page* 127)   Ditto E 185 Nádasdy Family B 1528, misc. Nádasdy F.

52 (*page* 127)   Ditto E 185, Nádasdy Family, B 1520, misc. Giczy.

53 (*page 127*) The component parts of the *kocsi* were mentioned in two documents:
1550: Budapest Archives E 185 Nádasdy Family B 1525 pall. 12 f. 1.
1750: Budapest Archives P 198 Esterházy Family Cseklész Accounts 604. f. 161.

54 (*page 129*) According to Bartoniek, Aczél rode into the water after the King, whereas Burgio rather implies, with *e intrato*, that he dismounted and waded or dived, which seems inherently more likely. (Bartoniek 1926.)

55 (*page 129*) Budapest Archives Dl. 24405. *Eodem die Johanni Warkony adulescenti Regie Maiestatis per Maiestatem Suam ad Moraviam pro abducentis equis armigeris misso pro expensis dati sunt in bona moneta per duas flos xxv.*—"The same day were paid His Majesty's esquire John Warkony, for going on His Majesty's errand to Moravia to fetch warhorses twenty-five florins, as his expenses, in good currency."

56 (*page 129*) The authorities for the content of the royal stables under Matthias and Vladislav II are Csánky, 1883, and Fogel, 1913.

The existence of a French saddle at the Court of Louis II indicates the prevalence of French customs there. The will of Miklós Balinszky, proved in 1515, bequeathed to the royal *dapifer* (cup-bearer) a horse 'together with a saddle made after the French manner' (*una cum sella in more francigerorum facta*). (Budapest Archives Filmtár, C. 267 Bártfa Váre Lt.-a 4563.)

57 (*page 130*) Burgio's account differs in many particulars from observations made on the spot. If the horse really refused the obstacle and threw the rider it would have been able to climb out on either bank, once loose, just as Aczél's and Czettricz's horses did. At this point the horse was at the exact place where according to the eye-witness Czettricz the weapons were found, and where the King must have lain. In contrast to Burgio's account, it therefore seems more probable that the horse reared up and came over backward, falling on the rider. But this is not part of the refusal behaviour. It is, of course, quite possible that the horse suddenly dropped dead of a wound previously received—but also most unlikely. When its strength fails a wounded horse falls forward. Rearing up and falling backward are the actions of a horse in full possession of its powers, but in a state of panic, mortal fear, and having lost its head. Taking all this into consideration, we must conclude that the horse was overtaxed and exhausted, and immersion in cold water brought on a heart-attack. There is supplementary evidence that a heavy horse was involved. The contemporary Italian chronicle of Marino Sanuto says that the King was drowned in a swamp by 'his fat horse' (*a cavallo grosse s'e impaludo*). Newcastle wrote of the Frisian horse in 1660: ". . . is apt for all exercise, save only for long gallops . . . it is of no use to urge them to gallop long, they have not the wind for it . . ."

Part V

58 (*page 139*) There are many records from the Arpad period of the hunting and sporting ability of Hungarian rulers. The Hildesheim Annals state that St Imre, only son of St Stephen, was mortally wounded out hunting by a boar. There are numerous accounts of the hunting of Géza I and St Ladislaus. (Gombos, p. 688.) A charter (Budapest Archives Dl. 5625) also mentions King Imre's death in the hunting-field. Endre II also refers in a charter of manumission to one of his youthful experiences while hunting: ". . . the spot where, when I was still a prince, I slew a wild bear and marked a cross on a tree". (Smiciclas.)

59 (*page* 139) General Csekonics comments thus:

Count Károlyi wanted to buy the mare on account of her great courage, but the owner refused all offers, though respectfully as became a subject of the Count . . . . He declared that great as the honour and favour that would accrue to him might be, if his horse were to enter His Lordship's stables, yet he would take neither money nor goods for it, and would no more think of parting with his grey mare than with his wife.

60 (*page* 140) Frederick II's book, besides its literary value, also affords useful source-material on the history of falconry in Europe. From it we learn that in contemporary England hawking was done on foot, although the Bayeux Tapestry shows the Normans about to invade England, some of them riding with hawk on fist, and that Spain in the thirteenth century was the true home of mounted falconry in the West, due to Moorish influence. Frederick himself brought falconers from the Arab world, chiefly from North Africa. The use of the hawk's hood or *capellum* originated there. But at the same time he employed austringers from other countries (*expertos huius rei tam de Arabia, quam de regionibus undecunque . . . redigere*). The real home of European falconry at that time was Hungary, of which there are many proofs. Hungarian annals often mention the Arpad dynasty hawking, *inter alia* a hawking party of Prince Almos at Szekesfehervar in 1106. (Szentpétery: *Scriptores Rerum Hungaricarum* I.S. 427.)

Frederick II had also personal ties with Hungary. As a boy of ten, under Papal pressure, he was betrothed to the widow of King Imre (who died in 1204), the Aragonese Princess Constance, ten years his senior. The wedding followed many years later, and in the bridal train there came to Palermo a large Hungarian household. Given the nature of Hungarian royal households at that time, and the large suite to which a Queen Dowager would be entitled, there can be no doubt that these will have included huntsmen and falconers.

61 (*page* 143) The encounter took place with much mounted pomp. The men presented a brilliant picture. There were all but a hundred cavaliers in ornate national costume, the bride escorted by the ban of Croatia and a bishop in a triumphal car drawn by six dapple greys with silver-mounted harness inlaid with purple, their manes and tails dyed blue. The Basket Hunt is described thus:

The basket was hunted near the village of Hesszurét, by five horsemen of the Prince (bridegroom) and one Turk of the Ban's (bride's father). The Prince's man mounted on a Turkish chestnut won the basket (Kelemen Kun), and the second prize, which was a length of scarlet cloth, was won by the Ban's horseman, although his mount collapsed at the winning-post; third came Szoboszlai on a bay horse which had already run in a race at Munkács.

(Budapest Archives R 224, 1666.)

62 (*page* 148) Budapest Archives 185 Nádasdy Family B 1530. Misc. Egerszeghy.

63 (*page* 150) Marco Polo says of the Mongol post system:

The post-houses are called Djam, and situated each twenty-five leagues apart. Foot couriers are relieved every three leagues, but express post is sent by horsemen. They cover two hundred or two hundred and fifty leagues in a day, horse and rider changing at every post-house, where fresh horses are always in waiting. Every town or village that lies near such a post-house is bound to furnish it with a certain number of horses. It is only in uninhabited places that the Emperor maintains the post-houses at his own charges.

64 (*page* 150) Budapest Archives Dl. 57632.

65 (*page* 150) 1. From Buda to Bia, on a half-blind horse, lame both sides before. 2. From Bia to Bicske, on a Hungarian farm-horse called Sólyom. 3. From Bicske to Bánhida, on a grey. 4. From Bánhida to Kóts, on a brown English half-bred mare. 5. From Kóts to Bábolna on a brown English half-bred mare called Princesse. 6. From Bábolna to Györ, by coach behind four bays from the Kezsthely stud (Count Festetic's) harnessed all abreast in the Russian style. 7. From Györ to Öttéveny on a Hungarian farm-horse called Kedves. 8. From Öttéveny to Mosony, on an English half-bred mare called Julianna. 9. From Mosony to Saida, on a Thoroughbred called Brigliadoro. 10. From Saida to Pahrendorf, on an English half-bred named Coquette. 11. From Parhrendorf to Schwechat, on an English half-bred named Restless. 12. From Schwechat to Vienna, on my own horse Bully. ['English half-bred' here means that the horse was partly Thoroughbred, the other part of its breeding had nothing to do with England. Tr.]

66 (*page* 151) "Then rode they four, being young and wilful, night and day, and when they would sleep they took to wagons; and you are to know they changed horses many times."

67 (*page* 151) Giovanni Sforza's ride in 1497 demonstrates the varying capabilities of Eastern and Western strains of horse. When he heard from his wife Lucrezia Borgia of the attack that Cesare Borgia was planning he mounted his Turkish horse in Rome and got to Pesaro 160 miles away in twenty-four hours. But his horse collapsed from exhaustion. This is equal to the average performance in the Budapest-Vienna long-distance ride.

68 (*page* 151) Horse-leaping was known among Orientals in antiquity. An inscription from Urartu of the eighth century B.C. mentions Arcibis, King Menua's horse, that could jump 22 cubits horizontally.

Source of Illustrations

Anglis: 114. E. Bacon: *Digging for History* (A. & C. Black, London, 1960): 22. E. Breuil and H. Obermaier: *La Cueva de Altamira* (Tipographia de Archivos, Madrid, 1935): 15. Bruckmann Bildarchiv: 40. W. Castelli: 81. Duke of Portland: *Memories of Racing and Hunting* (Faber, London, 1935): 86. H. Frankfort: *The Art and Architecture of the Ancient Orient* (Penguin, London, 1954): 19. M. Gábori: 10, 36, 65, 67. Giraudon, Paris: 4, 24, 30, 32, 41, 42. A. Godard, Paris: 31. A. Grote: 45. H. Hell: 14. Hutin, Compiègne: 93. Interfoto-Bilderdienst: 49. Keystone: 116. Kohalmy: 37. L. Ligeti: 12. W. Menzendorf: 99, 100, 106, 117. J. Molnár: 3, 26, 33–35, 39, 44, 50, 51, 69, 70, 72, 73–76, 82–85, 88, 90, 95, 96, 101, 103, 104, 111. W. Pruski: 16, 17, 89, 91. K. Salzle: *Tier und Mensch—Gottheit und Dämon* (BLV 1965): 119, 120. E. Schiele: 46–48, 55–61, 64, 98, 105. Solms-Laubach: *Die schönsten Reiterbilder aus europaischen Sammlungen* (Keysersche Verlagsbuchhandlung, Heidelberg and Munich, 1962): 1, 118, 121. W. Steinkopf: 92. Staatsbibliothek Berlin, Bildarchiv (Handke): 28. Süddeutscher Verlag, Bildarchiv: 52. Szalay: 11. G. Torlichen, Argentina. Chr. Belser Verlag, Stuttgart, 53, 54. E. Trumler: 6. Ullstein-Bilderdienst: 115. R. Viollet, Paris: 25. Zodiaque: 112.

Bibliography

The approximate English equivalents of German, Russian, Polish and Hungarian titles appear in roman after the titles in question. The insertion of an English equivalent title does not necessarily imply that a work has been translated into English.

AJTAI, E.: *A Magyar huszár* (The Hungarian Hussar), Budapest, 1936.

ALISTAI MÁTTYUS, J.: *A nemzeti lovag* (The National Horseman), Pest, 1828.

ALMÁSY, G.: *Vándorutam Ázsia szivében* (Rambles in the Heart of Asia), Budapest, 1903.

ANDRÁSSY, M. GR.: *Hazai vadászatok és sport Magyarországon* (Hunting and Sports in Hungary), Budapest, 1857.

Annales Hildersheimenses.

Anonymi Belae regis notarii: Gesta Hungarorum, ed. Gombos, No. 540.

Anonymi Descriptio Europae Orientalis anno 1308, ed. Gorka, Cracow, 1916.

APOR, P.: *Metamorphosis Transylvaniae.*

BAMM, P.: *Frühe Stätten der Christenheit* (Early Christian Sites), Munich, 1965.

BARTONIEK, E.: *Mohács Magyarországa* (The Hungary of Mohács), Budapest, 1926.

BELÉNYESY, M.: *Az állattartás a XV. században Magyarországon* (Cattle-breeding in Fifteenth-century Hungary), Ethnographic report, 1956.

BERGER, A.: *Die Jagd aller Völker im Wandel der Zeit* (International History of Hunting), Berlin, 1928.

BOESSNECK, J.: *Zur Entwicklung vor- und frühgeschichtlicher Haus- und Wildtiere Bayerns im Rahmen der gleichzeitigen Tierwelt Mitteleuropas. Studien an vor- und frühgeschichtlichen Tierresten Bayerns*, II (History of Prehistoric and Protohistoric Wild and Domestic Animals of Bavaria), Munich, 1958.

BÖKÖNYI, S.: *Die Haustiere in Ungarn im Mittelalter auf Grund der Knochenfunde. Viehzucht und Hirtenleben in Ost-Mitteleuropa* (Medieval Domestic Animals in Hungary from Skeletal Evidence), Budapest, 1961.

BOROSY, A.: *XI–XIV. századi magyar lovasságról* (Hungarian Cavalry of the Eleventh to Fourteenth Centuries), Military History Publications, 1962, II.

BRUNS, U.: *Ponies*, London, 1961.

CALKIN, V. I.: *Drevnyeje zsivotnovodsztvo plemjon vasztocsnoj Jevropu i szregynyej Azii* (Stockbreeding in Antiquity among East European and Central Asian Tribes), Moscow, 1966.

CARRUTHERS, D.: *Unknown Mongolia. A record of travel and exploration in North-West Mongolia and Dzungaria*, London, 1913.

CHLEDOWSKI, C. V.: *Der Hof von Ferrara* (The Court of Ferrara), Berlin, 1913.

Chronicon Budense, ed. Podraczky, J., Buda, 1838.

Chronicon Colmariense, ed. Gombos, No. 1290.

Corpus Juris Hungarici, I. 1000–1526, Budapest, 1899.

CSÁNKY, D.: *I. Mátyás udvara* (The Court of Matthias I), Budapest, 1883.

CSEKONICS, J.: *Praktische Grundsätze, die Pferde betreffend* (Practical Principles regarding the Horse), Pest, 1817.

DADÁNYI, G.: *Csordás voltam Paraguayban* (I was a Paraguayan Cowboy), Budapest, 1943.

DARKÓ, J.: *Turáni hatások a göröh-római hadügy fejlödésében* (Turanian Influence on the Development of Graeco-Roman Tactics), Military History Publications, Budapest, 1934.

DELBRÜCK, H.: *Geschichte der Kriegskunst im Rahmen der politischen Geschichte II.* (History of the Art of War in the Context of Political History), Berlin, 1921.

DENT, A. A. and GOODALL, D. MACHIN: *The Foals of Epona*, London, 1962.

Deutsche Fundgruben der Geschichte Siebenbürgens, I (German Sources for the History of Transylvania).

DIAKONOV: *Epigrafika Vostoka* (Oriental Inscriptions), 1951.

DIEM, C.: *Asiatische Reiterspiele* (Asiatic Mounted Sports), Berlin, 1941.

——: *Weltgeschichte des Sports und der Leibeserziehung* (World History of Sport and Physical Training), Stuttgart, 1960.

DIVÉKY, A.: *Zsigmond lengyel herceg budai, számadásai* (Prince Sigismund of Poland's Account-books at Buda), Hungarian Historical Research, 1914.

DOMANOVSZKY, S.: *Mázsaszekér* (The Wagon), *Fejérpataky Album*, Budapest, 1917.

DUBRAVIUS: *Historia regni Bohemiae*, Budapest, 1917.

EINHARD and NOTKER: *Two Lives of Charlemagne* (trans. Thorpe), Harmondsworth, 1969.

FEJÉR, G.: *Codex diplomaticus IV/2.*

FINTA, A.: *Herdboy of Hungary*, Washington, 1940.

FLADE, J. E.: *Das Araberpferd* (The Arab Horse) Wittenberg, 1962.

FOGEL, J.: *II. Ulászló udvartartása* (The Court of Ladislas II), Budapest, 1913.

FRAKNOI, V.: *Mátyás király levelei* (Letters of King Matthias II), Budapest, 1893–95.

Friderici Romanorum Imperatoris Secundi: De Arte Venandi cum avibus.

FROISSART, J.: *Chronicles.*

FUGGER, M.: *Von der Gestuterey* (Of Stud-farms), Frankfurt a/M 1584.

GÁBORI, M.: *Napfényes Mongolia* (Sunny Mongolia), Budapest, 1961.

GÁRDONYI, A.: *Budapest történeti emlékei* (Historical Memorials of the City of Budapest) Budapest, 1941.

Geneologia Comitum Flandriae, book 3, col. 402 z. von Du Cange.

GOMBOS, A.: *Catalogus fontium Historiae Hungaricae*, III, Budapest, 1938.

GORKA: *Anonymi Descriptio Europae Orientalis anno 1308*, Gracoviae, 1916.

GROUSSET, R.: *L'empire des steppes*, 1939.

GYÖRFFY, GY.: *Magyarok elödeiröl és a honfoglalasról* (Ancestry and Settlements of the Magyars), Budapest, 1958.

HALÁSZ, G.: *Telivérek* (Thoroughbreds), Budapest, 1943.

HANCAR, F.: *Das Pferd in prähistorischer und früher historischer Zeit* (The Horse in Prehistoric and Early Historical Times), Vienna, 1955.

HANKÓ, B.: *Székely lovak* (Székely Horses), Kolozsvár, 1943.

HAVARD, H.: *Dictionaire de l'ameublement et de decoration, depuis le XIII-e siècle jusqu'à nos jours*, Paris.

HEDIN, SVEN: *The Silk Road*, London, 1938.

IBN BATTUTA: *Travels in Asia and Africa 1325–54*, London, 1929.

ISTVÁNFFY, N.: *Regni Hungarici Historia*, ed. Coloniae, 1724.

KAKUK, Z.: *Az orkhoni felirat* (The Orkhon Inscription), *A magyarok elödeiröl, és a honfoglalásröl*, Budapest, 1958.

KEMALPASASZADE MOHÁCSNAME: *Török-magyarkori történeti emlékek* (Turco-Hungarian Historical Monuments), Turkish Historical Writings, I.

KEMÉNY JÁNOS: *Önéletrajzleirása* (Autobiography), Századok, 1959.

LAMING, A.: *La Signification de l'Art Rupestre*, Paris, 1959.

LÁSZLÓ, G.: *A koroncói lelet és a honfoglaló magyarok nyerge* (The Koroncó Find and the Saddles of the Hungarian Settlers), Budapest, 1943.

——: *A honfoglaló magyar nép élete* (Life among the Hungarian Settlers), Budapest, 1944.

——: *Kolzsvári Márton és György szobránák lószerszáma* (Saddlery in the Statue of St George), Transylvanian Scientific Institute Year Book, Kolozsvár, 1943.

László, J.: "Magyar huszárok idegen nemzetek szolgálatában" (Hungarian Hussars in Foreign Service), *The Hungarian Hussar*, Budapest, 1936.

Leo VI imperator dictus Sapiens (Philosophus) 886–912. *Tactica*.

Lestyán, S.: *Gróf Sandor Móric, az ördöglovas* (Count M. Sándor, the Devil's Horseman), Budapest, 1942.

Ligeti, L.: *Secret of the Mongols*, London, 1963.

Liliencron, R. v.: *Die historischen Volkslieder der Deutschen vom 13. bis. 16. Jahrhundert* (Historic German Folksongs, 1200–1600), Leipzig, 1865.

Magyar, K.: *Csekonics kapitány emlékirata* (Memorandum by Captain Csekonics), Hungarian Farmers' Union, 1936.

Makkai-Mezey: *Árpádkori és Anjou-kori levelek* (Correspondence of the Arpad and Anjou Periods), Budapest.

Masudi: *Murudzs adz-dzahab*, ed. Czeglédy, K.; *A magyarok elödeiröl és a honfoglalásról* (Ancestry and Settlements of the Magyars), ed. Györffy, Budapest, 1958.

Miskulin, A.: *Müvelödéstörténeti mozzanatok Giovani és Matteo Villani krónikdja alapján* (The Villani Chronicle as Historical Source), Budapest, 1905.

Moser, H.: *Durch Zentralasien* (Through Central Asia), Leipzig, 1888.

Nagy, G.: *A Magyar középkozi fegyverzet* (Weapons in Medieval Hungary), Ért, 1891.

Nestor monachus Kioviensis, *Annales Russorum*, ed. Kniezsa, I., Budapest, 1958.

Newcastle, Duke of: *Nouvelle Methode et Invention*, Antwerp, 1656.

Niederwolfsgruber, F.: *Kaiser Maximilians I. Jagd- und Fischereibücher* (Maximilian I's Books on Hunting and Fishing), Munich, 1965.

Oppyanos: *Kynegetika*, ed. Lehrs, Paris, 1846.

Pálffy János emlékezései, Magyarországi és Erdélyi urak (Memoirs of Hungarian and Transylvanian Noblemen), ed. Szabó T. Attila, Kolozsvár, 1939.

Perjes, G.: *Lóra termette-e a magyar?* (Is the Hungarian born to ride?) Life and Science, 1965.

Pest. Egy Tiszahdti Magyar's öszinte megjegyzései a'hazafiság, utánzási kór és nevelés felett (Honest observations of a Tisza-side Hungarian on Patriotism, Imitation and Training), Leipzig, 1846.

Pettko-Szandtner, T.: *A magyar kocsizás* (Hungarian Coaching), Budapest, 1931.

Pokorny, G.: *Skizzen zur Geschichte des Pferdes* (Sketches on the History of the Horse), Prague, 1878.

Pollay: *Neue Reitkunst, ein Reiterbrevier* (The New Art of Riding), Stuttgart.

Polo, Marco: *Travels*.

Pray, G.: *Annales veteres Hunnorum Avarorum et Hungarorum II.*, Vindobonae, 1761.

Pruski, W.: *Dzikie Konie Wschodniej Europy. Roczniki Nauk Rolniczych. 85. Der D.* (Horses of Eastern Europe), Warsaw, 1959.

Razin: *A hadmüvészet története* (History of the Art of War), II. ung. Ub., Budapest, 1961.

Ross, E. J.: *A Chalcolithic Site in Northern Baluchistan*, 1946, INES.

Rudenko, S. I.: *The Frozen Tombs*, London, 1970.

Salet: *Die Nachfolger Alexanders des Grossen in Baktrien und Indien* (Alexander the Great's Successors in Bactria and India), Berlin, 1879.

Sälzle, K.: *Tier und Mensch, Gottheit und Dämon* (Beast and Man, Deity and Devil), Munich 1965.

Schack, Gr., Adolf Friedrich: *Geschichte der Normannen in Sizilien, X.* (History of the Normans in Sicily).

Schadendorf, W.: *Zu Pferd, im Wagen, zu Fuss* (Riding, Driving, and Walking), Munich, 1961.

SCHULTZ, A.: *Deutsches Leben im XIV. und XV. Jahrhundert* (German Life in the Fourteenth and Fifteenth Centuries), Prague; Vienna, Leipzig, 1892.

SCHURIG, A.: *Die Eroberung von Mexico durch Ferdinand Cortes, mit den eigenhändigen Berichten des Feldherrn an Kaiser Karl, von 1520, und 1522* (The Conquest of Mexico by Hernan Cortés, with Holograph Reports . . .), Leipzig, 1923.

SCHWARZ, F. v.: *Turkestan, die Wiege der indogermanischen Völker* (Turkestan, Cradle of the Indo-European Peoples), Freiburg i. Br., 1900.

SHAW, H.: *Visits to High Tartary, Yârkand, and Kâshgar*, London, 1871.

SMIČICLAS, T.: *Codex Diplomaticus Regni Croatiae, Dalmatiae et Slavoniae*, IXX.

SOHNS-LAUBACH, E. GR. zu: *Die schönsten Reiterbilder aus europäischen Sammlungen* (Selected Equestrian Portraits from European Collections), Heidelberg; Munich, 1962.

STEIER, O. or Ottakar von Horneck: *Austrian Rhyming Chronicle*, ed. Gombos.

SZAMOTA, I.: *Travels in Ancient Hungary and the Balkan Peninsula*, Budapest, 1891.

SZÉCHENYI, GR. D.: *Eszmék a lovaglás és kocsizás köréböl* (Thoughts on Riding and Driving), Budapest, 1892.

SZENTPÉTERY, I.: *Scriptores rerum Hungaricarum*, Vol. I. Budapest, 1937.

SZILÁGYI, L.: *Az Anonymus kérdés reviziója* (The 'Anonymus' Question re-opened), Századok, 1937.

TAGÁN, G.: *A közlekedés módja és eszközei a baskiroknál és kirgizeknél* (Transport among the Bashkirs and Kirghiz), Budapest, 1938.

TAKÁCS, S.: *Régi magyar kapitányok* (Constables of Hungarian Castles), Budapest.

——: *Müvelödéstörténeti tanulmányok* (Studies in the History of Civilization), Budapest, 1961.

TELEKI, J.: *A Hunyadiak kora Magyarországon* (The Hunyadi Period in Hungary), Pest, 1852.

TOLSTOV, S. P.: *Az ösi Chorezm* (Ancient Khoresmia), Budapest, 1950.

TÓTH, Z.: *A huszárok eredetéröl* (On the Origin of Hussars), Közl, 1934.

VÁCZY, P.: *A hunok Europában* (The Huns in Europe), *Attila és hunjai*, ed. Németh, G., Budapest, 1940.

VÁMBÉRI, A.: *A török faj ethnologia és ethnografia tekintetében* (Ethnology and Ethnography of the Turks), Budapest, 1885.

VÁRADY, L.: *Késörómai hadügyek és társadalmi alapjai. A római birodalom utolsó evszázadai* (The Art of War in the Late Roman Period, and its Social Bases), Budapest, 1961.

VILLANI, G. and M.: *Historie Florentine.*

VITT, V. O.: *Loshadi Pazirskich Kuvganov* (The Horses in the Pazyryk Barrows), 1952.

WALDBAUER, H.-SÁROSSY, L.: *A messzelovaglás és a Budapest-bécsi distancverseny* (Marathon Rides and the Budapest-Vienna Ride), Pécz, 1909).

WENCZEL, G.: *Marino Sanuto világkrónikája* (The Chronicle of Marino Saluto), *Historical Magazine*, 1878.

WENKHEIM, J. FR. v.: *Ideen über eine Wiederherstellung der verfallenen ungarischen Pferde-zucht* (Ideas for the Reconstitution of Decadent Hungarian Horse-breeding), Pest, 1815.

WHYTE, J. C.: *History of the British Turf*, 1840.

WILLEMSEN, C. A.: *Die Falkenjagd* (Falconry), Leipzig, 1943.

WRANGEL, GR. G.: *Das Buch vom Pferde* (The Book of the Horse), Stuttgart, 1888.

——: *Die Rassen des Pferdes. Ihre Entstehung, Geschichtliche Entwicklung und charakteristische Kennzeichen* (Breeds of Horses, their Characteristics, Ancestry, and Historical Evolution), Stuttgart, 1908–9.

ZEUNER, F. E.: *History of Domesticated Animals*, 1962.

Index of Proper Names